D1601005

A Door Ajar

Contemporary Writers and Emily Dickinson

THOMAS GARDNER

OXFORD
UNIVERSITY PRESS

2006

OXFORD
UNIVERSITY PRESS

Oxford University Press, Inc., publishes works that further
Oxford University's objective of excellence
in research, scholarship, and education.

Oxford   New York
Auckland   Cape Town   Dar es Salaam   Hong Kong   Karachi
Kuala Lumpur   Madrid   Melbourne   Mexico City   Nairobi
New Delhi   Shanghai   Taipei   Toronto

With offices in
Argentina   Austria   Brazil   Chile   Czech Republic   France   Greece
Guatemala   Hungary   Italy   Japan   Poland   Portugal   Singapore
South Korea   Switzerland   Thailand   Turkey   Ukraine   Vietnam

Copyright © 2006 by Oxford University Press, Inc.

Published by Oxford University Press, Inc.
198 Madison Avenue, New York, New York 10016

www.oup.com

Oxford is a registered trademark of Oxford University Press

Library of Congress Cataloging-in-Publication Data
Gardner, Thomas, 1952–
A door ajar : contemporary writers and Emily Dickinson / Thomas Gardner.
p. cm.
Includes bibliographical references and index.
ISBN-13 978-0-19-517493-9
ISBN 0-19-517493-3
1. Dickinson, Emily, 1830–1886—Appreciation—United States. 2. American poetry—
20th century—History and criticism. 3. Poets, American—20th century—Interviews.
4. Dickinson, Emily, 1830–1886—Influence. 5. Influence (Literary, artistic, etc.) I. Title.
PS1541.Z5G374 2006
811'.4—dc22   2005016287

9 8 7 6 5 4 3 2 1

Printed in the United States of America
on acid-free paper

For Laura

ACKNOWLEDGMENTS ℛ

Jorie Graham, Susan Howe, Marilynne Robinson, and Charles Wright made major contributions to this book. My thanks to them. Their generous intensity, both during our actual interviews and in the back-and-forth of revision and expansion, was remarkable. My thanks as well to my friends and colleagues Esther Richey and Patty Raun, who were a first audience for much of this. I am grateful for a fellowship from the John Simon Guggenheim Memorial Foundation that helped me complete this book, and for sabbatical and travel support from Virginia Tech's Provost's Office and Department of English.

An early version of chapter 1 appeared in the *Emily Dickinson Journal* 10, 1 (2001). Versions of chapters 3 and 7 appeared in the *Kenyon Review* 26 (spring 2004) and *American Women Poets in the 21st Century*, ed. Claudia Rankine and Juliana Spahr (Middletown, Conn.: Wesleyan University Press, 2002). My thanks to the editors involved.

I am also grateful for permission to reprint the following material.

Excerpts from "Blaise Pascal Lip-syncs the Void" from *Negative Blue: Selected Later Poems* by Charles Wright, copyright © 2000 by Charles Wright, reprinted by permission of Farrar, Straus and Giroux, LLC.

Excerpts from "Yard Journal," "A Journal of English Days," "A Journal of True Confessions," and "A Journal of the Year of the Ox" from *The World of the Ten Thousand Things: Poems 1980–1990*, copyright © 1990 by Charles Wright, reprinted by permission of Farrar, Straus and Giroux, LLC.

ACKNOWLEDGMENTS

Excerpts from "Regalia for a Black Hat Dancer" from *Sun Under Wood* by Robert Hass, copyright © 1996 by Robert Hass, reprinted by permission of HarperCollins Publishers Inc.

Excerpts from "Vertigo" from *The End of Beauty* by Jorie Graham, copyright © 1987 by Jorie Graham, reprinted by permission of HarperCollins Publishers Inc.

Excerpts from "Picnic," "From the New World," and "Spring" from *Region of Unlikeness* by Jorie Graham, copyright © 1991 by Jorie Graham, reprinted by permission of HarperCollins Publishers Inc.

Excerpts from "In the Hotel," "Manifest Destiny," "Steering Wheel," "The Dream of the Unified Field," and "Subjectivity" from *Materialism* by Jorie Graham, copyright © 1993 by Jorie Graham, reprinted by permission of HarperCollins Publishers Inc.

Excerpts from "The Errancy," "The Scanning," Le Manteau de Pascal," "Untitled Two," "The Guardian Angel of the Private Life," "The Guardian Angel of the Little Utopia," and "The Guardian Angel of Self-Knowledge" from *The Errancy* by Jorie Graham, copyright © 1997 by Jorie Graham, reprinted by permission of HarperCollins Publishers Inc.

Excerpts from "from The Reformation Journal," "The Swarm," "The Veil," "Underneath (7)," "Underneath (9)," "2/18/97," "Underneath (Sibylline)," "Underneath (Calypso)," "Underneath (8)," "Probity," "Underneath (13)," and "Underneath (1)" from *Swarm* by Jorie Graham, copyright © 2000 by Jorie Graham, reprinted by permission of HarperCollins Publishers Inc.

Excerpts from "re:searches" from *Notes preceding trust*, 1987 in *il cuore: the heart (Selected Poems 1970–1995)* by Kathleen Fraser, copyright © 1997 by Kathleen Fraser, reprinted by permission of Wesleyan University Press.

Excerpts from *The Master Letters* by Lucie Brock-Broido, copyright © 1995 by Lucie Brock-Broido. Used by permission of Alfred A. Knopf, a division of Random House, Inc.

Excerpts from "Articulations of Sound Forms in Time" from *Singularities* by Susan Howe, copyright © 1990 by Susan Howe and reprinted by permission of Wesleyan University Press.

Excerpts from "= =" and "Immersion" from *Sensual Math* by Alice Fulton, copyright © 1995 by Alice Fulton. Used by permission of W. W. Norton & Company, Inc.

Emily Dickinson poems, reprinted by permission of the publishers and the Trustees of Amherst College from *The Poems of Emily Dickinson*, Thomas H. Johnson, ed., Cambridge, Mass.: The Belknap Press of Harvard University Press, copyright © 1951, 1955, 1979 by the President and Fellows of Harvard College.

Poem 1448 by Emily Dickinson, reprinted by permission of the publishers and the Trustees of Amherst College from *The Poems of Emily Dickinson: Variorum Edition*, Ralph W. Franklin, ed., Cambridge, Mass.: The Belknap Press of Harvard University Press, copyright © 1998 by the President and Fellows of Harvard College. Copyright © 1951, 1955, 1979, 1983 by the President and Fellows of Harvard College.

Excerpts from Emily Dickinson letters and prose fragments, reprinted by permission of the publishers from *The Letters of Emily Dickinson*, Thomas H. Johnson, ed., Cambridge, Mass.: The Belknap Press of Harvard University Press, copyright © 1958, 1986 by the President and Fellows of Harvard College.

Emily Dickinson manuscripts reproduced by permission of the Trustees of Amherst College.

CONTENTS ℬ

A DOOR AJAR ~

INTRODUCTION ✍

L
ucie Brock-Broido's 1997 collection *The Master Letters* is a powerful enactment of tensions within three well-known Emily Dickinson letters addressing an unknown "Master," found in draft form
after her death in 1886. The volume's fifty-two poems investigate, in Brock-
Broido's words, the way these "gracious, sometimes nearly erotic, worshipful
documents, full of Dickinson's dramas of entreaty & intimacy, her distances"
variously dramatize the speaker's relation to a "voicelessness" beyond her.
Dickinson's speaker shifts, in these letters, between the roles of "the Queen
Recluse, little girl, the mystic, the breathless renouncer," making use of "the
lyric density, the celestial stir, her high-pitched cadences, her odd Unfathomable systems of capitalization, the peculiar swooning syntax, the fluid
stutter of her verse." The letters, then, offer a particularly rich catalogue of
charged and innovative ways of speaking.[1]

Brock-Broido's "I Dont Know Who It Is, That Sings, nor Did I, Would
I Tell" is a striking example of how one might enact or put into play the tensions within another writer:

November

Master—

You say I have Misenveloped & sent you something Else. In the
middle of it all, my mind went blank, all the red notes of terror,
blinking. Please to tell me—have I unsettled you by this?

I told Ravi that a fear is not a temporal thing, the moment—now, is
Now. It is the next which harms him so. *I wonder how long we shall
wonder; how early we shall know.*

On the moors, all the russet weeds have grown there—always, they keep on going on. The rainstorm happens helplessly, like typhus, fills the mind's eye like the vacant oil lamps lighting like a lung with ochre liquid when the nighttime comes on, helplessly. Who is to leave here first, hooded in a yellow cape? *Where shall I hide my things?*

Suddenly, I am stammering in the face of Probability. I thought when the sparse trees began descent, that you would come to me. There is the thunder now; it gives the world a rampant tinge.

He has, after all, an ancient soul; he is unbent by Possibility as he walks sturdy in the rain, steady as a metronome's pendulum keeping—Time. No slicker. No hazard, no hood. If I lose him I will be insignificant. *What a privilege it is to be so insignificant.*

Bliss—is unnatural—

Your, L   (62)

In broadest terms, the poem works by crossing the rhetorical frame of Dickinson's three letters—particularly their charged play with the difference in scale between writer and recipient—with recognizable contemporary references. We see both at once. Dickinson's reply to her Master's apparent puzzlement about her poems—"You ask me what my flowers said—then they were disobedient—I gave them messages"—becomes Brock-Broido's "You say I have Misenveloped & sent you something Else. . . . have I unsettled you by this?" while Dickinson's "Could you come to New England—would you come to Amherst—Would you like to come—Master?" becomes "I thought when the sparse trees began descent, that you would come to me."[2]

Brock-Broido's speaker, signing herself "*L,*" recounts for *her* Master why her mind went "blank, all the red notes of terror, blinking," an experience causing her to send him "something Else" by mistake. That blank moment of fear was generated, it seems, by the thought of potentially "los[ing]" Ravi, the friend to whom the poem is dedicated, described as "walk[ing] sturdy in the rain, steady as a metronome's pendulum keeping—Time." If we look at the title and the three sentences Brock-Broido italicizes, we see that much of the speaker's language for what she fears is drawn from three other Dickinson letters written in the spring and fall of 1858. Save for one letter requesting a book, the entire series of letters the three are drawn from, 190 to 195 in Johnson's collection, forms a sort of sequence. All are written at night. Read together, they sketch a movement from early summer through late August, September, and November. Dickinson's "There is a smiling summer here, which causes birds to sing, and sets the bees in motion" (letter 190) becomes, as time passes, "Your going will redden the maple—and fringe the Gentian sooner, in the soft fields" (letter 192), which in turn becomes "Summer stopped since you were here" (letter 193), before finally returning to those now absent birds and bees: "You were not here in summer. *Summer*? My memory flutters—had I—was there a summer? You should have seen the fields go—gay little entomology! Swift little ornithology! Dancer, and floor, and cadence quite gathered away, and I, a phantom, to you a phantom, rehearse the story!" (letter 195).

Dickinson's sequence acknowledges our insignificance before the flow of time. It is a lament uttered in the dark. Working with its language, Brock-Broido reexperiences, or reenacts, Dickinson's confrontation with human limits. "My memory flutters," Dickinson writes, coming to grips with the fact that all things have been "quite gathered away." "Suddenly, I am stammering in the face of [the] Probability [of loss]," Brock-Broido echoes back. Her title is drawn from letter 190's account of sounds in the dark: "The day went down, long time ago, and still a simple choir bear the canto on. *I dont know who it is, that sings, nor did I, would I tell!*" (italics mine). The italicized sentence in the second stanza, in its original context, acknowledges that we have no firm idea what follows time's steady mowing: "Our man has mown today, and as he plied his scythe, I thought of other mowings, and garners far from here. *I wonder how long we shall wonder; how early we shall know*" (letter 190, italics mine). Dickinson's worry about her brother's typhus is the source of her stammering response to time in the third stanza: "Good-night! I can't stay any longer in a world of death. Austin is ill of fever. . . . Ah! democratic Death! . . . Say, is he everywhere? *Where shall I hide my thing*s?" (letter 195, italics mine). Finally, in the fifth stanza, the speaker's "insignificance" in the face of a probability she can't control is drawn from a sentence Dickinson sent to her sister-in-law Sue, complaining about not having heard from her: "I hav'nt any paper, dear, but faith continues firm—Presume if I met with my 'deserts,' I should receive nothing. Was informed to that effect today by a 'dear pastor.' *What a privilege it is to be so insignificant!*" (letter 194, italics mine). Dickinson's insignificance, pointedly accounting for why she doesn't "deserve" a response from her sister-in-law, plays, tongue in cheek, with the Calvinist notion that man, if he got what he deserved, would receive nothing from God but condemnation. "Insignificance" is a "privilege" because it opens one to this fact and thus to an accompanying experience of grace. It is a lack through which one receives, a blindness, once acknowledged, through which one sees.

What Brock-Broido's speaker has done, in gathering up Dickinson's references to not knowing and being in the dark, is both voice her own insignificance in relation to time's steady motion and claim that position's "privilege." Insignificance and uneasiness allow her to experience forces far beyond her that assurance and a settled position would overlook. Like Dickinson, then, "*L*" writes to her Master of her fearful encounter with insignificance, stammers in the face of it, because it opens her to her Master. Although he is unknowable, she in her brokenness, comes near. "*Bliss*," his world, "*is unnatural.*" "*L*" can only come into relation with the unnatural—becoming, as she signs herself, "Yours"—when she comes up against her "natural" limits and stands silent within them. Enacting a responsive insignificance by, as Gerald Bruns puts it about conversation, "picking up on the words in play" within Dickinson's letters, Brock-Broido's speaker gains a halting openness before her silent Master.[3]

What I investigate in this book is the way a significant number of contemporary writers have returned to just this moment in Dickinson's work—enacting for themselves, in their own terms, some aspect of the broken responsiveness before a world that can no longer be held in place that Dickinson puts into play.[4] In the interviews I've included here, Susan Howe speaks of this as Dickinson's "antinomian strain," Charles Wright as her "negative spirituality," and Marilynne Robinson as the way a Dickinson metaphor deliberately "ruptures the illusion that it has created." All of them, drawn, as Jorie Graham puts it, to Dickinson's "poems of enactment," attempt to act out, in their own terms, Dickinson's world-opening celebration of limits: "I dont know who it is, that sings, nor did I, would I tell!" Joyce Carol Oates, in a 1987 article in *Critical Inquiry*, praises Dickinson by asserting that "Dickinson of course has no heirs or heiresses. In the minuteness of their perceptions and the precision of their images one might think of Marianne Moore, Elizabeth Bishop, the early Anne Sexton, and, certainly, Sylvia Plath, but so far as the development of American poetry is concerned, Emily Dickinson really leads nowhere since she herself is the highest embodiment of the experimental method she developed. Genius of her kind is simply inimitable."[5] I would suggest that this is overstated and that, in putting into play or reenacting various aspects of Dickinson's encounter with the unknown, contemporary writers, rather than "imitate," demonstrate how her work might be extended or explored.

It's possible to describe Dickinson's side of this conversation fairly simply. First, as with Brock-Broido's Master and his association with "unnatural" Bliss, much of Dickinson is built on an awareness of a discontinuity between the human and the divine, the speaker and a lover, or the observer and the external world. Second, an awareness of that gap leads one, as with Brock-Broido's focus on insignificance, to an acknowledgment of the blindness or brokenness or fallenness of one's state in what Hart Crane would call "the broken world."[6] And third, that awareness turns one from ways of thinking or perceiving or mastering that refuse to acknowledge their limits and toward the revelatory power of brokenness, the "something Else" emboldening Brock-Broido's speaker to sign herself "Your L."[7] It's with this third category that contemporary writers are most forcefully engaged—often beginning with a Dickinson line or image or situation in order to investigate what sort of relationship with the indescribable brokenness makes possible. As we'll observe, they see Dickinson's responsive brokenness taking both linguistic and emotional or spiritual form. As Brock-Broido's stammering account suggests, fragmentation, discontinuity, use of pauses, shifting styles, bodily language, instability, opacity, wandering *and* loneliness, dread, uncertainty, silence, disorientation are equally, often simultaneously, explored as nontotalizing responses to what can never be grasped.

In her 1993 book *The Regenerate Lyric: Theology and Innovation in American Poetry*, Elisa New describes, in theological terms, the Dickinson that Brock-Broido and many other contemporary writers respond to. New focuses on what she calls "the instructive if irremediable gap between the subject and God" which she sees as an "abiding preoccupation" in American poetry. She argues that Dickinson's "chastened attraction to an unformed realm where she exercises little power to speak of" and the "blind and wandering language—as spiritual instrument" (6–7) that she develops in response produce one of the most powerful forms this preoccupation has taken. Confronted with "the withdrawn presence of a Calvinist universe" (192), Dickinson

> presses boundaries precisely to find that place where God marks his domain as the absence of the humanly intelligible . . . cultivat[ing] bluntness and abnegation, blind sight and dumb tongues; . . . practic[ing], in essence, an emptying of the articulate self for the sake of discerning the Other who needs not a Word. . . . Without discernible contour, He nevertheless exists, the proof of His existence strengthened rather than weakened by that indiscernibility. (153, 160)

An acknowledgment of "the hovering opacity of language" (192), then, or an unfolding of the "states of anticipation and dread, longing and uncertainty" (159) provide "route[s] of spiritual access" (192) because it is only in the display of difference that something outside human categories makes itself known. Only there does "divinity avail itself as 'possibility,' albeit a possibility never to be claimed in stable image or expression . . . poems *unwriting* themselves as poems, the better in their blindness to glimpse God" (181).

Such "an impulse . . . acutely aware of the [responsive] incompleteness of human language" (179) is, contemporary writing seems to argue, Dickinson's greatest legacy.

Although this pattern has theological roots, theology isn't the only way to describe it. Gary Stonum, for example, in *The Dickinson Sublime* (1990), uses the traditional term *sublimity*—an experience produced by "anguishing forces that rupture normal continuities of habit and belief" (118)—to get at the link, for Dickinson, between "idolatrously beloved Masters, internal psychic turmoils, and objective natural phenomena as various as sunsets and snakes. All are apprehended according to the magnitude of their affective intensity, and all are valued for precisely that" (68).[8] What Stonum adds, however, is that although an encounter with the sublime—say the beloved—typically moves from a normative through a traumatic to a reactive phase where "the subject experiences elevation, empowerment . . . a release from traumatic assault . . . [and] an influx of fresh resources" (69), the Dickinson sublime is a broken or "hesitant" (141) or "deferred" (188) one, turning aside from that last step. Dickinson's poetry, he writes, "isolates the traumatic moment of rupture and discontinuity . . . [suggesting that] access to an unequivocally conclusive power . . . lies beyond the space of the poem" (174).

Sharon Cameron, in *Choosing Not Choosing: Dickinson's Fascicles*, makes a similar point, focusing on the way Dickinson's variants turn aside from the claims of wholeness:

> Dickinson's poetry dramatizes the impossibility of wholeness understood as boundedness. It does so in its almost incomprehensible adherence to piecemeal utterance, in the refusal of the syntax to endorse resolutions marked by conventional grammatical pauses, connections, or punctuated units of sense. . . . Dickinson's language is language that is broken. . . . Most stunningly, Dickinson dramatizes the impossibility of wholeness by privileging variants as the essence of her poetry. . . . For the adequacy of words—or, to be more precise, the adequacy of certain words—to represent a stance in a definitive way is precisely what Dickinson's poetry disputes.[9]

As with New, Cameron suggests that Dickinson's "inability to settle on a phenomenon as a single entity or to represent it except variantly" records and preserves its still-potent possibility: "The single most prominent feature of Dickinson's poetry, then, is the opening up of spaces. It is the opening up of spaces allowed to remain open . . . illustrat[ing] the uncontainability of what is being represented" (184, 188).[10]

We should not be surprised that three different readers, focusing on theology, internal turmoil, and patterns of composition, come to similar conclusions about the power of Dickinson's wandering language, for it seems clear that to write about one is to write about the others. For Dickinson, to track one's experience with a beloved is no different from tracking one's encounter with poetry—both seem to share the same mysterious origin, and both seem to follow the same pattern of coming overpoweringly near and then moving inexplicably away.[11] In Dickinson's words:

> To pile like Thunder to its close
> Then crumble grand away
> While Everything created hid
> This—would be Poetry—
>
> Or Love—the two coeval come—
> We both and neither prove—
> Experience either and consume—
> For None see God and live—[12]   (J1247, F1353)

In "both" situations, we attempt to "prove," "experience," and "consume" the overwhelming object, and in "neither" (or, not in "either") are we successful. That lack of success, as what we are drawn to crumbles grand away, testifies, indirectly and linguistically, to having experienced God or the unknown or "Bliss" on the very border beyond which our eyes and senses don't reach. Poetry, love, and an encounter with the unknown share the same dynamic. To focus on one is to bring into play the other. This flexibility—the multiple ways Dickinson dramatizes our consuming only to be consumed—has a good bit to do with why, as we'll see, Dickinson's broken responsiveness has been fleshed out in various forms and genres, by writers working from often-opposed schools of thought.

Often, Dickinson lays out these issues in summary form, establishing rather than enacting her central problem. For example:

> This World is not Conclusion.
> A Species stands beyond—
> Invisible, as Music—
> But positive, as Sound—
> It beckons, and it baffles—
> Philosophy—don't know—
> And through a Riddle, at the last—
> Sagacity, must go—   (J501, F373)

Here is one source for Brock-Broido's "Invisible" Master, "stand[ing] beyond" but "beckon[ing]" and "baffl[ing]." To approach him, philosophy and sagacity must pass "through a Riddle" and acknowledge how much they "don't know"—exactly the process Brock-Broido enacts by revoicing the nighttime songs of "not knowing" found in Dickinson's letters. Consistently, in Dickinson, the agony of confronting one's distance from the beckoning invisible is also an experience of its nearness: "A nearness to Tremendousness— / An Agony procures— / Affliction ranges Boundlessness— / Vicinity to Laws" (J963, F824). This is also presented in summary form, although Dickinson's charged, flexible language—does agony produce a nearness to the tremendous or does a nearness produce agony? does affliction arrange the boundless near laws, or does it range freely through the boundless?—makes it a live, hesitant, mental act. Another well-known summary poem describes an openness to this baffling realm as "dwell[ing] in Possibility," a state in which one's occupation is "The spreading wide my narrow Hands / To gather Paradise—" (J657, F466). Narrow hands can't hold much; when they are spread wide, they let something go, but in letting go, they "gather," for they have become aware of a possibility beyond them, beckoning and baffling.

One could describe such an acknowledgment of bafflement or finitude as a willing taking on of flesh or mortality—in terms Brock-Broido and Dickinson share, counting it a "privilege" that language or gesture, bound in flesh, expire. As a powerful late poem, drawing on both the opening of the Gospel of John and the debate about eating Christ's flesh that follows the feeding of the five thousand in the same gospel, has it:

> A Word that breathes distinctly
> Has not the power to die
> Cohesive as the Spirit
> It may expire if He—
> "Made Flesh and dwelt among us"
> Could condescension be
> Like this consent of Language
> This loved Philology.   (J1651, F1715)

Giving up distinction and unchallenged coherence, "consent[ing]" to pass through the riddle and acknowledge that they do not know, words take on flesh. And if what inevitably follows from that act is brokenness and death, then—as the example of Christ demonstrates—it is a brokenness that may bring renewed life.

It would follow, then, as contemporary writers have realized, that Dickinson's most powerful poems are often those in which "this consent" to take on flesh and its expressive limitations is acted out in time rather than simply summarized. Many of these poems take place in the past tense, the poet reporting on an encounter with something that has shown itself to be unknowable. Poem 1084 (F1099) is a simple example. "At Half past Three" a bird propounds "a single term / Of cautious melody." "At Half past Four" the bird's "Experiment" seems to have passed whatever "test" it had ventured, and its "silver Principle" dominates the scene. But "At Half past Seven" the bird vanishes, and the observer finds herself banished from what had come close. In a sense, she dies back into a separate body: "And Place was where the Presence was / Circumference between."[13]

That bodily experience of coming to a halt, of being brought face to face with one's distance or limits, is, of course, just where things open up in Dickinson—as in this well-known poem, moving step by step into and through "insignificance":

> I saw no Way—the Heavens were stitched—
> I felt the Columns close—
> The Earth reversed her Hemispheres—
> I touched the Universe—
>
> And back it slid—and I alone—
> A Speck upon a Ball—
> Went out upon Circumference—
> Beyond the Dip of Bell—   (J378, F633)

Or here, the poet moving progressively deeper into a failure to comprehend until she finally finds herself in silence, "wrecked, solitary, here—":

> And then a Plank in Reason, broke,
> And I dropped down, and down—
> And hit a World, at every plunge,
> And Finished knowing—then—   (J280, F340)

Perhaps most interesting to contemporary writers are the present-tense poems where Dickinson actually describes such experiences—discovering "World[s]," finishing the project of "knowing"—as they are undergone. As Brock-Broido's casting her confrontation with Bliss as an act of finding—"Suddenly I am stammering in the face of Probability"—suggests, it is these poems, Dickinson displaying herself in the midst of broken consent, that most often prompt new enactings. In poem 160 (F132), for example, Dickinson pictures herself *just now* failing to enter a state of wholeness:

> Just lost, when I was saved!
> Just felt the world go by!

Just girt me for the onset with Eternity,
When breath blew back,
And on the other side
I heard recede the disappointed tide!

In poem 327 (F336), she wrestles with her experience of blindness "Today," drawing the reader along as she unfolds an "other way" of seeing, "with just my soul / Upon the Window pane." Or, the experience of feeling numb, being unable to take in what's become too much, not knowing if at this moment your hold on things is about to slide away completely—consenting to, inhabiting, this experience of bodily limits now, in the writing:

This is the Hour of Lead—
Remembered, if outlived,
As Freezing persons, recollect the Snow—
First—Chill—then Stupor—then the letting go—   (J341, F372)

Or, in poem 640 (F706), confronting an impossible boundary by speaking now, to a lover, from whom one will be forever apart:

So We must meet apart—
You there—I—here—
With just the Door ajar
That Oceans are—and Prayer—
And that White Sustenance—
Despair—

Or, to cite one last example, poem 777 (F877), where the poet acknowledges as she speaks that she is, in fact, possessed by "The Loneliness One dares not sound— / And would as soon surmise / As in its grave go plumbing / To ascertain its size":

I fear me this—is Loneliness—
The Maker of the Soul
Its Caverns and its Corridors
Illuminate—or seal—

In coming upon and holding itself before something it can't comprehend—something that might as easily seal her in silence as illuminate her soul—Dickinson's work points to the way brokenness opens one to possibilities outside the reach of "knowing." In pointing to this—and, most important, in enacting this—she hands those possibilities on to her best readers.

To suggest something of the breadth of her influence, let me look briefly at the way three other contemporary writers enact these Dickinson issues. Alice Fulton, who has written in detail about Dickinson's presence in her work, has, among other responses, quite deliberately extended her use of the dash. She comments: "The dash is an empty space, but Dickinson's syntactical deletions often asked to be filled in; they exist to be recovered. Recovering the deletions makes reading her a very active, reciprocal experience. You feel like you're building the poem with her as you read. Sometimes you can't recover the deletions. The phrases on either side of the dash remain non sequiturs."[14] Fulton notes that she drew this account of Dickinson's use of recoverable or nonrecoverable deletion from Cristanne Miller's *Emily Dickinson: A Poet's Grammar* (1987), and a brief look at Miller is quite useful in thinking about Fulton's work.[15] Miller writes that Dickinson's "deletion of part (or parts) of a sentence" (24), her "yoking of [contrasting] vocabularies" (40), and her use of dashes to isolate a word or a phrase in order to "call attention to the surprise of its relationship with others of the poem's terms" (53), "create a suggestion [of a] mind at work" (51) attempting "to express what was before inexpressible or unseen" (46). By "marking that some connection exists [between words on either side of the dash, or between contrasting vocabularies or parts of a sentence] but omitting to clarify it" (30), Dickinson's poems draw the reader (who both fills and fails to fill that "hole in meaning") into "the multiplying, rupturing aspect of creation over the positing, controlling one" (181). The dash, then, dramatizes meaning-making as a charged, tentative act; coming before the inexpressible or the unseen, it is never certain, continually fraying, always in process.

Fulton introduces her version of Dickinson's dash in *Sensual Math* (1995), inventing a sign she labels "The dash / to the second power = =."[16] Using the new sign as its title, "= =" is the fullest account of what she's trying to do. It begins:

It might mean immersion, that sign
    I've used as title, the sign I call a bride
after the recessive threads in lace = =
the stitches forming deferential
        space around the firm design.
        It's the unconsidered

mortar between the silo's bricks = = never admired
        when we admire

> the holdfast of the tiles (their copper of a robin's
>> breast abstracted into flat).
>
> It's a seam made to show,
> the deckle edge = = constructivist touch.   (56)

Dickinson's dashes, indicating connections without pinning them down, generate a sense of a work being built as we read, with much left unstitched as the mind pushes forward or prepares to reverse itself. In her work with the "bride" sign—drawing the term from the "deferential" or "recessive" stitches linking or bridging patterns in lacework—Fulton moves back a step, suggesting that one must first force the reader to take note of this space before exploiting its openness. So she uses a more visible sign than Dickinson's, drawing the reader's eye to the "unconsidered," "never admired" mortar between things—the very thing, another poem puts it, that normally "dissolves / under vision's dominion" (83). She "show[s]" the seam and she leaves untrimmed the "deckle edge" of her making in order to insist that connections or stitches or hinges are "constructed" rather than natural things. Someone paused here, the sign insists, and attempted to work out for herself, perhaps for the first time, something not before expressed and not unthinkingly assumed to be true.

Along with increasing the visibility of the space of the dash, Fulton also, with her two equal signs, calls more attention than Dickinson does to the act of joining. "It might mean immersion," she writes in the lines I've just quoted. "Metaphor is pure immersion," another poem suggests: "Pure sinking / one into another and the more / difference that's dissolved the more = = " (59). To insist on immersion while withholding the grounds for that connection is, as another poem adds in an echo of Dickinson's poem 501, to pass naming through a riddle:

> Yet immersion's also treason
> to a naming that's a nailing down.
> It's the barcode riddled down the middle
> so the product's up for grabs = =
> what no register can scan.   (68)

Unlike a comma, which "seems so natural, you don't see it / when you read" (57), such a sign "contests" the natural. As with Brock-Broido calling attention to her insignificance, Fulton's sign insists on itself as a tentative human gesture, a "letting go" or "spreading wide" before mystery:

> The natural is what
>
> poetry contests. Why else the line = = why stanza = = why

meter and the rest. Like wheels on snow

> that leave a wake = = that tread in white
> > without dilapidating
> > mystery = = hinging
> one phrase to the next = = the brides.　　　(57)

Such writing, "= =" concludes, is a form of not-knowing leaving "Mystery" intact—Fulton's mark attempting to make more visible one of Dickinson's most powerful habits of composition: "Thus wed = = the sentence cannot tell / whether it will end or melt or give / way to the fabulous = = ." Interestingly, while sketching the way the implications of Dickinson's dash might be more fully developed, Fulton doesn't, for the most part, actually *use* the mark to its fullest potential, as a glance at the lines I've quoted will confirm. The one exception, however, is quite powerfully expressive. In "Fuzzy Feelings," responding to her sister, whose twenty-one-year-old daughter had died the year before and who had asked whom her daughter most resembled, the speaker stumbles: "I think she = = you, I said / in some wrong tense" (61)— enacting exactly the Dickinson-like play between an opening of uncertain space and immersion that Fulton's other poems describe.

Kathleen Fraser's "re:searches," in *Notes preceding trust* (1987), a poem inscribed "fragments, after Anakreon, for Emily Dickinson," puts Dickinson's expressive brokenness into action in yet another way.[17] If Brock-Broido makes use of Dickinson's responsive "insignificance" and Fulton her refusal to "nail down," Fraser is drawn to Dickinson's rendering of what Fraser describes, in another context, as the "conditions of stammer, error, uncertainty, and ambivalence."[18] Fraser writes of a "'new music' inherited from Dickinson and further pioneered by the brave and highly imagined writings of the modernist women preceding us" (136), which "reinvent[s] language structures in order to catch one's own at-oddness with the presumed superiority of the central mainstream vision" (31).[19] Responsive to the "uncertainty and multiplicity in female experience" (135), drawn to "formerly inarticulate states of being" (175), such a music "foregrounds the investigation and pursuit of the unnamed" (175). "Emily Dickinson was, perhaps, the first woman poet to provide other women with a formal model of urgency and difference" (142), Fraser writes. Forcefully enacting "her 'inadequacy' in retaining a single wholeness of vision or rational sequence of thought" (143), Dickinson modeled for "contemporary women poets" an approach to "that marginal and unspoken region they've claimed as difference" (144).

"re:searches" was written while the poet was in Rome, as the radioactive clouds of the April 1986 Chernobyl accident "blew across Europe."[20] It was written as well, the poet has remarked, under the cloud of reading about the way Dickinson's brother Austin had mutilated some of her letters and poems after her death, eliminating references to his wife Susan. These two instances become for her an image for the sort of broken, damaged language the poet has been handed by society—mutilated, threatened with erasure. The first of the poem's twenty-three fragments combines these events:

inside
(jittery
burned language)
the black container   (36)

Here the nuclear plant's blown-open, blackened-inside release of radioactivity is crossed with the recent release of Dickinson's mutilated, broken language—and, I suppose, with the poet's own jitters. But what's fascinating about the poem is that, through an intricate play of sound, "radioactivity" becomes "radial activ- / ity" (40)—that is, the negative fact of the explosion and the "eee face ment" of Dickinson's work produces a new sort of language able to open itself to the unnamable in a more tentative and responsive way. Radial, outward-arcing, nonconsecutive spokes of memory and observation make "latent content" (36) visible through a language that has been shattered into something over which, like Dickinson's being simultaneously "pious   impious / reason could not take / precedence" (36).

Here are four early fragments:

"eee wah yeh
my little owlet"
not connected up
your lit-up exit

.

just picked
this red tumbling mound
in the bowl
this fact and its arrangement
this idea and who
determines it

.

this strawberry is
what separates her tongue
from just repetition

> .
> the fact of her
> will last only
> as long as she continues
> releasing the shutter, she thinks   (36–37)

A kind of thinking is going on here about how to use the "jittery / burned language" the poet has been handed. The childhood memory—"Little Owlet"
is a nursery song—of a parent singing and leaving through a door is, like the
precise taste of the strawberry "separat[ing] her tongue / from just repetition,"
most powerful because it is "not connected up."[21] Both facts, given a language
that continually "releas[es] the shutter" (or stutter) and continually starts over
again, can be presented free of "arrangement" and "determin[ation]." That is,
they can powerfully speak for one's inner and often inexplicable multiplicity
and difference, refusing the demand for "just repetition."

The poem continues (to simplify somewhat) by describing a series of
photographs—or events remembered as photographs—without articulat-
ing connections. The writer follows the "ee" sound of the nonsense song to
Rome ("E- / ternal city") and then to Dickinson:

> her separate person-
> ality, her
> father's neutrality
> ity
>
> .
> equalibrium
> (cut her name
> out of every
> scribble)
> hymn   himnal now, equal-
> lateral
>
> .
> pronounced with
> partially closed
> lips
>
> .
> pink pearl eraser
> erasing her face her
> eee face ment
> her face meant
>
> .
> he cut out

> of her, her name
> of each thing
> she sang
> each letter she
> hung, on line
> (divine)   (39)

The movement of sound here—personality, *e*qualibrium, *e*qual- / lateral, partiall*y*, *e*raser, *eee* face ment, h*e*, *e*ach, d*i*vine—allows Fraser to explore the forces against Dickinson (her father's neutrality, the family's fiercely enacted need for equilibrium, the brutal erasure of individual names and faces) but without having to make a consecutive argument. And what she demonstrates is that the cut-out language she has been handed is in fact brilliantly and fluently expressive—is in fact "(divine)." So, then, Fraser concludes, looking over her linguistic activity:

> not random, these
> crystalline structure, these
> non-reversible orders, this
> camera forming tendencies, this
> edge of greater length, this
> lyric forever error, this
> something embarrassingly clear, this
> language we come up against

The language she has come up against—erased, broken, mutilated—has in fact been shown, in action, to be deeply alive. The fragments are both precisely ordered, not random, crystalline rather than logical (a logical statement could be reversed) in their shapes, and strikingly individual: precise camera shots, nonequilateral edges, lyrics stubbornly clear and out of step. Dickinson's brokenness before a species standing beyond is here put to work to describe an internal world just as resistant to the demands to know for sure.

♫

In Robert Hass's meditation "Regalia for a Black Hat Dancer" from *Sun Under Wood* (1996), Dickinson's broken responsiveness is also put to work, suggesting that Dickinson's input isn't confined to either the experimental lyric or to women writers.[22] Hass's poem is an attempt to sort out a mixture of feelings associated with the end of a marriage:

> Walking down to Heart's Desire beach in the summer evenings
> of the year my marriage ended—
>
> . . .

> I don't think I could have told the pain of loss
> from the pain of possibility,
> though I knew they weren't the same thing.   (47)

These, of course, are very much Dickinson's terms—the pain of loss, and the pain of possibility. As we've seen, they are interrelated: pain in Dickinson bringing both an excruciating sense of distance and disorientation—it was "most, like Chaos—Stopless—cool— / Without a Chance, or Spar— / Or even a Report of Land— / To justify—Despair" (J510, F355)—and, at times, an accompanying openness to wider "possibility."[23] That Dickinson echo is confirmed near the middle of the poem when the poet reflects on his drive to nail down his feelings:

> There ought to be some single word for the misery of divorce.
> (What is the rhythm of that line? Oh, I see. Four and three,
> Emily's line!—
>
>> There ought to be some single word
>> For the misery of divorce.
>> It dines upon you casually
>> duh-dduh-duh-duh-dduh-fierce / remorse / pierce/)   (50)

Dickinson is on Hass's mind, then, not just because these are her issues but because her approach to something impossible to master—trying to nail a feeling down, and then being forced to leave it open and unsettled, choosing not to choose between variants—is what Hass finds himself enacting. Although divorce is not within the range of Dickinson's subject matter, and Hass's casual, circling meditation is not a form she would have used, Dickinson's expressive brokenness is clearly behind the acknowledgment driving the poem that there is no single word to pin the feeling down.

The first part of the poem talks about two ways of being "hollowed out by pain, / honeycombed with the emptiness of it." Walking down to the beach on summer evenings, he would first experience emptiness as a mixture of "pain and desire": "my throat so swollen with some unsortable mix / of sorrow and desire I couldn't swallow—." And then:

> I'd present my emptiness, which was huge, baffled
> . . .
> and most of the time I felt nothing,
> when the moment came that was supposed to embody presence,
> nothing really. There were a few buffleheads,
> as usual, a few gulls rocking in the surf.
> Sometimes a Western grebe diving and swimming

with its crazed eye.

So there were these two emptinesses: one made of pain and desire
and one made of vacancy.   (48)

Of the two painful emptinesses, the deeper of the two—being greeted not
with presence but with vacancy—is Dickinson's base line: "Place was where
the Presence was, / Circumference between." That base emptiness, he realized as he stood there baffled, made itself felt in a number of different ways.
One manifestation was the unsortable mix of sorrow and desire he felt then.
Related manifestations included his "mother ending her days in a hotel
room, / scarcely able to breathe" but insistently deluding herself, manag-
ing "I'm just lucky / I have my health"; his brother's account of coming
down from crack—"You got nothing left / but the lint in your pocket"; or
what he calls "The whole theater of the real: sadness, which seems infinite,
/ cruelty, which seems infinite, the cheerful one-armed guy / in the bakery
mornings—he puts his croissant between his teeth / and pours himself some
coffee; . . . the whole botched world—" (49, 50). All of these are faces of the
blind, fallen world. But somehow, perhaps through noticing, in that emptiness, the way "the pelicans / that settled in the cove in the late midsummer
dusk, / . . . [found] each other as the dark came on," he would also be led to
this different response: "I would go home, / make tea, call my children, some
piece of writing / that I'd started would seem *possible*" (51, italics mine). As
with Dickinson, these contradictory responses to an ungraspable emptiness
aren't sorted out—they simply float as variant possibilities.

The second half of the poem shifts to an account of climbing in Korea
and "coming to the cave of the Sokkaram Buddha," where he caught "perhaps a glimpse" of that deeper vacancy "Under sorrow . . . Under / the animal
sense of loss" (52). Unable to name it directly, however, he again resorts to
cataloging what floats above it:

> Looking at old frescoes
> from medieval churches in the Cloisters once, I wondered if,
> all over Europe, there were not corresponding vacancies,
> sheer blanks where pietas and martyrdoms of Santa Lucia
> and crowing cocks rising to announce the dawn in which
> St. Peter had betrayed his lord in sandstone and basalt
> and carnelian marble once had been. This emptiness
> felt like that. Under the hosannahs and the terror of the plague
> and the crowning of the Virgin in the spring.
> . . .
>   Under screams order, and under that—
> it must be the torturer's nightmare—nothing.

The nothingness he discovers in the cave—"I presented myself once more for some revelation. / Nothing"—just as it could be said to be all that lies beneath now-missing works of art, finally underlies all forms of order, even language, as the poem goes on to note. But its manifestations are multiple, he realizes, thinking of a new relationship, which, like the old one, is also based on nothing, but takes a strikingly different form:

> The way neither of us needed to hold back, think
> before we spoke, lie, tiptoe carefully around a given subject,
> or brace ourselves to say hard truths. It felt to me hilarious,
> and hilarity, springwater gushing up from some muse's font
> of crystal in old poems, seemed a form of emptiness. Look!
> (Rilke in the sonnets) I last but a minute. I walk on nothing.
> Coming and going I do this dance on air.
> . . .
>   Mornings—for how long—
> I'd wake in pain. Physical pain, fluid; it moved
> through my body like a grassfire spreading on a hill.
> (Opposite of touching.) I'd think of my wife, her lover,
> some moment in our children's lives . . .
> . . .
> I'd stare at the ceiling, bewildered, and feel a grief
> so old it could have been some beggar woman in a fairy tale.
> I didn't know you could lie down in such swift, opposing currents.
>   (56–57)

Following Dickinson, all four of these contemporary writers attempt to describe and enact forms of living in the emptiness or before stitched heavens and silent masters. For all of them, the forms are broken, multiple, and "not connected up." As with this poem, they lie down in "swift, opposing currents." In quite different ways, they stammer, exploit their "insignificance," and call attention to what it is that has forced knowing to acknowledge its limits. And yet all of them suggest, as Hass does in his conclusion, that, like "The Loneliness One dare not sound—" in Dickinson's 777, one can, through such broken forms, as she puts it, perhaps "ascertain the size":

> Private pain is easy, in a way. It doesn't go away,
> but you can teach yourself to see its size. Invent a ritual.
> Walk up a mountain in the afternoon, gather up pine twigs.
> Light a fire, thin smoke, not an ambitious fire,
> and sit before it and watch till it burns to ash
> and the last gleam is gone from it, and dark falls.

Then you get up, brush yourself off, and walk back to the world.
(57–58)

What follows are essays on and interviews with four of the strongest and most distinctive writers currently working to extend Dickinson's "emptying of the articulate self for the sake of discerning the Other who needs not a Word." In the essays, I focus on four quite different works—Marilynne Robinson's *Housekeeping*, a novel; Charles Wright's *Zone Journals*, a sequence of journal-poems; poet Susan Howe's experimental prose works *My Emily Dickinson* and *The Birth-mark*; and Jorie Graham's linguistically tormented book of poems *Swarm*. The interviews that follow each chapter are, by contrast, quite deliberately wide-ranging. Each writer sketches something of his or her history with Dickinson, but in the course of teasing out the charged, shifting relation between them, each writer goes his or her own way. One will find revelatory descriptions of the Roman forum and a family Bible, strikingly original readings of Dickinson poems and letters, and a general opening out of Dickinson in all sorts of directions. Giving some sense of the myriad ways her words have been "put into play" is my most basic goal here. As we'll see, Robinson's unfolding of the fragility of Dickinson's metaphors, Wright's reframing of her images as the brilliantly inadequate probes of memory and description, Howe's encountering of Dickinson's stutter in core colonial texts, and Graham's awakening to the body's powers in knowledge's moments of vertigo—all of these, when read together, insist that we are just beginning as a culture to understand the far-reaching implications of Dickinson's work. This volume attempts one part of that task.

ONE

ENLARGING LONELINESS

Marilynne Robinson's Housekeeping

In a short piece in the 1984 *New York Times Book Review*, the novelist Marilynne Robinson describes her interest in Dickinson, Melville, Thoreau, Whitman, and Emerson in these terms:

> Nothing in literature appeals to me more than the rigor with which they fasten on problems of language, or consciousness—bending form to their purposes, ransacking ordinary speech and common experience . . . always, to borrow a phrase from Wallace Stevens, in the act of finding what will suffice. I think they must have believed everything can be apprehended truly when it is seen in the light of an esthetic understanding appropriate to itself, whence their passion for making novel orders of disparate things. I believe they wished to declare the intrinsic dignity of all experience and to declare the senses bathed in revelation—true, serious revelation, the kind that terrifies.[1]

This is strikingly phrased. Stevens's "poem of the mind in the act of finding / What will suffice" is anticipated, for Robinson, in the display of "consciousness" in action found in their nineteenth-century work: the struggle to create an "esthetic understanding appropriate" to a world bathing the senses in revelation. Returning to this subject in a 1992 interview, Robinson, author of the much-discussed novel *Housekeeping* (1980),[2] refers again to these writers, but now laments: "There has been a rupture in the conversation of this culture . . . all sorts of things that were brought up in the early conversation were dropped without being resolved, and . . . nothing of comparable interest has taken their place." She adds, and it is this idea I want to explore here, "in writing *Housekeeping* I was consciously trying to participate in the conversation they had carried on and that I felt had been dropped."[3]

That conversation Robinson attempts to revive has to do with how one creates a form capable of responding to or engaging with a world that overwhelms the expectations one brings to it—a world "that terrifies." In the 1992 interview I have just cited, she calls attention to a characteristic pattern of American writing in which

> people go through a journey that leads to a kind of realization that is just at the limits of their ability to comprehend or articulate, and after that, there's an openness where earlier experience becomes impossible, and you're abandoned into a new terrain without being able to use your old assumptions about how to find your way. (6)[4]

That journey into a new terrain where old assumptions are abandoned and one is left with only their broken remains and an openness to the new allegorizes what Robinson calls

> the characteristic mode of thought of most of the classic American writers, which is based on the assumption that the only way to understand the world is metaphorical, and all metaphors are inadequate, and that you press them far enough and you're delivered into something that requires a new articulation. (6)

What Robinson is drawn to in these nineteenth-century writers is their peculiar combination of ambition and humility. For them, a form that acknowledges its own inadequacy or brokenness holds opens a door:

> what you're left with is an understanding that's larger than you had before, but finally it is a legitimate understanding because you know it's wrong or you know it's imperfectly partial. . . . What they are all trying to do is use language as a method of comprehension on the largest scale, at the same time using all the resources of language and absolutely insisting that language is not an appropriate tool.[5]

When Robinson criticizes current assumptions about writing in another recent essay, then, declaring that the contraction of imaginative language to strung-together "brand names, media phrases and minor expletives" amounts to a "notably ungenerous faith" in the ability of language to respond to experience, she is attempting to call contemporary writers back to that ambitious play with limits enacted in nineteenth-century American writing.[6] A contracted language is one comfortable with itself. It doesn't see itself as imperfectly partial or its metaphors as inadequate. It doesn't look beyond itself, and, as a result, the world it greets is a contracted one. In contrast, a language acknowledging its imperfect partiality stands poised to expand: its world is large and strange.[7] Robinson writes:

> I am as firmly persuaded as anyone that things can be explained, or usefully described, but I am convinced that our methods at this point are crude, and premature, and that they lead us to ignore such experience or intuition as cannot be accommodated by them. . . . We cannot in good faith sketch serpents in where the cartography of our understanding frays. But perhaps we can develop language that will acknowledge that it does fray, and where it does, and that those things we do not understand are not mere gaps to be closed by extensions of existing ways of thinking, but are sphinxes, riddles, their solutions likely to be astonishing and full of implication.[8]

How does *Housekeeping* bring back to life that abandoned conversation about language and limits and mystery? I've cited Gerald Bruns's suggestion that "a conversation is a good example of ungrounded talk." It is an "elucidation of the other [more] like picking up on the words in play . . . than like giving an interpretation of what someone means."[9] What *Housekeeping* does is very simple: its narrator Ruth, left on her own to make sense of the world around her by a series of deaths and losses, picks up on a series of images and situations first put into play by Emily Dickinson and speculatively re-creates her world through them. Ruth is quite literally "abandoned into a new terrain without being able to use [her] old assumptions about how to find [her] way." Robinson remarks:

> *Housekeeping* is meant as a sort of demonstration of the intellectual culture of my childhood. It was my intention to make only those allusions that would have been available to my narrator, Ruth, if she were me at her age, more or less. The classical allusions, Carthage sown with salt and the sowing of dragon's teeth which sprouted into men, stories that Ruthie combines, were both in the Latin textbook we used in Coeur d'Alene High School. My brother David brought home the fact the God is a sphere whose center is everywhere and whose circumference is nowhere. . . . Emily Dickinson and the Bible were blessedly unavoidable. There are not many references in *Housekeeping* to sources other than these few, though it is a very allusive book, because the narrator deploys every reference she has to try to make the world comprehensible. What she knows, she uses, as she does her eyes and her hands. She appropriates the ruin of Carthage for the purposes of her own speculation.[10]

Ruth, who mentions, at one point in the novel, reciting "I heard a Fly buzz—when I died—" in school (76–77), picks up or acts out a Dickinson fascinated by "subjects that resist" (J1417, F1440). Left blinded or starving or impoverished or homeless, as various poems put it, by a sense that the world is stranger or less knowable than "finite eyes" (J327, F336) have assumed, Dickinson at the same time pictures herself as feasting at a "Banquet of Abstemiousness" (J1430, F1447).[11] Ruth's tale of how she became a homeless, lyric-voiced drifter "cast out to wander" (209), "the perimeters of [whose] wandering are nowhere" (219), is, in many ways, simply a detailed fleshing-out of one of Dickinson's analogies: the account in poem J1382 (F1404) of being brought to a rich, wandering alertness by the inability to hold or recover an experience of joy.[12] Dickinson writes:

> It comes, without a consternation—
> Dissolves—the same—
> But leaves a sumptuous Destitution—
> Without a Name—
>
> Profane it by a search—we cannot
> It has no home—
> Nor we who having once inhaled it—
> Thereafter roam.

There is more, however, for Ruth not only unfolds Dickinson's analogy of wandering, homeless, through "a sumptuous Destitution," she also extends Dickinson's way of speaking, as in a conversation in which the gestures and intonations of one participant are reflected and varied and tested in those of another.[13] Abandoned into a new terrain and forced to rediscover how to speak, Ruth speculatively engages that terrain through a series of charged, only partially adequate analogies. She not only draws many of those analogies from Dickinson, she also employs them in a Dickinson-like manner, returning to Dickinson's earlier demonstration of "using all the resources of language [while] absolutely insisting that language is not an appropriate tool."

Let me begin with a single, extended example of the way her mind moves. Early in the novel, Ruth attempts to describe what she calls the strangeness of the ordinary—her sense of being "bathed in revelation." She sketches a scene, entirely speculative since it would have taken place before she was born, in which her grandmother, still in black after the death of her husband, "perform[s] the rituals of the ordinary," mutely testifying to a world and habits that once mattered to her. Think of the ordinary, Ruth instructs us, at that moment when her black-clad grandmother began to lose control of wet sheets in the wind:

One day my grandmother *must have* carried out a basket of sheets to hang in the spring sunlight, wearing her widow's black, performing the rituals of the ordinary as an act of faith. *Say* there were two or three inches of hard old snow on the ground . . . *and say* she stooped breathlessly in her corset to lift up a sodden sheet by its hems, *and say that* when she had pinned three corners to the lines it began to billow and leap in her hands, to flutter and tremble, and to glare with the light, *and that* the throes of the thing were as gleeful and strong as if a spirit were dancing in its cerements. (16, italics mine)

That scene—the lonely figure, sheets moving in the wind's suddenly visible breath—suggests another: the same wind, Ruth continues, "smell[ing] sweetly of snow, and rankly of melting snow," would have "called to mind the small, scarce, stemmy flowers that she and Edmund would walk half a day to pick" (16) high in the mountains, later, in other springs. What we realize, as we are drawn into the memory Ruth gives her grandmother of Edmund's ecstatic responses to those walks, is that Ruth is unfolding a connection between loneliness and the suddenly alive ordinary. These linked scenes are part of an "imperfectly partial" attempt to understand her own lonely world. That must be the order of things, Ruth speculates: as the world her grandparents shared each spring grew deeper and stranger, they would have each felt more and more alone. All shared responses that might have tamed or simplified that new world would have fallen away:

The rising of the spring stirred a serious, mystical excitement in him, and made him forgetful of her. He would pick up eggshells, a bird's wing, a jawbone, the ashy fragment of a wasp's nest. He would peer at each of them with the most absolute attention, and then put them in his pockets, where he kept his jackknife and his loose change. He would peer at them as if he could read them, and pocket them as if he could own them. This is death in my hand, this is ruin in my breast pocket, where I keep my reading glasses. At such times he was as forgetful of her as he was of his suspenders and his Methodism, but all the same it was then that she loved him best, as a soul all unaccompanied, like her own. (17)

Ruth continues her meditation on the strangeness of the ordinary by returning to the lonely widow and suggesting that her grandmother would also have sensed in the snapping sheets hints of long evenings spent outdoors, some time later in spring:

So the wind that billowed her sheets announced to her the resurrection of the ordinary. Soon the skunk cabbage would come up, and the cidery smell would rise in the orchard, and the girls would wash and starch and iron their cotton dresses. And every evening would bring its familiar strangeness, and crickets would sing the whole night long, under her windows and in every part of the black wilderness that stretched away from Fingerbone on every side. And she would feel that sharp loneliness she had felt every long evening since she was a child. It was the kind of loneliness that made clocks seem slow and loud and made voices sound like voices across water. Old women she had known, first her grandmother and then her mother, rocked on their porches in the evenings and sang sad songs, and did not wish to be spoken to. (17–18)

Continuing to employ the same configuration of terms, Ruth proposes that loneliness not only follows from a sense of the world's strangeness but seems to "sharp[en]" one's response to it. Those who understand the acuteness of insight that the loss of company provides would, of course, naturally wish to be left alone in order to enjoy the world's vast powers. And this thought prompts Ruth to turn the figure one last time—perhaps there is a kind of "comfort" (18) in loneliness, a comfort her grieving grandmother must have sensed when staring into the "calm inwardness" (19) of her daughters' faces. Unnoticed, she would have been "a soul all unaccompanied," the girls all but unconscious of her presence:

What was it like. One evening one summer she went out to the garden. The earth in the rows was light and soft as cinders, pale clay yellow, and the trees and plants were ripe, ordinary green and full of comfortable rustlings. And above the pale earth and bright trees the sky was the dark blue of ashes. As she knelt in the rows she heard the hollyhocks thump against the shed wall. She felt the hair lifted from her neck by a swift, watery wind, and she saw the trees fill with wind and heard their trunks creak like masts. She burrowed her hand under a potato plant and felt gingerly for the new potatoes in their dry net of roots, smooth as eggs. She put them in her apron and walked back to the house thinking, What have I seen, what have I seen. The earth and sky and the garden, not as they always are. And she saw her daughters' faces not as they always were, or as other people's were, and she was quiet and aloof and watchful, not to startle the strangeness away. (19)

As the "watery wind" filling the trees reminds us, this scene has grown out of the same wind that Ruth first imagined in her grandmother's sheets and then traced forward to her grandfather's stirring mysticism and the returning strangeness of deep spring nights. That is to say, this last scene, like the others, is entirely speculative. Working it out allows Ruth to explore the way loneliness opens one to the ordinary—proposing, in this last turn, that it is the tentativeness of one's impact, a lonely person being incapable of "startl[ing] the strangeness away," that prompts the ordinary to expand and show faces "not as they always were."

Ruth has built this meditation on traces of Dickinson's 1068 (F895), using it to voice and explore her own loneliness. Thinking about the "Druidic Difference / Enhanc[ing] Nature" when crickets celebrate their invisible, antique rituals, Dickinson describes their "unobtrusive Mass" in these terms:

> No Ordinance be seen
> So gradual the Grace
> A pensive Custom it becomes
> Enlarging Loneliness
>
> Antiquest felt at Noon
> When August burning low
> Arise this spectral Canticle
> Repose to typify

Robinson's old women and their sad songs, her newly strange ordinary sharpened and made visible by loneliness, seem to have grown from these lines. The crickets' late-August ceremony—pensive, melancholy, announcing to the world the cutting back of summer's expansion—is most powerful as it is most spectral. Like the eggshells or wasp nests carried in her grandfather's pocket, the sound of the crickets points toward a nonfamiliar world just at the reaches of human senses. Loneliness enlarges the world: the world opens out as things not familiar or known, perhaps not knowable, crowd in at the margin. Loneliness, in Dickinson, is like blindness or hunger. It is a bracing acknowledgment that the world is not available to us: it offers us no company and, like the daughters' faces, gives us no mind. But in that experience of slightness, Dickinson testifies and Ruth nods agreement, we sense a new terrain.

Robinson has traced her understanding of these Dickinsonian ideas in a number of essays. In "My Western Roots," for example, she writes that growing up she heard "the word 'lonesome' spoken in terms that let me know privilege attached to it" and recalls:

> I remember when I was a child at Coolin or Sagle or Talache, walking into the woods by myself and feeling the solitude around me build like electricity and pass through my body with a jolt that made my hair prickle. I remember kneeling by a creek that spilled and

pooled among rocks and among fallen trees with the unspeakably tender growth of small trees already sprouting from their backs, and thinking, there is only one thing wrong here, which is my own presence, and that is the slightest imaginable intrusion—feeling that my solitude, my loneliness made me almost acceptable in so sacred a place. (167–68)

Similarly, in an essay entitled "Psalm Eight," she remarks that, as a child, "when the presence of God seemed everywhere and I seemed to myself a mote of exception, improbable as a flaw in the sun, the very sweetness of the experience lay in that stinging thought—not me, not like me, not mine."[14] Dickinson, then, would have given Robinson's Ruth a way of coming to terms with loneliness—arguing that a world "not like me," a world not comfortably housed in familiar terms, is at the same time an enlarged world.

But, along with developing the links poem 1068 makes between loneliness and strangeness and largeness, these passages also experiment with Dickinson's *way* of speaking. Robert Weisbuch's book *Emily Dickinson's Poetry* (1975), a text available at the time Robinson was working on *Housekeeping*, succinctly describes the voice that Ruth extends.[15] Weisbuch sees Dickinson's work as poised at a boundary between the finished and the yet-to-be (xi). Continually drawn toward "the ungraspable" (175) only to fall back into an acknowledgment of the limits of her perceptual powers, Weisbuch's Dickinson "celebrates her insufficiency" because it shatters the notion that the world can be "confidently known" (67) and thus "elevate[s] experience . . . mak[ing] the world strange and new again" (68). One banquets on abstemiousness, then, because "only by the act of our limited perception do we learn how limited it is, how far the real is situated outside the mind's circumference" (161). But not only do Dickinson's poems celebrate insufficiency, Weisbuch claims, they also enact it at the level of language. Dickinson's "sceneless" analogies, he claims, make use of a language whose authority has been shattered, "merging . . . terms from ordinarily discrete realms of experience" (13) in a speculative series of propositions that are "not mimetic but illustratory, chosen, temporary" (16).[16] Uncovering, through a confrontation with their own limits, a world beyond mimesis, Dickinson's analogies represent, for Weisbuch, a "deepening and expansion of the meanings of language" (71).[17]

This is exactly what we see in the Robinson passages. Ruth's four versions of the newly strange ordinary—wind in a sheet, ruin in a hand, voices across water, faces not as always—are paired with four variations on the idea of being abandoned: the widow in black, a soul unaccompanied, solitary rockers, a presence too indistinct to be noticed. Stripped bare like this, the phrases resemble a Dickinson poem, and for the same reason: Ruth is at the edge of what she is able to pin down, and she too is venturing a series of possible figures. Robinson's paragraphs are "not mimetic, but illustratory"— "temporary" formulations in a series that has no stable resting point save the abandoned Ruth making sense of new terrain. Ruth's language everywhere acknowledges that it frays: say my grandmother walked out in black one spring, what would that have been like? Look at it this way, what would *that* have been like?[18] As with Dickinson, the tentative, cascading analogies remind us that something hovers just outside her mind's circumference. They pursue what Robinson in another essay calls "hint[s]." They are awakened by "the continuous sense of failure, of falling short, that makes meaning float beyond the reach of language."[19]

↪

As I've suggested, *Housekeeping* can be understood as Ruth's account of reading herself from within the terms of a Dickinson analogy: beset by many losses, she in time finds herself at peace within a "sumptuous Destitution," wandering and deeply alive within a strangeness in which she cannot be at home. And it tells the story of how Ruth came to read and speak herself in such an extraordinary way—how, words fraying in her hands, she became capable of making use of fragments of Dickinson and other writers in the way I've just described. Ruth tells that tale by unfolding a series of analogies in which, as with the series of figures linked to the black-clad window struggling with flapping sheets, one set of terms generates another, the real standing just outside each "chosen, temporary" formulation. As Ruth inhabits and gives voice to analogies, she both builds a world for herself in a place of abandonment and extends, by reenacting the manner of speaking, a conversation Dickinson had begun.

Ruth is quite literally abandoned and cut-off and lonely. She has never met her grandfather, dead in a spectacular train derailment years before she was born. Her father has vanished; her mother, returning from Seattle with Ruth and her younger sister Lucille, drowns herself in the same Idaho lake Ruth's grandfather died in; her grandmother, who raises her alongside that same lake after her mother's suicide, dies early in the novel; even her sister, companion through those lonely years, slips away in search of a more stable environment by the end of the book. All of that destitution is behind Ruth's voice when, early in the novel, she describes her grandfather's wreck: "The disaster took place midway through a moonless night. The train, which was black and sleek and elegant, and was called the Fireball, had pulled more than halfway across the bridge when the engine nosed over toward the lake and then the rest of the train slid after it into the water like a weasel sliding off a rock" (6). Because "the darkness was impenetrable to any eye" (6), there were no real witnesses, and though divers searched for hours in the nearly freezing water, the train was never located. Only a seat cushion, a suitcase, and a head of lettuce were recovered: "no relics but three, and one of them perishable" (7). With the coming of morning, Ruth imagines, ice would have begun to form:

> The sun rose higher, and the sky grew bright as tin. The surface of the lake was very still. As the boys' feet struck the water, there was a slight sound of rupture. Fragments of transparent ice wobbled on the waves they made and, when the water was calm again, knitted them-selves up like bits of reflection. . . . [Soon] the water was becoming dull and opaque, like cooling wax. Shivers flew when a swimmer sur-faced, and the membrane of ice that formed where the ice was torn looked new, glassy, and black. All the swimmers came in. By evening the lake had sealed itself over. (7–8)

Although these events happened years before her birth, Ruth keeps return-ing to them in the course of the novel, reconfiguring their elements in an attempt to think through her condition: a sudden disaster shatters the world; inexplicable vistas blink open and then vanish as the disturbed surface heals itself; ordinary things, to those with eyes to see, become relics—weightless, perishable, sodden with loss, charged by what they have brushed against.

Dickinson's work is demonstrably behind the series of analogies Ruth spins out of the derailment and its aftermath. Dickinson's term for that membrane knitting itself up at the limit of what can be known and seen is "Circumference"—her poetry a continual probing of that boundary in an attempt to discover and pass on "Odd secrets of the line" (J160, F132).[20] In poem J1084 (F1099), for example, a poem we looked at in the introduction, she charts the same predawn hours we've just seen Ruth sketch, describ-ing a single bird testing the silence with a "cautious melody" at "Half past Three" and then fully sounding its "silver Principle" at "Half past Four." She concludes, much as Ruth does, with the same scene, hours later, stripped of song and singer:

> At Half past Seven, Element
> Nor Implement, be seen—
> And Place was where the Presence was
> Circumference between.

In the same way, Ruth's sense that the ordinary is a charged relic, cut off from what really matters, can be understood as a version of Dickinson's insistence on the flimsiness of the apparently stable givens of our the world.

Left behind by Presence's vanishing, one inhabits in Dickinson a suddenly weightless ordinary—an experience other poems describe as "Philosophy" acknowledging its "baffle[ment]" or seeing acknowledging its blindness. Perhaps closest to Ruth's disappointed "no relics but three, and one of them perishable" is a Dickinson poem I have already referred to—160 and its notion of being abandoned on *this* side of the divide, the tide of Eternity washing back and leaving one with only the shore's tangles of ruins:

> Just lost, when I was saved!
> Just felt the world go by!
> Just girt me for the onset with Eternity,
> When breath blew back,
> And on the other side
> I heard recede the disappointed tide!
> . . .
> Next time, to stay!
> Next time, the things to see
> By Ear unheard,
> Unscrutinized by Eye—

Ruth first uses the "imperfectly partial" figures of wreck, sealed-over ice, and fragmentary relics to think about the effect of her grandfather's disappearance on the family he left behind. She imagines the sense of quiet that settled over the family for five years until all three daughters abruptly left home:

> One year my grandmother had three quiet daughters and the next year the house was empty. . . . Perfect quiet had settled into their house after the death of their father. That event had troubled the very medium of their lives. Time and air and sunlight bore wave after wave of shock, until all the shock was spent, and time and space and light grew still again and nothing seemed to tremble, and nothing seemed to lean. The disaster had fallen out of sight, like the train itself, and if the calm that followed it was not greater than the calm that came before it, it had seemed so. And the dear ordinary had healed as seamlessly as an image on water. (15)

The shock passed, "next time" receded from view, and the boundary between worlds seemed so permanent that the ordinary became all there was. Her grandmother was shocked at her daughters' departure, Ruth speculates, because she had been "lulled . . . into forgetting what she should never have forgotten" (13): that the ordinary was a surface phenomenon, no more stable or permanent than an image on water.

Ruth's mother Helen is one of the daughters who suddenly leaves home. She marries and eventually ends up raising two daughters, on her own, in Seattle. When, seven and a half years after leaving, she returns to the family home in Fingerbone, deposits her children on her mother's porch, and drives off a steep bank into the lake, her suicide in turn disturbs the medium of the ordinary in which Ruth and Lucille must live. Their grandmother, in Ruth's re-creation of the scene, is bewildered at being forced to relive what must have seemed an already vanished day with her own daughters and refuses this time to trust that healed-over surface:

> Indeed, it must have seemed to her that she had returned to relive this day because it was here that something had been lost or forgotten. She whited shoes and braided hair and fried chicken and turned back bedclothes, and then suddenly feared and remembered that the children had somehow disappeared, every one. How did it happen? How might she have known? . . . And it must have seemed, too, that she had only the frailest and most inappropriate tools for the most urgent uses. Once, she told us, she dreamed that she had seen a baby fall from an airplane and had tried to catch it in her apron, and once that she had tried to fish a baby out of a well with a tea strainer. (24–25)

When her grandmother dies, Ruth inherits that same sense of the charged fragility of the everyday and returns once again to the book's opening images to describe her own sense of alarm. The town takes note of her grandmother's death by revisiting, with a black-bordered feature in the local paper, the spectacular derailment of her grandfather's train:

> it was considered an impressive tribute to her and was expected to be a source of pride to us. I was simply alarmed. It suggested to me that the earth had opened. In fact, I dreamed that I was walking across the ice on the lake, which was breaking up as it does in the spring, softening and shifting and pulling itself apart. But in the dream the surface that I walked on proved to be knit up of hands and arms and upturned faces that shifted and quickened as I stepped, sinking only for a moment into lower relief under my weight. The dream and the obituary together created in my mind the conviction that my grandmother had entered into some other element upon which our lives floated as weightless, intangible, immiscible, and inseparable as reflections in water. She was borne to the depths, my grandmother, into the undifferentiated past, and

her comb had no more of the warmth of a hand about it than Helen of Troy's would have. (41)

Ruth powerfully reimagines her world by means of the figures of wreck, ice, and relics here. This last disaster, reminding her of a world beyond circumference, insists that the ordinary is no more than a fragile skin or reflective play of light temporarily settling over "some other element" deeper and more alive than the "weightless" and "intangible" images floating on its surface. The stirred up, constantly reforming reflections that make up her world will never settle or grow stable; "inseparable" from that other world they speak so glancingly for, they are also "immiscible"—never fully a part of what they float upon.

Growing up in the wake of these losses, then, Ruth comes to understand herself as abandoned, left behind in the trembling ordinary to sort through shards and fragments. She refuses to fall back into the sleepy dream life she had imagined for her grandmother. Circumference doesn't reassure her about this world; it torments her with rumors of another. The flooding of the town one spring pictures what is for her a permanent transformation of the ordinary:

> During those days Fingerbone was strangely transformed. If one should be shown odd fragments arranged on a silver tray and be told, "That is a splinter from the True Cross, and that is a nail paring dropped by Barrabas, and that is a bit of lint from under the bed where Pilate's wife dreamed her dream," the very ordinariness of the things would recommend them. Every spirit passing through the world fingers the tangible and mars the mutable, and finally has come to look and not to buy. . . . So Fingerbone, or such relics of it as showed above the mirroring waters, seemed fragments of the quotidian held up to our wondering attention, offered somehow as proof of their own significance. (73)

The flood's charged, once-significant but now abandoned relics are for Ruth ways of visualizing both her inner and outer worlds. Haunted by half-held memories and always shifting thoughts about her vanished mother, Ruth is tormented by the ordinary work of thinking and remembering—by their weightless and fragmentary inability to grasp what dances just beyond them. She is, as Dickinson puts it in an elegy for *her* mother, "Homeless at home" (J1573, F1603). Memories, she knows, even ones like the treasured and passed-down tale of the train wreck or the glimpse of her grandmother at her wash we began with, "are by their nature fragmented, isolated, and arbitrary as glimpses one has at night through lighted windows" (53). Thoughts are equally fragmentary, bewilderingly so:

> For why do our thoughts turn to some gesture of a hand, the fall of a sleeve, some corner of a room on a particular anonymous afternoon, even when we are asleep, and even when we are so old that our thoughts have abandoned other business? What are all these fragments for, if not to be knit up finally? (92)

Her gradual acknowledgment, as the novel goes on, that these fragments will never be knit up leaves Ruth feeling tricked by the world. It is no wonder that, at times, she yearns, like her mother, to free herself permanently from the deceptive and accidental and arbitrary:

> Everything that falls upon the eye is apparition, a sheet dropped over the world's true workings. The nerves and the brain are tricked, and one is left with dreams that these specters loose their hands from ours and walk away, the curve of the back and the swing of the coat so familiar as to imply that they should be permanent fixtures of the world, when in fact nothing is more perishable. *Say* that my mother was as tall as a man, and that she sometimes set me on her shoulders, so that I could splash my hands in the cold leaves above our heads. *Say* that my grandmother sang in her throat while she sat on her bed and we laced up her big black shoes. Such details are merely accidental. Who could know but us? And since their thoughts were bent upon other ghosts than ours, other darknesses than we had seen, why must we be left, the survivors picking among flotsam, among the small, unnoticed, unvalued clutter that was all that remained when they vanished, that only catastrophe made notable? Darkness is the only solvent. . . . it seemed to me that there need not be relic, remnant, margin, residue, memento, bequest, memory, thought, track, or trace, if only the darkness could be perfect and permanent. (116, italics mine)

Abandoned, weightless, cut off from a world that seems truer and more permanent than hers, Ruth is overwhelmed with a sense of her own finitude. At the limits of knowing, thoughts and memories and bits of poems seem as fragile and "accidental" as debris on a shoreline. Who could be satisfied with such clutter? "Next time" seems never to come. Oh that it could be otherwise, Ruth laments. The reason Ruth doesn't give into that yearning and follow her mother's lead, I want to suggest, is because she gradually works out a Dickinsonian response to the residue and relics that make up the sealed-off ordinary. Becoming aware of the fragility of "memory, thought, track, or trace," that "small, unnoticed, unvalued clutter," not only closes off one way of speaking, it opens up another. In Robinson's phrase, Ruth is "delivered into something that requires a new articulation." And it is in working with a second set of Dickinson images that Ruth feels her way toward this new response to Circumference's promises and torments.

This new articulation is modeled for Ruth by her Aunt Sylvie, who returns to Fingerbone to raise the two girls after the death of their grandmother. An incurable wanderer, Sylvie is an embodiment of Dickinson's notion of being "Homeless at home." Her habits, Ruth remarks "(she always slept clothed, at first with her shoes on, and then, after a month or two, with her shoes under her pillow) were clearly the habits of a transient" (103) and suggest that houses are fragile and impermanent and arbitrary. The two sisters react in different ways to Sylvie's embrace of fragility. Lucille eventually turns her back on it, while Ruth is drawn to what it produces—in Dickinson's terms, a "Susceptive" ear, responsive to "Reportless Measures" (J1048, F1118) outside of normal earshot. Even in her early days with the girls, Sylvie's ease with the eroding of boundaries pulls them in different ways, as when the first floor of the house floods: "Sylvie took me by the hands and pulled me after her through six grand waltz steps. The house flowed around us. Lucille pulled the front door open and the displacement she caused made one end of the woodpile in the porch collapse and tipped a chair, spilling a bag of clothespins" (64).

In undermining what we might call the "premise" of stability, Sylvie introduces a more open sort of housekeeping. Soon after she arrives, leaves and scraps of paper begin to gather in corners of the house:

> She had to have been aware of them because every time a door was opened anywhere in the house there was a sound from all the corners of lifting and alighting. I noticed that the leaves would be lifted up by something that came before the wind, they would tack against some impalpable movement of air several seconds before the wind was heard in the trees. Thus finely did our house become attuned to the orchard and to the particularities of weather, even in the first days of Sylvie's housekeeping. (85)

Sylvie also "liked to eat supper in the dark," rapt before a window luminous in the evening. Reminding one of Dickinson's blinded speaker who, "with just [her] soul / Upon the Window pane" (J327, F336), sees in an extraordinarily sensitive "other way," Sylvie demonstrates for the girls a way of seeing that embraces the house's permeability:

Opposite her was a window luminous and cool as aquarium glass and warped as water. We looked at the window as we ate, and we listened to the crickets and nighthawks, which were always unnaturally loud then, perhaps because they were within the bounds that light would fix around us, or perhaps because one sense is a shield for the others and we had lost our sight. (86)

In refusing to shore up the house or to make herself comfortable within its ordinarily accepted claims to shelter or wall out, Sylvie embraces its finitude or brokenness:

She seemed to dislike the disequilibrium of counterpoising a roomful of light against a worldful of darkness. Sylvie in a house was more or less like a mermaid in a ship's cabin. She preferred it sunk in the very element it was meant to exclude. We had crickets in the pantry, squirrels in the eaves, sparrows in the attic. [When we came home] Lucille and I stepped through the door from sheer night to sheer night. (99)

At the turning point of the novel, when Lucille and Ruth separate after a night spent nearly in the open under a collapsing structure they build alongside the lake, Ruth explicitly aligns herself with Sylvie's notion of an attuned, permeable house. Even as Lucille spends the night doggedly refusing to accept "that all our human boundaries were overrun" (115), Ruth discovers herself exhilarated by that loss, "the darkness in the sky becom[ing] coextensive with the darkness in my skull and bowels and bones" (116), and it becomes clear that the sisters have chosen different paths:

It seemed to me then that Lucille would busy herself forever, nudging, pushing, coaxing, as if she could supply the will I lacked, to pull myself into some seemly shape and slip across the wide frontiers into that other world, where it seemed to me then I could never wish to go. For it seemed to me that nothing I had lost, or might lose, could be found there, or, to put it another way, it seemed that something I had lost might be found in Sylvie's house. . . . It seemed to me that what perished need not also be lost. . . . Sylvie, I knew, felt the life of perished things. (123–24)

Sylvie, to cite the Dickinson poem behind all of this, feels the life of perished things because she dwells in their continuing possibility:

I dwell in Possibility—
A fairer House than Prose—
More numerous of Windows—
Superior—for Doors—

Of Chambers as the Cedars—
Impregnable of Eye—
And for an Everlasting Roof
The Gambrels of the Sky—

Of Visitors—the fairest—
For Occupation—This—
The spreading wide my narrow Hands
To gather Paradise—   (J657, F466)

Robinson remarks in an essay that "to the degree that [Sylvie] has not taken the impress of society she expresses the fact that human nature is replete with nameless *possibilities*, and, by implication, that the world is accessible to new ways of understanding" (italics mine).[21] To choose the world of prose, as Lucille does when she goes to live with her home economics teacher, is to accept "the impress of society"—"some seemly shape" (123). It is to have crossed "wide frontiers" into a settled world where, Ruth suspects, "nothing . . . lost . . . could be found" (123). To dwell in possibility is to be attuned to the impalpable (possibility's house has numerous windows, and its roof is the sky) and yet to feel secure enough for the most intimate growth (its house has superior doors and impregnable chambers). One's time is occupied, in possibility, in "spreading . . . narrow Hands / To gather Paradise." As Robert Weisbuch notes, narrow hands are limited.[22] Like Sylvie's house "sunk in the very element it was meant to exclude," narrow hands can't grasp or hold anything that matters, but as they spread wide and let "paradise" slip through, they are attuned to its existence, alert to its gathering possibility.[23]

To follow Sylvie's lead and dwell in possibility, Ruth must develop her own way of living within limits. She must learn to use her own narrow hands. Which is to say, no longer comfortably at home within the play of memory and observation—homeless, in fact, within a world continually tormenting her with glimpses of her mother in the face of a woman staring out of a passing train or in the posture of a melting snow statue or in her aunt's absent-minded angling of her head before a mirror—Ruth must nonetheless learn to dwell within the possibilities they open up. For Ruth, such thoughts and memories and observations are "as weightless, intangible, immiscible, and inseparable as reflections in water" (41). They are fragments, relics, and are as fragile as Sylvie knows houses to be. In working out an attuned way of speaking that allows her to dwell in them like Sylvie in her darkened kitchen, then, Ruth unfolds a version of Dickinson's attuned poetics.

After her sister leaves her, Ruth is taken by Sylvie across the lake to a valley trapped between steep hills where Sylvie is convinced that lost children play near a ruined house. There, a powerful drama is staged. The scene is established slowly. When the two arrive, having crossing the lake in a stolen boat, everything is white with frost—locked up and dead. They wait until noon, at which point the light coaxes "a flowering from the frost, which before seemed barren and parched as salt" (152). Barrenness flowing into new life plays before Ruth as a tantalizing vision:

> Imagine a Carthage sown with salt, and all the sowers gone, and the seeds lain however long in the earth, till there rose finally in vegetable profusion leaves and trees of rime and brine. What flowering would there be in such a garden? Light would force each salt calyx to open in prisms, and to fruit heavily with bright globes of water—peaches and grapes are little more than that, and where the world was salt there would be greater need of slaking. For need can blossom into all the compensation it requires. To crave and to have are as like as a thing and its shadow. For when does a berry break upon the tongue as sweetly as when one longs to taste it, and when is the taste refracted into so many hues and savors of ripeness and earth, and when do our senses know any thing so utterly as when we lack it? . . . So whatever we may lose, very craving gives it back to us again. (152–53)

Ruth's description of the rich play of light picks up on Dickinson's "Success is counted sweetest / By those who ne'er succeed. / To comprehend a nectar / Requires sorest need" (J67, F112)—lines at the heart of Robinson's conversation with Dickinson. Dickinson's insistence that an acknowledgment of need or failure or narrowness destroys a settled view of the world and opens up the possibility of a larger view is just what Sylvie has been modeling with her permeable house "sunk in the very element it was meant to exclude." It is enacted here in the exuberant blossoming of the seemingly salt-parched landscape. "Need can blossom into . . . compensation," this scene suggests, because "crav[ing]" reveals facets and hues and savors that mere "hav[ing]" knows only the "shadow" of. Craving, like loneliness or like the acknowledgment of the flimsiness and partiality of memory, enlarges the world.

As Ruth marvels, Sylvie disappears. Alone, sitting on a log, Ruth remarks: "I knew why Sylvie felt there were children in the woods. I felt so, too, though I did not think so" (154).[24] Why is that? The word that gives her access to what follows when one has "finished knowing—" is Dickinson's *loneliness*—the word we traced through Ruth's meditation on her mourning grandmother. Loneliness, she senses—mother, grandmother, sister, and now her aunt all gone—has left her without a visible or stable set of premises in which to dwell, but it has also, like Sylvie rapt in the darkened house, opened up a world otherwise lost:

> Having a sister or a friend is like sitting at night in a lighted house. Those outside can watch you if they want, but you need not see them. You simply say, "Here are the perimeters of our attention. If you prowl around under the windows till the crickets go silent, we will pull the shades. If you wish us to suffer your envious curiosity, you must permit us not to notice." Anyone with one solid human bond is that smug, and it is the smugness as much as the comfort and safety that lonely people covet and admire. I had been, so to speak, turned out of house now long enough to have observed this in myself. Now there was neither threshold nor sill between me and these cold, solitary children who almost breathed against my cheek and almost touched my hair. (154)

Revealing our essential homelessness, loneliness erases thresholds and sills; it eliminates the smug, solid sense that the lit world—the world above the ice, or on this side of circumference—is all there is. Now Ruth sees that "roomful of light" as simply an illusion. She is adrift in a different, larger, and more terrifying world: "Loneliness is an absolute discovery. When one looks from inside at a lighted window, or looks from above at the lake, one sees the image of oneself in a lighted room, the image of oneself among trees and sky—the deception is obvious, but flattering all the same. When one looks from the darkness into the light, however, one sees all the difference between here and there, this and that" (157–58). Having been out in the dark, Ruth knows there is something beyond the limits of the lit world: call it a "Druidic Difference" (J1068), a world "not me, not like me, not mine." It almost breathes against her cheek, almost touches her hair.

What does Ruth make of that insight? How does she employ her narrow hands in that enlarging world? How does she dwell in Possibility? Simply put, she takes Sylvie's story of lost, abandoned children and plays it out. Staring at the ruins of a collapsed homestead near where she sits, Ruth commits herself to the possible presence of the invisible children. It is as if she says, with her body, "*Say* there were children living in this fragile house":

> I began pulling loose planks out of the cellar hole, the right corner at the front. . . . I began to imagine myself a rescuer. Children had been sleeping in this fallen house. Soon I would uncover the rain-stiffened hems of their nightshirts, and their small, bone feet, the toes all fallen like petals. . . . I imagined myself in their place—it was not hard to do this, for the appearance of relative solidity in my grandmother's house was deceptive. It was an impression created by the piano, and the scrolled couch, and the bookcases full of almanacs and Kipling and Defoe. For all the appearance these things gave of

substance and solidity, they might better be considered a dangerous weight on a frail structure. (158–59)

This is an extraordinary moment. Ruth, like Robinson's nineteenth-century models, has been quite literally "delivered into something that requires a new articulation" and responds by speculatively imagining her participation in a new form of reality. Of course, she knows the inadequacy and partiality of her metaphor—knows that it crumbles in the face of the open world it holds itself before: "And despite the stories I made up to myself, I knew there were no children trapped in this meager ruin. They were light and spare and thoroughly used to the cold, and it was almost a joke to them to be cast out into the woods, even if their eyes were gone and their feet were broken" (159).

And what does Ruth gain from this new, hands-on way of "speaking"?

I thought, Sylvie is nowhere, and sometime it will be dark. I thought, Let them come unhouse me of this flesh, and pry this house apart. It was no shelter now, it only kept me here alone, and I would rather be with them, if only to see them, even if they turned away from me. If I could see my mother, it would not have to be her eyes, her hair. I would not need to touch her sleeve. There was no more the stoop of her high shoulders. The lake had taken that, I knew. It was so very long since the dark had swum her hair, and there was nothing more to dream of, but often she almost slipped through any door I saw from the side of my eye, and it was she, and not changed, and not perished. She was a music I no longer heard, that rang in my mind, itself and nothing else, lost to all sense, but not perished, not perished. (159–60)

Ruth has entered into the world of Possibility. Her fraying language (herself as rescuer of lost children) has allowed her to enter into a deeper and larger reality where her mother, although "lost to all sense," has "not perished." Her language and her actions are attuned to that reality because she is "unhoused." There are no longer any conventional assurances for her to dwell in. They have been stripped away and discarded.

Ruth finally articulates what has in fact been visible throughout the novel. Cut off from her mother who can no longer be touched or known or even dreamed of, Ruth has been catching glimpses of her everywhere. Her mother has become enlarged—a "taste refracted into so many hues and savors" that "often she almost slipped through any door I saw from the side of my eye." Unhoused, Ruth discovers that her mother has become "gigantic and multiple . . . extraordinary by [her] vanishing" (195), "not perished."

In fact, Ruth muses as she and Sylvie spend that night on the water, making their way home from that ruin-filled valley, the world is filled with thousands of such weightless images.[25] Call them relics. Call them the ordinary and the accidental—the given. None of them is capable of mastering or reflecting or bringing back what is moving or lost to us—a fact obscured by the well-lit rooms we normally inhabit, but visible to loneliness—and yet, in the hands of the right sort of housekeeper, their glancing presence speaks of a world slipping free of their narrow hands:

> What is thought, after all, what is dreaming, but swim and flow, and the images they seem to animate. . . . They mock us with their seeming slightness. If they were more substantial—if they had weight and took up space—they would sink or be carried away in the general flux. But they persist, outside the brisk and ruinous energies of the world. I think it must have been my mother's plan to rupture this bright surface, to sail beneath it into very blackness, but here she was, wherever my eyes fell, and behind my eyes, whole and in fragments, a thousand images of one gesture, never dispelled but rising always, inevitably, like a drowned woman. (162–63)

Thought animates such weightless, accidental images, Ruth sees—and in seeing this, is able to pass beyond her mother's final rejection of the finite world. As she discovered in the frost-covered valley, thought, in committing itself to such fragments, flows through them, stirs their bright surfaces. It takes up residence within dead images and makes them into permeable, responsive, attuned houses.

When Ruth puts into words what she has learned from Sylvie's modeling, then, we understand that she is talking about having learned to think and handle the world's insubstantial images, sunk in the very world they had been thought to be excluded from: "I dreamed that Sylvie was teaching me to walk under water. To move so slowly needed patience and grace, but she pulled me after her in the slowest waltz, and our clothes flew like the robes of painted angels" (175). That this is in fact a description of the slow patient style of Ruth's own narration—her voice, in its speculative *says* and *imagines*, an example of New's "blind and wandering language," a slow waltz through a vast world of fragments, none of which offers a permanent home—becomes clear near the close of the novel, when Ruth formalizes what she has taken from Sylvie and what the retrospective voice of the novel has in fact all along been demonstrating.[26] After Ruth's and Sylvie's night on the lake has convinced the people of Fingerbone of Sylvie's instability and set in motion a plan to place Ruth under the care of the state, the two burn a great pile of accumulated papers and magazines in a last attempt to convince the town of their seriousness about proper housekeeping. Consumed pages, "the print and the dark parts of pictures turned silvery black" (199), swirl above the fire and explode in "cinders and motes" (200). Completing her book-length meditation on the weightlessness and insubstantiality of images and memories, family bonds and houses, Ruth remarks on the fragility of words: "It had never occurred to me that words, too, must be salvaged, though when I thought about it, it seemed obvious. It was absurd to think that things were held in place, are held in place, by a web of words" (200). Words, in their fragility, have become Ruth's way of wandering and eating in the dark. They are the narrow hands she spreads wide, their very limits opening a world of possibility.

Night descends, they cover the ashes with dirt, and then Ruth drifts away from Sylvie back into the dark orchard. They play a sort of a game, Sylvie calling "Come in where it's warm" and Ruth staying just out of reach. At one point, Ruth gazes from the dark at their house and remarks: "The house stood out beyond the orchard with every one of its windows lighted. It looked large, and foreign, and contained, like a moored ship—a fantastic thing to find in a garden. I could not imagine going into it" (203). All lit up, that house is an image of stability and confinement—an illusion, Ruth knows, not to be trusted. But then an interesting thing happens: Ruth tells herself a story about the threatening house. She turns to her newly freed language and spins out a fable that releases her from the house's power. She enters the house with her words and, quite literally, wanders through it—standing blind before its bright windows, experiencing the loss of everything that matters. She sketches an analogy—a speculative figure "not mimetic but illustratory, chosen, temporary"—and at that moment formally takes on her broken, lyric voice with which she'll go on to produce the novel we are reading:

> Once there was a young girl strolling at night in an orchard. She came to a house she had never seen before, all alight so that through any window she could see curious ornaments and marvelous comforts. A door stood open, so she walked inside. It would be that kind of story, a very melancholy story. . . . She would be transformed by the gross light into a mortal child. And when she stood at the bright window, she would find that the world was gone, the orchard was gone, her mother and grandmother and aunts were gone. . . . And those outside would scarcely know her, so sadly was she changed. Before, she had been fleshed in air and clothed in nakedness and mantled in cold, and her very bones were only slender things, like shafts of ice. . . . And now, lost to her kind, she would almost forget

them, and she would feed coarse food to her coarse flesh, and be almost satisfied. (203–4)

The "moored" house—initially "foreign, and contained"—has been refigured as an aspect of Ruth's meditative house of possibility. This is exactly what Ruth has done in entering the figure of her mourning-clad grandmother or in working with the weightless, fragmentary memories of her mother. No longer taken in by the smug, warm rooms of conventional agreements about the world, aware that its images and terms and major voices are weightless relics, she has nonetheless learned to dwell within them, "homeless at home" and attuned through their brokenness to what's "not me, not like me, not mine." She has accepted the cold and her loneliness, having come to see how much could be made of the fact that "the combined effects of cold, tedium, guilt, loneliness, and dread sharpened our senses wonderfully" (79). As Ruth puts it now:

> I learned an important thing in the orchard that night, which was that if you do not resist the cold, but simply relax and accept it, you no longer feel the cold as discomfort. I felt giddily free and eager, as you do in dreams, when you suddenly find that you can fly, very easily, and wonder why you have never tried it before. (204)

It should come as no surprise, then, that one of the weightless relics that Ruth animates in this little fable is a Dickinson poem, for it is Dickinson's fraying voice, alive "at the limits of [her] ability to comprehend or articulate," that Ruth is most in conversation with. Dickinson's 579 (F 439) is also a liberating fable about going inside a house whose windows the speaker had hungrily peered through for years:

> I had been hungry, all the Years—
> My Noon had Come—to dine—
> I trembling drew the Table near—
> And touched the Curious Wine—
>
> 'Twas this on Tables I had seen—
> When turning, hungry, Home
> I looked in Windows, for the Wealth
> I could not hope—for Mine—

As with Ruth's story, the speaker here is also changed by actually gaining what she had yearned for—another "melancholy story." Ruth's "mortal child" "feed[ing] coarse food to her coarse flesh," no longer "clothed in nakedness and mantled in cold," is a fleshing-out of Dickinson's satiated, no longer gifted or responsive speaker:

The Plenty hurt me—'twas so new—
Myself felt ill—and odd—
As Berry—of a Mountain Bush—
Transplanted—to the Road—

Nor was I hungry—so I found
That Hunger—was a way
Of Persons outside Windows—
That Entering—takes away—

What Dickinson gives Robinson, I have been suggesting, is not just the basic terms of many of Ruth's analogies but a way of employing them—"no longer feel[ing] the cold as discomfort" (204), moving freely through the boundless spaces cold or loneliness or partiality open up. To have learned to say "Say she stooped breathlessly in her corset to lift up a sodden sheet by its hems" (16) is to proclaim "What have I seen, what have I seen" (19) and glory in your limits.

TWO

INTERVIEW WITH
MARILYNNE ROBINSON

TG: In an interview in the *Iowa Review* a number of years ago, speaking about Dickinson and Emerson and Melville, you said a fascinating thing: "There's been a rupture in the conversation of this culture. All sorts of things that were brought up in the early conversation were dropped without being resolved." Could you go on with that thought? What issues do you have in mind?

MR: Well, for me the germinal issue is the issue of perception and metaphor. I took a course at college in nineteenth-century American literature, and it was good and interesting. The professor talked a great deal about Melville's metaphysics and metaphors, and Thoreau's, and so on, and it seemed to me that I didn't understand the intellectual culture that surrounded what they did. In a certain way I've spent a lot of years trying to figure out what it was—trying to restore the larger context that made them turn to metaphor so consistently with the assumption that they would be able to make meaning of the highest order from the lyrical. It's not ornamental. Their metaphorical writing is never ornamental. In fact, it draws attention to itself in order either to rupture the illusion that it has created because of the intrinsic beauty of making a good metaphor, or it draws attention to itself by awkwardness or improbability, as Emily Dickinson does so often. There was something in the intellectual culture that was yielding use of language and use of perception at very high levels of sophistication. It had to do with what, I suppose, one has to describe as the individualism of the culture, in the sense that the individual sensorium was assumed to be a sort of sacred place and to be a sufficient revelation of whatever there was to be understood. At a certain point, the culture turned to talking in terms that were much closer to sociology than to metaphysics.

TG: And so metaphor dropped out?

MR: It ceased to be exploratory. When Frank Norris uses a metaphor, it works more like allegory. The point being to make clear, unmistakable structures for the reader. There's an element of didacticism.

TG: Because he knew what he thought already?

MR: He knew what he thought already. It wasn't a way of thinking. It was a way of instructing—two very different things. I think that the impulse to instruct and to make historical pronouncements rather than individual discoveries became more and more characteristic. In the best writers, this is never characteristic. Faulkner uses the sensorium in very much the same way that the earlier writers did. So does Hemingway at his best. So does Eudora Welty at her best. But as an acknowledged project of understanding, it seems to me to have passed out of the culture. For someone like Walt Whitman, of course, perception is meaningful in the sense of being integrative; it is not a report on reality but it is the primary locus of reality itself.

TG: Perception is the primary locus of reality?

MR: Yes. The idea that being is addressed to us. It is not something that exists independently of us upon which we report. It goes back to Puritanism. Puritanism is one of the things I'm trying to excavate because it seems to me that there is now a very reductionist understanding of it. It is very strange. I was reading something that Isaac Newton wrote about the fact that his understanding of planetary motion did not align with biblical arguments. He said that the Bible wasn't written for scientists and mathematicians; it was written to be meaningful in terms of the understanding of ordinary people, to be meaningful in terms of perception. Of course, Isaac Newton was a mystic and a Puritan also. As was John Locke. In saying this, in giving this account of the double nature of the universe, he's quoting Calvin. That comes from Calvin's commentary on Genesis. It means that, on the one hand, there's more to reality than we perceive, and on the other hand, what we perceive is also a language through which things are communicated to us. Something that can be understood scientifically or intellectually, and something that can be understood simply at the level of perception, exist side by side without contradiction.

TG: Double nature?

MR: Of being. When you read Dickinson, one thing that is very striking is that she moves back and forth over time between the language of learning, good science in terms of the time, and the language of perception.

TG: In "A Light exists in Spring," she writes about a quality of light that "Science cannot overtake / But Human Nature feels."

MR: Exactly. Doubleness is characteristic of her writing. Her poems almost always set one mode of perceiving against another, not canceling either, and I think that's very important. Reality is something that is available to us to know and to sense, and on the other hand it is emblematically meaning-ful—how it appears also communicates. This frees science, for one thing, because there is no objective reality more powerful than experiential reality, even though the two are not at odds with each other.

TG: Because experiential reality is a doorway?

MR: Here is a paragraph I use fairly often when I'm teaching. It's a passage from Jonathan Edwards's "Doctrine of Original Sin Defended":

> It will follow from what has been observed, that God's upholding of created substance, or causing of its existence in each successive moment, is altogether equivalent to an *immediate production out of nothing*, at each moment. Because its existence at this moment is not merely in part from *God*, but wholly from him; and not in any part, or degree, from its *antecedent existence*. . . . So that this effect differs not at all from the first creation, but only *circumstantially*; as, in the *first* creation there had been no such act and effect of God's power *before*: whereas his giving existence afterwards, *follows* preceding acts and effects of the same kind, in an established order. . . . And there is no identity or oneness in the case, but what depends on the *arbitrary* constitution of the Creator; who by his wise sovereign establishment so unites these successive new effects, that he *treats them as one*, by communicating to them like properties, relations, and circumstances; and so, leads *us* to regard and treat them as one. When I call this an *arbitrary constitution*, I mean, that it is a constitution which depends on nothing but the *divine will*; which divine will depends on nothing but the *divine wisdom*. In this sense the whole *course of nature* with all that belongs to it, all its laws and methods, constancy and regularity,

continuance and proceeding, is an *arbitrary constitution*. For it does not at all *necessarily* follow, that because there was sound, or light, or colour, or resistance, or gravity, or thought, or consciousness, or any other dependent thing the last moment, that there shall be like at the next. All dependent existence whatsoever is in a constant flux, ever passing and returning; renewed every moment, as the colours of bodies are every moment renewed by the light that shines upon them; and all is constantly proceeding from God, as light from the sun. *In him we love and move and have our being.*

This phrase of his, "the arbitrary constitution of the universe," means that things are the way they are because that's how God created them and sustains them.

TG: Why is the word *arbitrary* in there?

MR: He's saying in effect that there's not a mechanistic causality in things—that things are the way they are because they express the will of God. The ongoingness of things is not sustained out of material necessity. His conception is Newtonian. The old commentators on Edwards saw that. Of course Newton said that the planets were kept in their orbits by the grace of God, which other people call gravity, which he called gravity—but nevertheless, the idea that there was nothing inevitable in it, that there was an intrinsically arbitrary quality, is Newtonian. The Blakean idea, which people have taken very seriously, is that Newton's thinking was purely mechanistic. But this is a misunderstanding of Newton. A good deal of Puritan thought comes out of an extremely sophisticated understanding of the best then-contemporary science, or is completely at home in it. This sort of thinking reconciles better with current physics than does virtually any other theological understanding of reality. For whatever reason that's true, it's too valuable a thing to let go. The idea that the Puritans had a simple or rigid conception of anything is wrong. And I think you have to understand Dickinson in terms of the real sophistication of the intellectual culture she came from to actually understand what she's doing.

TG: Let's focus a bit on metaphor and perception. Can you talk about differences in metaphorical thinking in Dickinson, Thoreau, and Melville? Differences in how they build and cancel metaphors?

MR: To a certain extent, there's a difference in subject. In the case of Melville, he's actually casting nets, trying to get some part of the cosmos in them. He's after very big game. He's trying over and over again. It's extraordinarily beautiful. He sees something about the world that is overwhelmingly beautiful to him; he develops a description of it which would seem to be a comprehension of it; then everything changes—this utter mobility of being, this utter plasticity. The feeling of exaltation in that book is so wonderful: I can do anything. But the point is always that it doesn't work. The cosmos shifts and shows another side, and what had been erected collapses. In a way, it reminds you of prophetic writing in the Old Testament where every vision is pulled down. The burden of it for the prophet is to invoke an order of being much higher than what is actual. That is pretty much what Melville is doing also. I think that he is agnostic, relative to the others, that he doesn't know what he is describing.

I think that Thoreau probably fits intellectually into the interest at that time in imagining a way of living ethically, in the world. He starts out talking about economic theory in *Walden*. In contemporary British and European writing there was a great deal of talk about subsistence, because the assumption was that the poor would always drift down to the level of subsistence and you'd have to make subsistence tolerable. In America, the issue was how to develop without developing all the dreadful things that were aspects of the elaborated economies of Europe: the wretchedness of the working class, starvation. I think that *Walden* is about a life at the level of subsistence, which is utterly the level of the sensorium. In other words, it's a stripping away of the world in terms of hierarchy or luxury or attainment, where the sole resource is perception and reflection. The point of the book is that these things by themselves are fully sufficient. In England at the time, the grounds for depriving people of political rights were that they were degraded by poverty. Economic inequalities were used to justify social and political inequality—for example, restriction of the right to vote. That has nothing to do with Thoreau's meaning. His meaning is that people who live at whatever degree of simplicity are still the primary locus of reality, whose experience is still utterly meaningful. It is possible for people to subsist, materially, while retaining their full humanity. There is no diminution of human brilliance or dignity as a result. Quite the opposite. Thoreau makes the point that the "subsistence" of the economists can be the "simplicity" of the mystics—or the transcendentalists. Again, going back to Newton, even though what Thoreau says comes through the mind of a naturalist and a Harvard grad, it also functions at the same level of the inner man. It's meaningful to know whatever you can know, but it's equally meaningful or even privileged to see how things look, to perceive without special understanding.

TG: Does Thoreau let his metaphors go in the same way Melville does?

MR: I don't think so. In a certain way, there's flux. The given of the world-view is that everything is continually made new, a new world is being spoken all the time, but . . . I think that Thoreau is basically a more peaceful spirit; he's at peace with what he feels and discovers, and does not characteristically do that.

TG: And Dickinson?

MR: She is always talking about change in states of consciousness. How to describe it? You know that revival that went through Mt. Holyoke when she was there? The culture was very, very full of that sort of thing. It's one of the uncapturable things about American cultural history. The Second Great Awakening was basically many people having visionary experiences—people like Charles Grandison Finney and George Washington Gale, and so on. They would have these visions, and it is interesting to read about them; they would normally be visions of Jesus, and what Jesus told them was "Free the slaves." It had the authority of occurring in the intellectual classes and having strong Abolitionist credentials. These revival experiences were simply assumed to be valuable, assumed to be essential in a way. I think, when she's moving back and forth, in terms of imagining the transformation of consciousness, that this is at least a major metaphor for her. In terms of the culture, it meant stepping over a threshold. The assumption was that you were radically changed and your perception would not be the same afterwards as it was before. What you perceived after this experience was . . . like those texts in Paul's letters where things are simultaneously part of the world to come and part of present experience. That's the sort of text they would use.

TG: Would you call this a conversion experience?

MR: They used the word *conversion* in a very special sense. They didn't mean that you were converted to a Methodist from a Presbyterian. It tended to be a visionary experience, some kind of overwhelming experience. It took you from normal religiosity or normal piety into something much more intense. For example, you understand on the one hand that the world is quotidian, but then something else leads you to think, well, it's a complete anomaly relative to anything else we know about in the universe. It's utterly fragile, it's utterly peculiar to itself. For a moment, you can see that, but you can't sustain the understanding. What we call reality is a great distraction from everything we know to be real, and I think in a way she is talking about that, except that reality for her has the other charge, that secondary Newtonian charge, of also being meaningful as perceived.

TG: So, that's a central pattern to how her poetry works. But oddly, she didn't claim this experience herself. How does it come to be so central?

MR: It was something that probably everyone in her surroundings would have called the essential experience of life. I assume that people who felt this were very observant of themselves. The assumption was that it was something that befell you, not something that you did, and that it would befall you as an alteration of consciousness. Inevitably, if this was an issue in one's mind, then experience would be tested continuously relative to the question of whether a change in consciousness was merely wished for or was in fact real. I have respect for this religious mentality. It did worlds of good, it was brilliant in many of its manifestations, but I don't want to reduce her thinking to that either. But I do think this pattern in the culture directed attention intensely to inward experience and to the fact that we do actually stand apart from our inward experience.

TG: She sometimes breaks the figures of her poems down into Me and Myself.

MR: Exactly. There's often a tone of parody: I thought this, and I did that, and then . . . And it's as if she's watching herself from a distance and whenever delusion may have led her to see something in a certain light, she seems to be conscious of it, and at the same time she sees that even the delusion has a great dignity. I think that she's a profound student of her own consciousness and that breaking it into parts is a mode of understanding. She watches herself think and feel with such utter care and objectivity.

TG: Would you describe your own history with Dickinson?

MR: I think I came across Emily Dickinson in the usual way, originally. She was in textbooks and I had to do reports on her poems in high school. And then my brother brought me home a copy of her collected works at Christmas. He said that he had given it to me because I had also "feasted on abstemiousness," which I thought was an interesting insight.

TG: And do you read her regularly now, or in spasms of attention?

MR: Spasms of attention. It's funny, I pick up a book and read one of her poems and I think this is such an amazing poem that I will never forget it. And then I read twelve of them and think these are twelve poems I'll never forget. In the oddest way, unless I utterly memorize them, they always seem new to me. There are very few of them that I feel I have "appropriated" at all. Her great impact on me was the fact of her building such a complete autonomy out of her self and her circumscribed life. In a way, she does what Thoreau does, except her economy is an aesthetic one rather than a material one. His is, too, but in a greater degree hers is strictly aesthetic rather than something generalizable in the way that his is. She does a thing, which I think is also very Puritan, of assuming that everything is full of meaning. You know the thing that Blake said about the universe in a grain of sand, which is literally true: if you could understand a grain of sand, you'd understand a lot. Apparently, she's been criticized for not quoting, not alluding, but in a way what she's doing is developing a kind of complete autonomy. I don't know why it has such meaning for me, it just seems like some kind of purity and honesty. I don't even know why. God knows I allude. I've said before that when I wrote *Housekeeping* I tried not to make allusions that Ruth couldn't make. I think that that was something Dickinsonian in my mind, the declaration of the fact that art, which is actually composed experience, composed perception, is not something that you learn like a trade but actually has its essence, its basic origins, in individual experience. That's just a statement. I don't know if it's true. But I think she wishes to demonstrate that. I don't like received art.

TG: Received art?

MR: The basic model of culture which assumes that people are modified by preexisting assumptions and aesthetics rather than that there's something overwhelmingly individual, involving the discovery of the syntax of one's own being, in all great art.

TG: When we first corresponded, you mentioned that you didn't have Dickinson in front of you when you were working on *Housekeeping*, so that there wasn't a conversation going on that level. But there are obviously quite a number of Dickinson poems moving beneath the text. Were you surprised when I pointed this out?

MR: I was sort of surprised. I couldn't say that you were wrong. If those poems, and others, lurk there, I couldn't say that that's not true.

TG: Would you say something about such conversations then, based on your work in this book?

MR: It's a strange thing. You live in a world so saturated with interpretation. If you interpret the world by extending what you take to be the vision of earlier writers, you can in some degree legitimize your interpretation of your tradition. The writers that I love, I really love, as if they were relatives. And I want to declare fealty, if not kinship. And that's what a lot of alluding and so on is actually about. And also the fact, with those writers particularly, that I do feel they were doing something radical, not of a second order by any means. And I would like to see it continued.

TG: What part of Dickinson would you say you were attuned to? Or that *Housekeeping* is?

MR: Stripping down to the essence of perception. That terrible phrase of Emerson's, the transparent eyeball—too bad he couldn't come up with something better—but, nevertheless, the sort of pure perception without anything accidental being of more interest or more importance than perception itself. The "I am nobody" posture.

TG: An "unaccompanied soul" is how you put it in *Housekeeping.*

MR: Yes. Again, it's the project of Thoreau's I was talking about. It has everything to do with the fact that the great, wonderful, brilliant observer on the *Pequod* is the lowest ranking sailor and not the first mate or the captain. This almost-disappearing man in terms of his obscurity, not a hero.

TG: This seems to me to connect to Dickinson's phrase "enlarging loneliness." You know her cricket poem:

Further in Summer than the Birds
Pathetic from the Grass
A minor Nation celebrates
Its unobtrusive Mass.

No Ordinance be seen
So gradual the Grace
A pensive Custom it becomes
Enlarging Loneliness.

Antiquest felt at Noon
When August burning low

Arise this spectral Canticle
Repose to typify

Remit as yet no Grace
No Furrow on the Glow
Yet a Druidic Difference
Enhances Nature now.

Loneliness runs through *Housekeeping* and a number of your essays. Can you talk about why loneliness enlarges the world, or the soul?

MR: I truly grew up in a culture, as I think I said somewhere, where loneliness is considered a privileged condition . . . I have always found it to be true. But since it wasn't a discovery for me . . . The contingency of relationship, which is inevitable, means that even in your own thinking there's a tendency to negotiate. You try to negotiate your sense of reality with somebody else's sense of reality, and if you do that in good faith, you're continuously trying to modify your own sense of reality.

TG: It's what we're doing right now.

MR: Exactly.

TG: But there are gains.

MR: There are. And of course, loneliness by itself is not sufficient. But on the other hand, when you have no contingency of that kind, you actually find out what you think. You become aware of your consciousness as a mysterious other. It's very beautiful and it's very privileged. If you have a reasonable tranquility and a good eye and have acquired enough knowledge to furnish your observations, it's a beautiful experience. And that fact by itself is a large comment on the meaning of human life.

TG: It seems to happen for Dickinson when she's shut off from the world—from the mass of the crickets. Why would that be?

MR: Well, to be secluded was . . . For example, the conversion experience we were talking about before would have meant to her, among other things, assimilation into the society that surrounded her, because this way of thinking was so common. On the one hand she feared default, and on the other, she feared success. When she's rejected, she's thrown back on herself and she's loyal to herself. The I here, that solitary thing, is utterly privileged in a way: it's not anything else. Something else is going on besides sadness or rejection or any of those other things. It's being thrown back on some essential being of her soul toward which she is in fact reverent.

TG: Along with being thrown back on your self there is the experience of "Druidic Difference." In one of your essays you speak about the experience you had as a child of something "not me, not like me, not mine." Can you talk about that? Isn't there also an experience of something utterly other than you?

MR: Absolutely. The difference between what you perceive as utterly other and yourself is a sense of proportion, among other things. This is something again that runs all through mysticism and also Calvinism—the sense that the smallness of the self is a celebration of the utter vastness of the other. Whatever happens, this difference cannot be mitigated. It's a feeling of discomfort, because what you're doing when you have that feeling is apprehending a certain grandeur. I don't know quite what this means, except that the privileged position is, one might say, the cricket, the disappearingly small.

TG: That's clearly where Ruth gets to in *Housekeeping*, isn't it? A good bit of the book is her experience of having things stripped and becoming weightless and understanding how flimsy thought or house or self or memory is. But the end result is a wide opening up of experience.

MR: A very nice reading. Yes.

TG: In a sense, the experience of the weightlessness of self or language is an entrance into this larger world. Can you say more about that?

MR: It's part of the "arbitrary constitution of the universe." There are many things I can say that I take to be true and I have no idea why they are true. There is the great element of arbitrariness in existence. This is the assumption of mysticism. When you look at science, for example, there is an ethic of objectivity, ideally the observer will disappear—the idea that the self clouds perception, that the self is a historical accident from God's perspective I think is very much acknowledged by science or math, and by theology and mysticism, and by virtually nothing else. The Dickinsonian ambivalence of consciousness. If you yourself are the primary object of interest in the sense of "What do I own, am I admired," then that is the theater of your consciousness. It's an either/or sort of thing. If you give a significant part of your consciousness to that kind of understanding of the world, the other comes close to you, and I think that's why the living-in-the-desert-on-locust-and-honey understanding is so authoritative. The fact that she apparently almost always dressed in white . . . she wanted the things that were true for her to be always true. It was as if she didn't want to have an ordinary life.

TG: Was she a mystic in the way that you're using the term?

MR: That's an interesting question . . . She adopts a mystic posture. Is there such a thing as ironic mysticism? Again, I'm very interested in Calvinist culture, and obviously she's a major figure in that culture. Calvin was contemporary with Theresa of Avila and St. John of the Cross, and it is interesting to read them side by side. But what the Spanish mystics did was, in a sense, mortify the flesh and proceed by that means to visionary experience. But for Calvin, right in the beginning of the *Institutes* he talks about this, the first thing you have to do in order to know God is to know yourself. And then he talks about how you develop this idea of your failures and shortcomings—this inverse definition of the self generates the idea of God as its obverse.

TG: Because your neediness shows that God is someone who fills needs, or your hunger shows you why Jesus was feeding people?

MR: Exactly. For him the insufficiency of people is the great gift of God's grace. A wonderful thing goes on despite us, really. But you don't overcome yourself in order to attain a vision of God; you actually become incredibly aware of yourself. And it seems to me that if she's a mystic, she's a mystic in that tradition, because there's never any rapture or transport or anything. The sense of herself and her smallness and so on is always painfully present.

TG: In one of your essays on Calvin, you say: "His theology is compelled and enthralled by an overwhelming awareness of the grandeur of God, and this is the source of the distinctive aesthetic coherency of his religious vision, which is neither mysticism nor metaphysics, but mysticism as a method of rigorous inquiry and metaphysics as an impassioned flight of the soul. This vision is still very present in writers like Melville and Dickinson." So Dickinson's mysticism, if we use that word, would be worked out through that rigorous self-analysis or inquiry.

MR: Yes, definitely. The thing that is very beautiful about Calvin's mysticism over against Spanish mysticism is that he always refers you to the world. He calls the universe God's shimmering garment and it's forever a mirror, the things that reveal God without revealing him, or that reveal him while concealing him. But nevertheless, there's the democracy of all this, the idea that all perception is meaningful if it's approached with the assumption that it is. Basically, experience is saturated with the presence of God.

TG: That's like the Edwards quotation.

MR: Exactly. When you read something like Thoreau or Melville, it's— there's a word I want I haven't thought of all afternoon . . . the gracefulness, the continuously self-transforming quality of their thinking . . .

TG: It's attended to, they are utterly alert. There's a passage in *Walden* where he says we shouldn't put up a door or foundation without first considering what these things are about.

MR: I just read a book—I suffer constantly because people always say bad things about the Puritans—talking about the famous dropping of the cup. The journals of the Puritans often report tiny moments and say these signify such and such—they reminded me of my sinfulness or reminded me of my mortality. But of course, Dickinson's aesthetic comes right out of that habit of mind. The man whose book that was ridicules the idea that God would have time to concern himself on that level. Which is really a very reductionist idea of God. It's much less grand actually than this kind of model, like Edwards's, which assumes that God saturates reality and that he is actually communicated relative to every human being. That's the old grandeur . . .

TG: I'd like to move to the novel now. One of the things I've been thinking about in *Housekeeping* is Ruthie's voice and where it comes from. The novel in part is the story of how she develops that voice, I think. One of the distinctive things about her voice is the use of analogy: "Say [my grandmother] stooped breathlessly in her corset to lift up a sodden sheet by its hems, and say that when she had pinned three corners to the lines it began to billow and leap in her hands, to flutter and tremble." Or, "Say that water lapped over the gunwales, and I swelled and swelled until I burst Sylvie's coat." Where does that sort of language come from?

MR: Well, Ruth, as I understand her, has lost many things and she in effect creates a complete reality out of the things she's lost. Either on the one hand by memory or on the other by imagination. She knows that in a sense what she's saying is true because she knows her grandmother, but at the same time she knows it's not true. She's making reality. Nobody told her this. She knows what the wind is like, and she knows what the frozen ground is like, and she knows how her grandmother hung clothes. And so in a way she's created things that haven't been in reality. And of course what that does is put reality in question, in a way, puts it in suspense one might say. What is real, what is remembered, what is hypothesized? How do they relate? This is a way of asserting her aloofness from conventional understandings of reality.

TG: Because reality is grander than that? Within these stories she seems to find room to move around. She starts with the wind, but then she moves from that to "In a month she would not mourn, because in that season it had never seemed to her that they were married" and then from that to the two of them being most themselves alone and then to the paragraph on the pleasures of loneliness. So, she doesn't just remember, she . . . thinks with it?

MR: How would I describe that? I don't quite know how to describe it. She takes meaning from the lives she sees around her. There's a nexus of lives that she finds herself within. She's in a sense moving into the mind of her grandmother. One of the things that is most mysterious about consciousness is that we don't know what's in there. You can know someone, but they're so complex that even while you apprehend them, even while you appreciate them, it's as if there is a very dense center of being that you never really know, and you have to represent that to create the wholeness of a character.

TG: And Ruth discovers it as she talks?

MR: Yes.

TG: When that comparison starts, we're to assume she doesn't know where she's going with it.

MR: Absolutely.

TG: Do you remember when and how you wrote it? You've said before that you wrote a lot of this while you were doing your dissertation to prove you could write other things. Was this section one of them?

MR: Yes. The character of Sylvie actually came rather late. When I started writing about Sylvie I didn't know anything about her except that her hands were cold and she wore a raincoat. And as soon as I knew that I knew an enormous amount about her.

TG: Do you remember anything else that came early?

MR: The early part of the book—the grandfather's painting, and then the train wreck. That had a strange genesis. I was walking across campus at the University of Massachusetts and I met a man who was on the faculty and he told me he'd been reading some fiction from a graduate student, and I said, "I used to write fiction." And he said, "Well, get me some, I'd like to see it." So I went right into the library. I had a spiral notebook. I sat down and I fell profoundly asleep. It was very strange. And then I wrote the train wreck, virtually from beginning to end. It was not at that point something that I thought of necessarily as part of the novel. It was about itself.

TG: There are a number of other passages I'd love to ask about. Near the end of the book they burn old magazines out in the orchard. Ruth drifts away into the dark and Sylvie turns on all the lights and says, "Come in where it's warm." Ruth tells a story: "Once there was a young girl strolling at night in an orchard." That for me is the moment where she discovers the voice we've been talking about.

MR: There's a sort of exaltation about that passage. It's the pure experience of oneself by stepping out of oneself, in a certain sense. It's an exultant escape that is a self-rescue.

TG: Here's another. She and Sylvie have taken the boat trip across the lake and are looking for the children. Sylvie leaves her alone, and Ruth pulls together the threads about loneliness and being alone without a sister and then, after a page and a half, there's a lovely passage where she talks about her mother. She doesn't have her literally, but her mother is present, not perished. In between are a couple of paragraphs where she goes into that broken-down house and messes with it, tries to rescue the children, and then identifies with it—says my house could as easily fall. Why couldn't she have gone from Sylvie missing and no stable bonds to the vision of her mother? Why did she have to go into the house and do that with her hands?

MR: I think that signified or accomplished a sort of transition in her thinking. She goes from accepting these mythical children of Sylvie, and then she tries to do something that is real to her, splintery and difficult. And in the course of thinking about it, the children become very real, and the idea of their being abandoned in that house, needing rescue, which is of course thematic, God help me. And then after that . . . she goes from accepting them as something in the peripheries of her attention, to thinking of them as something she has contact with as their individual rescuer, to putting herself among them. I don't want to schematize, but it goes from that house to her house and she then becomes like the children, in the sense that the house fell.

TG: In a way, her house has already fallen.

MR: Well, in the sense of where she goes back to, the house is still standing. She's seeing herself in the loss of that house. And then after that, she's in the position of the children themselves, they being the needy watchers. And then by the end of it, when she imagines her mother, she's the needy watcher, she's the avid child.

TG: So, that business in the cellar is a little bit like the act of writing—doing something with your hands, standing away from yourself, studying yourself.

MR: Well, like Dickinson, like many other people, the idea of the sacramental quality of reality—the great riddle of, the great fascination in the sense that the materiality of things can be understood as a part of contact with something utterly beyond the material . . . The strange, dreamlike good faith of her wishing to accept the reality of the children and what they mean for her is acted out physically by participation, one would call it, in sacramental language.

TG: Let's talk about a few of Dickinson's poems. Do you know "I saw no Way—The Heavens were stitched"?

> I saw no Way—The Heavens were stitched—
> I felt the Columns close—
> The earth reversed her Hemispheres—
> I touched the Universe—
>
> And back it slid—and I alone—
> A Speck upon a Ball—
> Went out upon Circumference—
> Beyond the Dip of Bell—

It's one of the great poems.

MR: Very great. I don't know if I know that poem.

TG: I wondered if you could show me what you bring to the page, what issues arise for you as you read a poem like this. Do you want to look at this one, or pick another?

MR: Well, I'll look at that one. A poem that I think illustrates that double perception of the kind I was talking about as being central to her is that one "I should have been too glad, I see," the one with "that Scalding prayer—Sabachthani."

TG: Let me read it:

> I should have been too glad, I see—
> Too lifted—for the scant degree
> Of Life's penurious Round—
> My little Circuit would have shamed
> This new Circumference—have blamed—
> The homelier time behind.
>
> I should have been too saved—I see—
> Too rescued—Fear too dim to me
> That I could spell the Prayer
> I knew so perfect—yesterday—
> That Scalding One—Sabachthani—
> Recited fluent—here—
>
> Earth would have been too much—I see—
> And Heaven—not enough for me—
> I should have had the Joy
> Without the Fear—to justify—
> The Palm—without the Calvary—
> So Savior—Crucify—

MR: She uses that image of elevation that she associates with crucifixion. At the beginning, it means elevation, but since she falls short of what she thought, what she thought would happen, it falls back into the unachieving consciousness. Then the image goes from elevation to crucifixion.

TG: Oh, in a way she is crucified.

MR: Yes. "So Savior—Crucify" is the last line, which implies, of course, that the suffering she feels is the means to the elevation she is promised. So it's dynamic in that sense. It's a great poem.

TG: See if the one I quoted touches this.

MR: Well, in terms of bringing to the page, it seems to me as if legitimately one could think about this in terms of the mystery of the interaction between noetic awareness and experience. Of course, I'm thinking of Newton—the idea of the physicality and the geometric nature of the world. It seems to me that she's talking about heaven perceived as closed . . . the enclosure that's implied by the ultimate meeting of the thing perceptually, i.e., if you imagine columns of a sufficient height you imagine them closing, because they would become narrower. When you look down a road it seems to become narrower. And she goes here from a perception of herself in the world, in effect, physically speaking, to a perception of herself in the universe. She overwhelms the reality of earth. And these are both highly intellectual. Nevertheless, she does this Calvinist thing we were talking about where she reduces herself— relatively, to a speck upon a ball—but in the act of reconceiving reality into larger terms that diminish her, she's broken out of an entrapment. . . The thing that's interesting to me and I think so important for understanding her . . . This is very satisfactory as image, the second quatrain, at the same time that it's completely an intellectual construct. She's talking about the world as she knows it, a learned conception of the world. The simplicity of it is entirely apparent. What she is doing is reconceiving the world as something in the universe rather than thinking of herself as something in the world, and feeling liberated by moving away from an immediacy and toward a different kind of intellectual construct.

TG: And that's important for what reason?

MR: Well, for one thing, it makes the point that she's a highly intellectual poet. It's also important because it illustrates the liberation of diminution that we were talking about before—that what would, to many people, seem like an enormously threatening thing, the loss of relative significance, is her break from entrapment.

TG: There are nature poems that are similar. Here's one:

> A Bird came down the Walk—
> He did not know I saw—
> He bit an Angleworm in halves
> And ate the fellow, raw,
>
> And then he drank a Dew
> From a convenient Grass—

And then hopped sidewise to the Wall
To let a Beetle pass—

He glanced with rapid eyes
That hurried all around—
They looked like frightened Beads, I thought—
He stirred his Velvet Head

Like one in danger, Cautious,
I offered him a Crumb
And he unrolled his feathers
And rowed him softer home—

Than Oars divide the Ocean,
Too silver for a seam—
Or Butterflies, off Banks of Noon
Leap, plashless as they swim.

MR: It's really beautiful. It's just amazing. She's earning some reversal. Even in the course of hearing it, you think, What's she going to do? That's the transformative vision—things that are charming and minor, however freshly observed, and then—what out of this is to be perceived, where is the mystery? And then, of course, the mystery is . . . Strange analogy between ocean and ether, implying no doubt further analogy. The transition she makes is difficult to understand. She estranges things, rowing on the ocean and seeing the butterflies as swimming. It's estranging in the sense that, in the first place there's a sort of anthropomorphic convention operating, dealing with the bird, stopping at a convenient blade of grass and so on, and then when the bird startles and refuses, everything is changed, but it is not changed beyond the limits of our ready comprehension. She is telling us to look at things in a way that we've never done before, but all you say is "that's true," not "that's threatening." Do you know what I mean? The strangeness is true and therefore doesn't abandon . . . which simply makes the point, I suppose, that the world is available to being seen very differently from the way we ordinarily see it. That is probably the point of every writer, particularly writers who feel that conventional seeing is at odds with the project of comprehension, which I would say certainly includes Emily Dickinson.

TG: Do you have other favorites?

MR: There's a poem I was thinking of. I love the one about her dropping thoughts like a ball of yarn. Or, I felt a plank in reason break. It's so beautiful.

TG: Let's do that one:

> I felt a Funeral, in my Brain,
> And Mourners to and fro
> Kept treading—treading—till it seemed
> Than Sense was breaking through—
>
> And when they all were seated,
> A Service, like a Drum—
> Kept beating—beating—till I thought
> My Mind was going numb—
>
> And then I heard them lift a Box
> And creak across my Soul
> With those same Boots of Lead, again,
> Then Space—began to toll,
>
> As all the Heavens were a Bell,
> And Being, but an Ear,
> And I, and Silence, some strange Race
> Wrecked, solitary, here—
>
> And then a Plank in Reason, broke,
> And I dropped down, and down—
> And hit a World, at every plunge,
> And Finished knowing—then—

MR: This is such a great poem. Gee: "Some strange race wrecked, solitary, here." Hmm, this poem was probably in my mind. One of the things that I think is so wonderful about this kind of consciousness I've been talking about is that it values everything. Even in the course of saying that something is conventional or artificial, it values it also as another meaningful artifact of consciousness. When she starts saying "I felt a Funeral, in my Brain," it's like the crickets having their mass in the other poem. She talks about things that are conventional, but they are conventional in the sense that they are emblematic also—they are deeply significant human behaviors. They are embedded in the world. She is writing as if this is something that she is hearing, but there is nothing to make you feel that anything is going on simultaneously with her experience. In other words, the funeral in her brain need not have anything that it refers to in the outside world. She is implying that there are orders of consciousness that are simply necessary, in the way that human beings act out loss and death and so on and ritually acknowledge things, wordlessly. It's so intrinsic, in that it is something that everyone experiences as subjective, that it is meaningful to describe as an isolated subject of experience. And it's really interesting because it is as if people are intruding on her, the treading and the heavy boots and all the rest of it . . .

TG: But isn't it for you a mental experience she is describing through the analogy of the funeral?

MR: Yes, but at the same time something that is very much conditioned by the experience of funerals.

TG: She's gone through them with her eyes open.

MR: The idea that the heavens are a bell and being is an ear . . . I was talking before about the communication between being and consciousness. It *is* a bell, perception *is* an ear.

TG: It's overwhelming, too, isn't it? All of heaven directed toward a single ear.

MR: Yes. That assumption is elaborated here—the consequences of that vision of being are described in this poem. She's very Melvillean, only more so perhaps, in the sense that she's perfectly willing to embrace the implications of this vision of reality, in terms of the fact that it exposes human solitude to the vastest available order of being. And that's the thrill of it in a way, the beauty of it, and the terror of it also. Notice also, as we were saying before, the self is not lost. She's "wrecked, solitary." Perception follows what is to be perceived, and expands to fill this expanded apprehension. But at the same time, there is a sense of the self abandoned. It's like those poems she has about the sense of herself dead, which clearly assume "not dead," because she sees the moss grow over her lip. To look back on a lost self is still to retain that identification. The "finished knowing" is very interesting, because it can be interpreted in so many ways. If you move beyond the possibility of not-knowing, you finish knowing. It's like Paul, "Now we know, then we know . . ." On the one hand knowing, because it's an encapsulated experience, is done with. On the other hand, knowing insofar as it could expand to what is to be known is also finished. In the sense that Jesus uses the word *finished*.

TG: I see. This seems to take us back to Emily Dickinson reading her consciousness as cresting in and out of the conversion experience. Is that how you put it?

MR: Yes, I think that she watched her consciousness in effect to find out what was being enacted in it.

TG: And what did she learn here as she watched it?

MR: I think that her preoccupation with death is very much related again to her religious and metaphysical culture, because the assumption was, of course, that you simply passed from this life into a state of comprehension. The circumstance of this life is not to know—again it's Paul, "We see in a glass darkly." There's a relationship between what we know and what is real, but it's an extremely problematic and attenuated relationship. And so whatever she thinks about death, virtually whatever she does, she thinks about it in terms of a door opening onto this level of apprehension, before which none of the customary methods of understanding will be salient. And of course, being on this side of it, she can't know what that change will be. But the thing about it is, if you say that experience is partial, then you are saying that it has many of the essential qualities of real experience, and it is highly corrupted by one means or another, because of fallibility, of which the Puritans were notoriously aware. So, you can watch it with the intention or with the hope of discovering what is essential in it, not assuming that you can do that analytically or do it once for all, because the assumption is that you are always being instructed, that it will always change. This assumption does not allow you to disallow anything. And it doesn't allow you to trust anything either. I think that she makes the assumption that lots of people do, that meaning is, in a sense, affirmed by beauty. And the originality of her aesthetic comes very much from the idea that if you subscribe to an inappropriate notion of the beautiful then the beauty that would affirm other kinds of truth is lost to you.

TG: When we corresponded, you wrote: "I would suggest that the famished I, the I stripped to its marrow, is a question . . . I think it's an underreading of Dickinson, and I hope of my book as well, not to entertain the question, or at least spread the table for it and hope it will appear." Would you say a bit more about that?

MR: I think that this I is a discipline, a kind of ecstatic discipline, and that its absolute character is openness. Being at the highest degree of exposed sensitivity—not sensitivity like "oh me," but sensitivity to what is being shown to me . . . a dis-encumbering of self. I think one of the poignant things about human beings is that they're so undefended, physically. And that there's an absolute relationship between that defenselessness and everything that's impressive about them. I think a lot of us would like to be turtles and porcupines, and I think that in a way one of the impulses of human beings is to defend themselves in a way that nature did not. But I think the other impulse is to just love the experience with nothing to protect oneself, and actually feeling in fact no barrier. People know about their mortality in a way that we can't know that any animal knows. They know about Earth being a ball in space. Intelligence of the high human sort could be translated as defenselessness, because we can know many things that are very hard to bear. It's that fierce humanness of feeling, the character of feeling, that is sought out by people like Dickinson and Melville. In this particular cultural moment there may be a tendency to see the self as rather pathetic—to understand it not as a sort of brave experiment, the only kind of self-conception that can actually confront the cosmos. And I think that the people who have done it well have brought back news.

TG: So, that "famished I" is a disciplined receptivity.

MR: Exactly. Instead of meaning "I am a victim"—which is the way that this wonderful person has been read—it means "I have extraordinary courage," "I have privileged apprehension." As a corollary, it means, "This is not about me." She's not writing about herself in any sense. She's writing about the universal mystery of metaphor and perception.

December 11, 1999
Iowa City

THREE

RESTRUCTURED AND RESTRUNG

Charles Wright's Zone Journals

In a 1987 essay, "A.P. and E.D.," Charles Wright points to Emily Dickinson as

> the only poet who, when I read her, I feel as though I understand, I know, and have heard before, somewhere, what she is trying to tell me. . . . Emily Dickinson is the only writer I've ever read who knows my name, whose work has influenced me at my heart's core, whose music is the music of the songs I've listened to and remembered in my very body.[1]

What he is drawn to, Wright continues, is the way Dickinson's poems echo and extend the music of his childhood, most notably the songs of A. P. Carter and the Carter family:

> traditional and oddly surreal at the same time . . . [written from] the point of view of someone watching, from inside, the world go on outside, and always aspiring to something beyond that world that waited as surely as sunrise. . . . Dickinson's poems, in their surreal simplicity and ache, are without question the artistic high ground, the city of light, in this uniquely American landscape. (H, 53–54)

What Wright calls Dickinson's ache, watching the world while aspiring to something unknowable beyond it, is what I've been describing as her broken responsiveness. For Wright as well, brokenness is a ladder potentially connecting one with what waits beyond, a road leading outward:

She sat in her room and the galaxy unrolled beneath her feet. She sat in her room and the garden and orchard outside her windows took on the ghostly garments of infinity. . . . Her poetry was an electron microscope trained on the infinite and the idea of God. Such distances under her fingertips! Inside the tube of the climbing rose, the River of Heaven flowed. Under the oak's throat, the *broken* ladder to Paradise waited for reassembly. . . . Her poems are immense voyages into the unknowable" (Q, 39–40, italics mine).

Although a number of Dickinson's phrases and poems echo through Wright's books, the most prominent is the well-known 258 (F320), a poem notable for its simplicity and ache:

There's a certain Slant of light,
Winter Afternoons—
That oppresses, like the Heft
Of Cathedral Tunes—

Heavenly Hurt, it gives us—
We can find no scar,
But internal difference,
Where the Meanings, are—

None may teach it—Any—
'Tis the Seal Despair—
An imperial affliction
Sent us of the Air—

When it comes, the Landscape listens—
Shadows—hold their breath—
When it goes, 'tis like the Distance
On the look of Death—

What do we see here? A slant of light "comes," heralding the possibility of a world other than the unbroken gray of a winter afternoon, and then it "goes," an experience Wright's poems repeatedly refer to. In his terms: "Something infinite behind everything appears, and then disappears" (W, 79). When the light comes, the landscape it touches and those who view it come alive, listening and holding their breath in intense concentration on that other world the slant seems to dart out from and invite entrance into. When it goes, that possibility goes with it. The world we inhabit is left for dead as the other world recedes and turns its back. The slant of light is heavy and "oppress[ive]," dealing out "Heavenly Hurt" and "imperial afflic-tion," because, while it declares the existence of depth and intensity, it and the world it emanates from cannot be held or known. Bonnie Costello, in an article on Wright's response to landscape, describes such an experience as an example of "a Dickinsonian countersublime rather than an Emerso-nian sublime . . . not . . . the confirmation of being in the infinite but [the] alienation of being *from* the infinite."[2] The slant is not "teach[able]"; it has a mind of its own, coming and going at will. It stands before us as a vacancy, insisting that we are blind to the world it speaks from, wounded by its lack: "Something inhuman," in Wright's words, "something you can't know" (C, 83). At the same time, even as the slant of light painfully brings us up against what is sealed off from us, we are changed—made different "internal[ly]" by that contact and, as with Robinson's abandoned Ruth, forced to confront new "Meanings." Testifying to a world that can't be spoken for or reached, the slant of light, for both Wright and Dickinson, functions, paradoxically, as a "lifeline to the unseen."

I draw that phrase from Wright's description of the Italian artist Giorgio Morandi, whose dissolving bottles and doorways, Wright claims, highlight "the presence / Of what is missing, keeping its distance and measure" (W, 199).[3] Like Dickinson's slant that comes and goes, speaking of a world invis-ible to us—insisting on its "distance" and its set-apart nature—Morandi's work also draws our eyes to what isn't there, a world corrosively other. Read-ing Wright's comments, one thinks of Robinson's train sliding like a weasel off a rock:

> Morandi's late line is always on the point of disappearing, of not *seeming* to be there. . . . The famous bottles and compote dishes begin to be drawn back into the paper, becoming larger the more they dis-semble. It's almost as though they are drawn on the air, that masterly, and in that instant starting to be borne away. . . . The windows into the invisible are lit; . . . what is not there is at least as powerful and tactile as what is. It is an art in transition, between here and there. [His late drawings] are full of wonder and singularity, lifelines to the unseen. (H, 8–9)

Throughout his work, Dickinson's slant of light has been for Wright a way of calling attention to these issues, at least in part because of her stress on the "Heavenly Hurt" of the encounter with that dissolving "lifeline." Consider these lines from "Blaise Pascal Lip-syncs the Void":

December. 4 p.m.
            Chardonnay-colored light-slant

Lug weight in the boned trees.
　　　　　　　　　　　　Squirrel dead on the Tarmac.
Boom-boxing Big Foot pickup trucks
Hustle down Locust,
　　　　　　　light pomegranate pink grapefruit then blood.
We take it into our hearts.　　　　(N, 35)

As with Dickinson, the rapidly disappearing "light-slant" of a winter afternoon, shifting from Chardonnay to pomegranate to pink grapefruit to blood,
once taken "into our hearts," speaks of a world other than Charlottesville's
Locust Street and its dead squirrels and pickup trucks. But its speech is a
"Lug weight" in the "boned trees" it cuts through, as heavy and ultimately
unbearable as Dickinson's cathedral tunes. Her "Seal Despair," bringing us
up against and closing us off from the invisible, seems here to have become
a lug nut spun and tightened, and yet, with both writers, it is a despair that
calls one to reread the world.

Wright has consistently described his own pursuit of the unknowable in
Dickinson-like terms: "We live in two landscapes, as Augustine might have
said, / One that's eternal and divine, and one that's just the back yard, / Dead
leaves and dead grass in November, purple in spring" (N, 163).[4] Wright's back
yard, as numerous commentators have noted, is shot through with both the
fleeting, borne-away traces of another world offered by light, shadow, and
seasonal change and with the similarly elusive traces left behind by memory
and reading.[5] What his poems ask is if anything can be made of that painful
"affliction / Sent us of the Air," that moment when "the Landscape listens" as,
underneath the noise of boom boxes and pickup trucks, "Something infinite
behind everything appears, and then disappears" (W, 79). Robinson asked
this question by creating a character who explored the "homeless," "sumptuous Destitution" one finds oneself in after the infinite vanishes. Wright asks
it by returning time after time, in progressively extended forms, to poem
258's "imperial affliction": the moment when something in a landscape trig-
gers a painful, revelatory sense of being cut off from what matters—call it
"an otherness inside us / We never touch, no matter how far down our hands
reach. / It is the past" (W, 48); or "A city I'll never remember, its walls the
color of pure light, /. . . a landscape that keeps my imprint / Forever, and
stays unchanged, and waits to be filled back in" (W, 54–55).

"The great ones," Wright remarks, seem to "always write as though from
the other side" (H, 180). Responding to Dickinson, then, is responding to
that painful sense of another world that she brings to the surface for him:

I write for the ghost of Thomas Hardy and Hart Crane, for Emily
Dickinson and Arthur Rimbaud. When you say you write for the

angels, for the dead, for that which is beyond you, you write for that part of yourself that is better than you are, for all of those things that are in this imaginary, mythical, still, brightly lit center of attention at the heart of the universe. (H, 128–29)

Wright is no more able to answer and control Dickinson's slant than Dickinson was originally. She brings to his back yard a world he is blind to and calls him to listen. That world can't be "taught" or held; it can only be suffered and "take[n] into" the heart as difference. Wright's pursuit of it, then, like Robinson's (and like Dickinson's before them both), "at the same time us[es] all the resources of language and absolutely insist[s] that language is not an appropriate tool."[6] He remarks:

> When Joyce talks about his epiphanies, when Hopkins talks about his inscape, when other people talk about their revelation of intellect at a given moment, when they first saw what a certain object meant to them, what a certain passage meant to them, when they saw a certain memory exfoliate into its full meaning, they're all talking about the same sensation. . . . I believe in that sort of thing, and I believe in trying to get there through language. That impossibility. . . . But then, of course, the only job that's worth doing is the one which can never be finished. (S, 44–45)

The impossibility of this job is what drives Wright's work.

Zone Journals, published in 1988 and to my mind Wright's most important work, is also, perhaps not accidentally, the work in which Wright's "never . . . finished" confrontation with poem 258's vacant, unteachable slant of light is most fully played out.[7] As Mutlu Konuk Blasing notes, Wright in an interview has suggestively linked the "zones" this book explores with the blank or the unwordable:

> There's a passage I came across in the letters of Paul Cézanne in which he says that colors were to him numinous essences beyond which he *knew* nothing—"the diamond zones of God remaining white." For me if you replace the word *colors* with *words* and *white* with *blank*, you would get how I try to find out what those "zones" are. I admit that I think they exist; I'm just not very sure of them.[8]

As we'll see, the journal form that the volume explores—in particular, its built-in rhythms of finding and losing—is his fullest answer to Dickinson, a way to show "I'm listening." It is a form that acknowledges, in its dogged blindness, "That no one could answer back from the other side. / Still, I'd like to think I've learned how to speak to them, / I'd like to think I know how to conjugate 'Can you hear me?' and 'What?'" (W, 91–92).[9]

Zone Journals is made up of a single year-long journal, "A Journal of the Year of the Ox," forty pages in length, and a number of shorter journals. The early, shorter journals work with "There's a certain Slant of light" in fascinating ways. The first piece, "Yard Journal" (W, 121–23), begins by recalling Dickinson's notion of "Circumference"—the edge of what can be known—drawing particularly on her notion in poem 802 (F858) that the knowable edge continually expands and contracts, making itself felt "By Processes of Size":

> Strange how the light hubs out and wheels
> > concentrically back and forth
> After a rain, as though the seen world
> Quavered inside a water bead
> > swung from a grass blade

As the light, catching the moisture in the air, shifts back and forth, it seems to establish and abandon a series of "concentric" boundaries, as if the yard were a droplet suspended within a larger, unseen world. Each time the light shifts, the boundaries between the seen and the unseen, droplet and larger world, are reestablished, leading to a sense that movement from one to the other is possible. A second entry returns to this possibility, musing about what waits beyond the concentric circles of the visible. The scene is evening; the sky seems to have established a shell or "carapace" overhead:

> —Deep dusk and lightning bugs
> > alphabetize on the east wall,
> The carapace of the sky blue-ribbed and buzzing
> Somehow outside it all,
> Trees dissolving against the night's job,
> > houses melting in air:
> Somewhere out there an image is biding its time,
> Burning like Abraham in the cold, swept
> > expanses of heaven,
> Waiting to take me in and complete my equation:

Outside the carapace and the rapidly contracting boundaries of the seen, "out there" beyond the reach of the alphabet, "an image is biding its time," seemingly waiting to show him how "all things fit together." Borders give way—houses melting in the twilight, trees dissolving—but for now what's outside simply waits, still inaccessible.

Dickinson's slant of light, coming and going according to its own "imperial" whims, gives Wright a way to think about the seen world's brushes with what's beyond it. The third entry begins:

—Blue jay's bound like a kangaroo's in the lawn's high grass,
Then up in a brushstroke
              and over the hedge in one arc.
Light weights down the azalea plants,
. . .
Wax-like flowers of sunlight drift
              through the dwarf orchard and float
Under the pygmied peaches and pears
All over America,
       and here, too, the blossoms
Continuing down from nowhere, out of the blue.
The mockingbird's shadow is burned in the red clay below him.

The light drifts down "from nowhere," from outside circumference, in luminous blossoms and flowers. Like Dickinson's slant of light, there is a disturbing "heft" to the unknowable light—it "weights down the azalea plants." Its eventual vanishing is predicted by its comparison to "wax-like flowers"—recalling the abandoned landscape's "look of death"—and the framing images of the disappearing blue jay and mockingbird. What the light brings with it is a sense of what's missing, the "nowhere" it has drifted down from:

—Exclusion's the secret: what's missing is what appears
Most visible to the eye:
          the more luminous anything is,
The more it subtracts what's around it,
Peeling away the burned skin of the world
             making the unseen seen:
Body by new body they all rise into the light
Tactile and still damp,
That rhododendron and dogwood tree, that spruce,
An architecture of absence,
         a landscape whose words
Are imprints, dissolving images after the eyelids close:
I take them away to keep them there—
         that hedgehorn, for instance, that stalk . . .

As with Dickinson, the light is so "luminous" that it seems to draw our eyes away from the world. It makes us aware of "what's missing"—what is "unseen" or excluded from view. It "subtracts" or "peel[s] away" some portion of the visible as we become aware that the visible is only part of the story and attempt to look beyond it.[10] As the rhododendron, dogwood, and spruce of this final scene rise up, "body by new body" in the morning light, Wright imagines that glowing, unseen world they appear, for a moment, to be drawn from. His back yard takes on "an architecture of absence." Like glowing, dissolving "images after the eyelids close," the various parts of the landscape imprint themselves so fiercely that they seem to be last luminous traces, brief windows on that other world they are dissolving back into. Description becomes deeply charged, the poet seemingly in possession of "the secret" and able to reproduce, on the page, that painful, luminous dissolving: "I take them away to keep then there—that hedgehorn, for instance, that stalk . . ."

A second journal, "A Journal of English Days" (W, 124–34), also responds to Dickinson's poem 258, but in a more painful, less confident way. It begins with two September scenes in London's Kensington Gardens and concludes, by way of a flashback, with another September scene in the courtyard of the Victoria and Albert Museum. All three framing scenes are marked by full sun—"slick, unseasonable sunshine" (124)—and a suggestion in the air of the "Weightlessness of the world's skin" (134). In each scene, the world seems as if it could be seen through, the flesh becoming so weightless that the difference between flesh and spirit seems no longer absolute:

> One of those weightless, effortless late September days
> As sycamore leaves
> > tack down the unresisting air
> Onto the fire-knots of late roses
> Still pumping their petals of flame
> > up from the English loam,
> And I suddenly recognize
> The difference between the spirit and flesh
> > is finite, and slowly transgressable . . .
> (125)

In September, such movement seems possible, but the sunlight is soon erased in "the slow swish of the English rain, / . . . The rain lying like loose bandages over the ground, / . . . The comforting slide of darkness edging like deep water / Back through the afternoon" (125–26). The poet struggles in October with what Ezra Pound called "the cold soup of the English mind" (129), and in November finds himself drained of all vitality, his lines erased and dwindling away, making contact with nothing:

> > water and earth
> And air all bleared to the same color, an indiscriminate estuary

Shoaling into the landscape, nobody here but me
Unspooling to nothingness,
>line after line after latched, untraceable line . . .
(130)

What happens next is fascinating. "[P]ared" and "unspooled," the poet finds himself, late in the year, returning to the places where the weightless light of September had once greeted him. Now he feels for himself Dickinson's "homesick" yearning for a world outside her reach, having experienced on his own skin the painful weight of that brief, imperial play of light, opening and closing entirely free of his control:

—I keep coming back, like a tongue to a broken tooth,
Kensington Church Walk,
>late afternoon,
Pigeons in bas-relief and frieze on the building's edge—
There is no sickness of spirit like homesickness
When what you are sick for
>has never been seen or heard
In this world, or even remembered
>except as a smear of bleached light
Opening, closing beyond any alphabet's
Recall to witness and isolate . . .   (131–32)

Rather than recreating Dickinson's poem from a position of confidence—as he did in "Yard Journal," asserting "I take them away to keep them there"— the poet finds himself thrust into a position of brokenness. He doesn't take radiant parts of the landscape away and reproduce them on the page; rather, he loses them, he aches, he suffers the limits of his "alphabet." Pulled back to her "smear of bleached light," he testifies now to its scouring retreat. September's "weightless light," in memory, bears down "like the Heft / Of Cathedral Tunes." The difference between the spirit and flesh seems absolute.

The final journal in this sequence, "A Journal of True Confessions" (W, 138–46), extends the poet's personal encounter with the alphabet's limits. It begins with a description of a West Coast fishing trip that, like the weightless world of possibility opening the two previous journals, establishes a scene in which a hidden world seems all but accessible, the invisible fishing lines standing as ideal versions of the poet's own probing lines:

—Power rigs drift like lights out past the breakwater,
>white, and florescent white,
The sea moving them up and down
In the burgeoning dawn,

up and down,
White as they drift and flicker over the salmon run,
. . .
The day's great hand unfolding
Its palm as the boats drift with the tide's drift:

All morning we slipped among them,
. . .
Watching the rods as their almost-invisible lines
Trailed through the boat's wake,
                              waiting for each to dip:
And when it came
We set the drag and played him,
                              the salmon jumping and silver,
Then settled like quick foil in the net's green . . .   (138)

But, as the poet acknowledges (or "confesses," as his title has it) a month
later, that brief slant of vision is quite different from what he actually accomplished in the seventeen years he previously spent writing on that coast:

—Lashed to the syllable and noun,
                              the strict Armageddon of the verb,
I lolled for seventeen years
Above this bay . . .
Trying to get the description right.
                              If nothing else,
It showed me that what you see
                              both is and is not there,
The unseen bulking in from the edges of all things,
Changing the frame with its nothingness.

Its blue immensity taught me about subtraction,
Those luminous fingerprints
                              left by the dark, their whorls   (139)

He was never able to master the scene. He was blind. His lines unspooled.
Failing "to get the description right," he experienced the "blue immensity"
overpowering his lines, blotting them out or "subtract[ing]" them as simply
beside the point. He produced something like a Morandi drawing, his over-
powered lines charged with the painful sense of something "not there" that
he remained blinded to—their "luminous" erasures almost readable as the
unseen's "fingerprints."

The journal's confessions continue as the poet contrasts his own descriptive
failures with other more powerful voices: that of a ship's captain ("His sweet

invective lotioning my right ear"); the Italian poet Dino Campana; Leonardo da Vinci's games of "artifice, beauty and fear"; the lines of great painters:

> Morandi's line
> Drawn on the unredemptive air, Picasso's cut
> Like a laser into the dark hard of the mystery,
> Cézanne with his cross-tooth brush and hook,
> And sad immaculate Rothko,
>
> whose line was no line at all.   (143)

Although he continually anticipates some sort of breakthrough—"When the right words are found I will take them in and be filled / through with joy" (141); "The new line will be like the first line, spatial and self-contained, / Firm to the touch / But intimate, carved, as though whispered into the ear" (142)—he finally must acknowledge that the search seems never ending. He seeks an ideal "cadence," he admits to a friend's memory, but he hasn't found it. Rather than creating his own version of Dickinson's charged landscape— "tak[ing] them away to keep them there" in "Yard Journal," finding "the measure we talked about" (143) here—he is himself measured and shown to be inadequate. At his best, he simply returns to the broken tooth of her "slice of sunlight" and its imperial ways, nothing more:

> I look for it, Desmond, I look for it constantly
> In the long, musical shape of the afternoon,
>
> in the slice of sunlight pulled
> Through the bulge of the ash trees
> Opening like a lanced ache in the front yard,
> In the sure line the mockingbird takes
>
> down from the privet hedge
> And over the lawn where the early shade
> Puddles like bass chords under the oak,
> In the tangent of 4 p.m., in the uncut grass,
>
> in the tangle and tongue-tie it smooths there . . .
>
> But our lines seem such sad notes for the most part,
> Pinned like reliquaries and stopgaps
>
> to the cloth effigy of some saint
>
> (143–44)

In a final entry a month later, however, a different note crosses the poem. Perhaps *his* line is the circuitous path traced over the previous four months— not the fishing trip and its morning dream of access to the invisible; not Dickinson's precise, luminous account of the loss of such dreams; but the process traced by the journal itself, returning again and again to that broken tooth:

The song of white lights and power boats,
      the sails of August and late July devolve
To simple description in the end,
Something about a dark suture
Across the lawn,
     something about the way the day snips
It open and closes it
When what-comes-out has come out
       and burns hard in its vacancy,
Emerging elsewhere restructured and restrung,
Like a tall cloud that all the rain has fallen out of.   (145)

Like this poem in which July's songs of possibility have "devolve[d]" to "simple description," Wright's journals, in their various attempts to rework Dickinson's poem 258, finally only testify to a suture opening and closing. For Wright, "what-comes-out" "burns hard in its vacancy" and cannot be known; it constantly slips away and reformulates itself, leaving poetry increasingly aware of its blindness in vacancy's wake. To know that as a writer is to be prodded into constant motion. Elisa New writes that Dickinson's poems take place at

> a limit distinctly outside the boundaries of what we can grasp. . . .
> Her sojourns on the limit traced by circumference yield poems that
> chronicle, in "feet" increasingly "hobbled" and "blind," the wander-
> ings of the poet as disoriented theologian who affirms God's knowl-
> edge through her own lack thereof.[11]

Rather than recreate a Dickinson landscape, then, Wright has unfolded her poems' wandering potential—in his words, putting "Emily Dickinson on Walt Whitman's open road, kinetic compression within a more open-ended space" (Q, 172).[12] The wandering lines of his journals, continually coming back to that broken tooth of possibility as it is variously "restructured and restrung," are Wright's versions of Dickinson's broken-off glimpses or Morandi's "dissembling" lines. In their own way, they testify to a world they are excluded from.

It's no surprise, then, that the year-long "A Journal of the Year of the Ox" (W, 150–90) uses images of exile, process, and pain to describe itself. It opens in January, the poet peering through branches at a world that, like the light of Dickinson's poem 258, comes and goes: "Thursday, purgatorial Thursday, / The Blue Ridge etched in smoke through the leaded panes of the oak trees, / There, then not there" (150). A July entry, meditating on a set of frescoes in the Schifanoia Palace of the dukes of Este in Ferrara, returns to this notion of the speaker as a pilgrim moving through a sort of purgatory—an "in-between" (155).[13] The frescoes detail three levels of existence: "scenes of everyday life"; the inner lives of those struggling through that life ("the dark allegory of the soul"); and the world beyond them, which, through that struggle, they are, perhaps, being prepared for—"the white light of eternity," "the third realm . . . Of pure Abstraction and pure Word" (170, 171–72). In purgatory, then, Wright's pilgrim is continually confronted with and wounded by that just-out-of-reach third realm, brought up against "the carapace of the sky"—its outer shell. The poem, he comments, "deals with circumference, as Emily said her business was. It's mine, too, the outer boundary" (Q, 116). Like Dickinson, Wright's pilgrim is called to a deeper world only to have his apparent means of access continually swept away:

> Pity the poor pilgrim, the setter-forth,
> Under a sweep so sure,
> > pity his going up and his going down.
>
> Each year I remember less.
> This past year it's been
> > the Long Island of the Holston
> And all its keening wires
> > in a west wind that seemed to blow constantly,
> Lisping the sins of the Cherokee.
>
> How shall we hold on, when everything bright falls away?
> How shall we know what calls us
> > when what's past remains what's past
> And unredeemed, the crystal
> And wavering coefficient of what's ahead?   (150)

In Wright, memory is a luminous window, seemingly opening onto a lost, whole self—that other realm where "an image bid[es] its time, / . . . Waiting to take me in and complete my equation" (121). But it is like Dickinson's slant of light, for, when one examines and follows it back, it fades and "falls away." "Brightness falls from the air," writes Thomas Nashe—in this case the past that "remains what's past" and is never redeemed or bought back out of captivity, its crystal shape hinted at but remaining unavailable to the present. "Heavenly Hurt," Dickinson called her experience of that inaccessible world. "Sifting" or "scouring" are Wright's terms for the same confrontation. He remembers—the island of his childhood, for example—but remembers only how little he now recalls. Like Dickinson, he is "alter[ed] . . . utterly"

(that is, brought to "internal difference") by the purgatorial "imperial affliction" of a world that, in memory, comes close but "stays hidden":

> What sifts us down through a blade-change
> > stays hidden from us,
> But sifts us the same,
> Scores us and alters us utterly:
> From somewhere inside and somewhere outside, it smooths us down.
> (151)

What the journal traces, then, is a year's worth of that continual sifting,
exploring the ways in which the speaker is changed as he is drawn to and
disappointed by the luminous brokenness of memory.

One of the repeated observations of this journal is that the poet is not
alone on his pilgrimage. It's caught here in the phrase "sifts us the same,"
which one first takes to mean that although the corrosive force is hidden, it
"sifts us, all the same; sifts us, nevertheless," but then comes to understand
as "sifts us the same way, sifts us all." That notion is picked up in a February entry in which the poet notes that we are all in the same situation.
Brought to the "green gates" of the natural world that promise access to
the "unseen," we find ourselves with only words or images, tangible things,
rising in response—"substitutes for the unseen" or "stand-ins against the
invisible":

> —We stand at the green gates,
> > substitutes for the unseen
> Rising like water inside our bodies,
> Stand-ins against the invisible:
> It's the blank sky of the page
> > —not the words it's never the words—
> That backgrounds our lives:
> It's you always you and not your new suit
> That elicits solicitude:
> The unknown repeats us, and quickens our in-between.
> (154–55)

All of us are "in-between," simultaneously stripped and "quicken[ed]" by the
unknown which, overwhelming our words, opens us to the "blank sky"—
Cézanne's "diamond zones." Dickinson calls this an experience of "internal
Difference." We hear the same note later in the month: "One, one and by
one we all sift to a difference / And cry out if one of our branches snaps or
our bark is cut. / The winter sunlight scours us, / The winter wind is our
comfort and consolation" (156).[14] The fact that the corrosive pilgrimage is

shared means that there are others for Wright's speaker to turn to in this scoured space, other figures who "quicken our in-between" by embodying for a moment, like Dickinson's slant of light, the continually "restructured and restrung" forms the unknown takes, "burn[ing] hard in its vacancy" (145).

A revealing portion of that pilgrimage in which Dickinson plays such a role for Wright begins in March. As with many strands of the journal, the meditation comes only slowly into view, assembling itself across a number of different entries that, in the manner worked out in "A Journal of True Confessions," can be usefully read as the poet coming back, over and over, to the same "broken tooth" or "limit." Wright describes this as returning to the "*strada sottonarrativa*" of the journal: "the undernarrative road" (Q, 169); "a constant thread that you sometimes [see] and sometimes [don't], but [is] always there" (Q, 118). Wright begins this portion of the journey by remembering Verona:

> I remember a woman I saw there once,
>   in March,
> The daylight starting to shake its hair out like torch flames
> Across the river,
>   the season poised like a veiled bride,
> White foot in its golden shoe
> Beating the ground, full of desire, white foot at the white threshold.
> She stared at the conched hillside
>   as though the season became her,
> As though a threshold were opening
> Somewhere inside her, no woman more beautiful than she was,
> No song more insistent than the beat of that white foot,
> As she stepped over,
>   full of desire,
> Her golden shoe like a sun in the day's deep chamber.
> I remember the way she looked as she stood there,
>   that look on her face.
>
> (157–58)

This would seem to be an example of "the difference between the spirit and flesh" becoming "finite, and slowly transgressable" (125). The season, "poised like a veiled bride," seems just at the "threshold" of opening itself utterly while the woman, equally "full of desire," senses the same stirrings inside her. She "stepped over." The memory, for the poet, is a slant of light; it brings the unknown almost within reach. Juxtaposed, the next month, is an account of the Cherokee who once lived on the Long Island of the Holston River near where Wright grew up, being forced to give up, in 1806, the land most sacred to them. Parallels between the two scenes—both sets of figures stand there, ceremonially garbed, staring across a river dancing in sunlight –suggest that we are in the presence of the journal's undernarrative: the Cherokee lost everything the woman in Verona stepped forward into. The poet, weaving this sequence out of memory and imagination, is scoured as well. The possibility of stepping over, which he had felt himself called to by one memory, is abruptly dashed by another. "I remember the way she looked as she *stood there*," he begins; "Imagine them *standing there* in full headdress and harness / Having to give it all up" (italics mine), he goes on:

> Imagine them standing very still,
> Protecting their families, hoping to hang on to their one life.
> Imagine the way they must have felt
> > agreeing to give away
> What wasn't assignable,
> The ground that everyone walked on,
> > all the magic of water,
> Wind in the trees, sunlight, all the magic of water.   (160)

The Dickinson echo—"giv[ing] away / What wasn't assignable" recalling her well-known "I willed my Keepsakes—Signed away / What portion of me be / Assignable" (poem J465, F591)—leads him, in May, to remember a visit to her house in Amherst "A decade or so ago / One afternoon toward the end of winter." Again, a repeated phrase—the Cherokee "standing very still" (160), the poet in Dickinson's cupola "sat very still" (162)—reminds us that we are in the presence of the "Heavenly Hurt" and "broken tooth" of the journal's undernarrative and suggests that Wright is continuing to explore the purgatorial space between "stepping over" and "giv[ing] it all up." Remembering the visit, and behind it the displaced Cherokee and the woman of Verona, he is exploring the nature of that "in-between" space.

He sought Dickinson, but of course he didn't find her. When several friends left him alone in her Amherst cupola, he waited expectantly, but:

> nothing came up through my feet like electric fire.
> And no one appeared in a white dress
> > with white flowers
> Clutched in her white, tiny hands:
> No voice from nowhere said anything
> > about living and dying in 1862.
> (161)

And yet, he continues, something did happen:

> I liked the view down to the garden.
> > I liked the boxwood and evergreens

And the wren-like, sherry-eyed figure
I kept thinking I saw there
                         as the skies started to blossom
And a noiseless noise began to come from the orchard—
And I sat very still, and listened hard
And thought I heard it again.
                         And then there was nothing, nothing at all,

The slick bodice of sunlight
                         smoothed out on the floorboards,
The crystal I'd turned inside of
Dissembling to shine and a glaze somewhere near the windowpanes,
Voices starting to drift up from downstairs,
                         somebody calling my name . . .

(161–62)

The phrases "wren-like, sherry-eyed" are from Dickinson's description of herself in a letter to T. W. Higginson in 1862, which suggests that, although she was gone and "No voice from nowhere said anything about living and dying in 1862," a few shards of her voice were left as she was borne away.[15] The blossoming skies and noiseless noise are from a second letter to Higginson later in the same summer: "I think you would like the Chestnut Tree, I met in my walk. It hit my notice suddenly—and I thought the Skies were in Blossom—Then there's a noiseless noise in the Orchard—that I let persons hear" (letter 271). Handling those luminous shards, Wright's speaker is prompted to "listen hard" to the "noiseless noise" of the world she had been swept into. It is as if she speaks to him for a moment, drawing him into the circle of those she "let[s] . . . hear." Dickinson's phrases, and before that the memories of Verona and the Long Island of the Holston, function like Morandi's "borne away" lines or "Yard Journal"'s blossoms of light, or poem 258's "imperial affliction." "Luminous," they "peel away the burned skin of the world, making the unseen seen." Or they almost do. They draw the poet to a world that is "missing," before which his only response is to "listen hard." "Listen hard," in fact, seems to be what not only Dickinson but all Wright's broken-off memories say as they fall away. They don't give us the unknown. Rather, they scour us and draw us away from certainty. As with "A Journal of True Confessions," in time everything "dissembles" or "devolves / To simple description in the end," and the poet is left only with the sense that something has come, "burned hard in its vacancy," and vanished, poised to reemerge "elsewhere restructured and restrung." The poet's mark of "internal Difference" is that he has learned to "listen hard" to Dickinson's half-caught voice—that he has been alert as, just for a moment, something of that other world crystallized, dissembled, and then drifted away.

The first half of the journal draws to a close with a June entry in which this notion of moving in the company of other voices is developed further. Another connecting phrase—"I thought I heard" (162, 164) invisible music or noiseless noise— links this scene to the undernarrative of the previous three I've examined. Still in Charlottesville, Wright notes:

—Horn music starts up and stutters uncertainly
                                        out of the brown house
Across the street: a solo,
A duet, then three of them all at once, then silence,
Then up and back down the scale.

This uncertain music leads the poet back, in his mind, to Italy:

Where was it I heard before
Those same runs and half-riffs
                            turned through a summer morning,
Come from one of the pastel buildings
Outside the window I sat in front of looking down
As I tried to practice my own scales
                            of invisible music
I thought I heard for hours on a yellow legal pad?
Verona, I think, the stiff French horn
Each weekend echoing my own false notes
                            and scrambled lines
I tried to use as decoys to coax the real things down
Out of the air they hid in and out of the pencils they hid in . . .
(164)

What he was doing as he wrote—listening to "invisible music" and trying to "coax" it down with his inadequate "scrambled lines" and clumsy "scales"— was just what he was doing in Dickinson's cupola, listening hard to a "noise-less noise." Just as he was drawn to this music by the few still-echoing phrases remaining after her work had been borne away, so the "stiff" French horn player and the "stutter[ing]" trio across the street, echoing his "false notes," draw him toward the "invisible music" overwhelming their own. In fact, some of those uncertain notes hanging in the air are once again Dickinson's; "invisible music" is her phrase—half erased but still calling him to listen:

This World is not Conclusion.
A Species stands beyond—
Invisible, as Music—
But positive, as Sound—

It beckons, and it baffles—
Philosophy—don't know—
And through a Riddle, at the last—
Sagacity, must go—   (J501, F373)

What all of these "uncertain" voices call him to is the music they are in the process of being borne back into: a music that both "beckons and . . . baffles," subverting philosophy and passing all "sagacity" through a "Riddle." That music measures us and find us wanting—scouring us, stripping away our "substitutes for the unseen," and ridding us of the assurance that we are able truly to hear anything. "Heavenly Hurt, it gives us":

Silence again. For good, now,
I suspect, until next week,
                    arduous harmony,
Unalterable music our lives are measured by.
What will become of us, the Italian French horn player,
These players, me, all of us
                    trying to imitate
What we can't see and what we can't hear?
Nothing spectacular, I would guess, a life
Scored more or less by others,
                    smorzando here, *andante* there:
Only the music will stay untouched,
Moving as certainly as the wind moves,
                    invisible in the trees.   (165)

If he is "Scored more or less by others" who, being borne away, have left, in memory, a few lines and images as a score to be followed out, he is, at the same time, most deeply scored—that is, scraped, chastened, measured, and opened—by the music they allow him to glimpse, which can never be touched and can never fully be heard.

The journal moves to Italy for the summer, and the idea of scored listening as a response to vacancy comes to full development. Wright begins with a quite literal account of being scoured by the wind:

—North wind flows from the mountain like water,
                    a clear constancy
Runneling through the grapevines,
    . . .
                    backwashes against the hillsides
And nibbles my cheeks and hands
Where I stand on the balcony letting it scour me.   (165)

That scouring is linked to a scene a few days later in which, at evening, the departing light drains away, flowing back along the same route the north wind had come in on. Scouring becomes the loss of the luminous. As the repetition of a phrase—"sat still"—from his visit to Dickinson's house suggests, Wright has again returned to the broken tooth experienced at Amherst. Fragments of voice or glimmers of light, barely heard or seen, once again pull away:

> I sat on the stone wall as the white shirts of my son and friend
> Moved through the upper yard like candles
> Among the fruit trees,
>   and the high voices of children
> Sifted like mist from the road below
> In a game I'd never played,
>   and knew that everything was a shining,
> That whatever I could see was filled with the drained light
> Lapping away from me quietly,
> Disappearing between the vine rows,
>   creeping back through the hills,
> That anything I could feel,
>   anything I could put my hand on—
> The damasked mimosa leaf,
> The stone ball on the gate post, the snail shell in its still turning—
> Would burst into brilliance at my touch.
> But I sat still, and I touched nothing,
>   afraid that something might change
> And change me beyond my knowing   (167)

What he is forced to confront, painfully, is his distance from that other world. He is chastened and scored by his inability to act. The language here is much like Dickinson's poem 160 (F132), in which a similar failure to step across is described in terms of a receding tide:

> Just lost, when I was saved!
> Just felt the world go by!
> Just girt me for the onset with Eternity,
> When breath blew back,
> And on the other side
> I heard recede the disappointed tide!

That image, I think, explains why, some days later, the poet's uneasiness about his failure to step over and be "change[d] . . . beyond my knowing"

generates a vision of Dante in that same "night garden," speaking "in disap-
proval" as if from Dickinson's receding, "disappointed tide":

> Who else could it be,
>   voice like a slow rip through silk cloth
> In disapproval? *Brother*, he says, pointing insistently [toward a
>   statue of the Madonna on a nearby hillside],
> A sound of voices starting to turn in the wind and then disappear as
>   though
> Orbiting us, *Brother, remember the way it was*
> *In my time: nothing has changed:*
> *Penitents terrace the mountainside, the stars hang in their bright courses*
> *And darkness is still the dark:*
>   *concentrate, listen hard,*
> *Look to the nature of all things,*
> And vanished into the oncoming disappearing
> Circle of voices slipstreaming through the oiled evening.
> (168–69)

What the disappointed tide always says—Dante, Dickinson, and the other
voices turning in the wind and disappearing—is "concentrate, listen hard." As
they vanish, they take our eyes to what isn't there. That desire to hear and see,
of course, is an impossible-to-complete task in purgatory where, as another July
entry has it, the only music we are sure of is the screeching of brakes and the
moaning of tires as trucks rumble down the Italian mountainside: "A music of
sure contrition that troubles our ears / And shudders the farmhouse walls. . . . /
But everyone suffers the music. / We all sway to the same tune" (169). What we
suffer is "Heavenly Hurt," exclusion from what we know to be there.

Purgatory, this world between, seems in fact filled with penitents strain-
ing to hear:

> Volcanic originally, the Euganean hills
> Blister a tiny part,
>   upper northeast, of the Po flood plain.
> Monasteries and radar stations
> Relay the word from their isolate concentration,
> Grouped, as they are, like bread mold
>   and terraced like Purgatory.
> . . .
> Outside my door, a cicada turns its engine on.
> Above me the radar tower
> Tunes its invisible music in   (170)

All of this comes to a head during an August thunderstorm. As lightning strikes, the statue of the Madonna and the radar dishes seem to successfully tune in that invisible music. Though the poet is still on this side of that great tide and storm, he understands what he is seeing:

> Dog fire: quick singes and pops
> Of lightning finger the mountainside:
> > the towers and deep dish
> Are calling their children in, Madonna is calling her little ones
> Out of the sky, such fine flames
> To answer to and add up
> > as they all come down from the dark.
> In the rings and after-chains,
> In the great river of language that circles the universe,
> Everything comes together,
> No word is ever lost,
> > no utterance ever abandoned.
> They're all borne on the bodiless, glittering currents
> That wash us and seek us out:
> > there is a word, one word,
> For each of us, circling and holding fast
> In all that cascade and light.
> Said once or said twice,
> > it gathers and waits its time to come back
> To its true work:
> > concentrate, listen hard.   (176)

"[F]ine flames" of vision—things, writes Dickinson in poem 160, by the "Ear unheard / Unscrutinized by Eye"—are for the moment all around him. They are, I would suggest, versions of the searing insights of Dickinson or the childhood scenes whose fragments draw and trouble Wright. We could think of them as the powerful but ultimately untouchable slants of light that Wright has been examining through this entire series of journals. Seeing them, he feels called "To answer to and add up" their influence. But how is he able to do that when the lightning flashes only for a moment and recedes, leaving at best a "dissolving image after the eyelids close"? That is the question *Zone Journals* continually returns to. And here, a moment of insight occurs. Although those voices are "borne [away] on the bodiless, glittering currents" of the unknown that "wash us and seek us out," painfully demonstrating that we can't hold or pursue the brief insights they offer, "No word is ever lost." The unknown they recede back into is a real world, he speculates: a "great river of language that circles the universe / [Where] everything comes together."[16] And its "one word, / For each of us" "waits its time." He "answers" or responds, then, by "listening hard" for that word, a process, as we've seen, that involves moving and losing, remembering and setting aside, being scoured and moving on—Elisa New's "hobbled or blind . . . wanderings." We find him a few days later at the end of the Italian entries, in the same night garden:

> No scooters or trucks,
> No voices of children, no alphabet in the wind:
> Only this silence, the strict gospel of silence,
>
> > to greet me,
>
> Opened before me like a rare book.
> I turn the first page
> > and then the next, but understand nothing,
> The deepening twilight a vast vocabulary
> I've never heard of.
> I keep on turning, however:
> > somewhere in here, I know, is my word.
>
> (177)

To listen, this suggests, is to "keep on turning." Such a process is exactly what the journal form is designed to foreground.

The final entries of the poem, set back in Virginia, begin to expand that sense of connection with those of us on this same, continuous pilgrimage. Poets, musicians, relatives, readers: in Wright, we all embrace a similar uncertainty, echoing each other as we strive to hear a music beyond us. Driving down the Shenandoah Valley and puzzling over the way his "mother's mother's family" has "For generations . . . sifted down / This valley like rain out of Clarke County, seeping into the red clay / Overnight and vanishing into the undergrowth / Of different lives as hard as they could" (178), Wright comes to see the family's embarrassing wanderlust as a response to, an inadvertent tracking of, the unknown's continual sifting and erasing of what we would otherwise cling to and grow falsely comfortable with:

> What makes us leave what we love best?
> What is it inside us that keeps erasing itself
> When we need it most,
> That sends us into uncertainty for its own sake
> And holds us flush there
> > until we begin to love it
> And have to begin again?
> What is it within our own lives we decline to live
> Whenever we find it,

> making our days unendurable,
> And nights almost visionless?
> I still don't know yet, but I do it.   (179)

A last reference to Dickinson's slant prompts this description of those on Wright's pilgrimage:

> Afternoon light-slant deep weight
>   diluting to aftermath on the lawn,
> Jay immobile and fluffed up,
> Cloud like a bass note, held and slow, now on the sunlight.
> The disillusioned and twice-lapsed, the fallen-away,
> Become my constituency:
>   those who would die back
> To splendor and rise again
> From hurt and unwillingness,
>   their own ash on their tongues,
> Are those I would be among,
> The called, the bruised by God, by their old ways forsaken
> And startled on, the shorn and weakened.   (184)

"Twice-lapsed" gets at this in an interesting way. Wright's "constituency" is those, like himself, who have fallen away from a sense of the everyday and then have, in time, fallen away from the insight prompting that awakening. As the tide recedes, such figures "die back" to an acknowledgment of "splendor" they can't touch, only to "rise again" when a glimpse returns to tantalize. Hurt by heaven, such figures are both "called" and "bruised." Having lost their "old ways," they are "startled on" to a life of continuous movement.

The final, December entry is quite firm in its confession that the pilgrim hasn't yet stepped over the edge of circumference. Wright begins with David's great line in Psalm 22, the psalm recalled by Christ on the cross, and acknowledges that he hasn't been struck by *that* bolt of the invisible music:

> —*I am poured out like water.*
> Who wouldn't ask for that *lightning strike,*
>   the dog's breath on your knee
> Seductive and unrehearsed,
> The heart resoftened and made apt for illumination,
> The body then taken up and its ghostly eyes dried?
> Who wouldn't ask for that light,
>   that liquefication and entry?

What he is left with instead are the questions driving this book: "What is a life of contemplation worth in this world? / How far can you go if you concentrate, how far down?" (190). Of course he doesn't know. But what he has seen is how continually the question might be returned to and acted on. Emily Dickinson comes back one more time, and this time he separates himself from her, to a degree, perhaps in the name of continually looking and listening and wandering. In the journal's last lines, Wright recalls poem 303 (F409): "The Soul selects her own Society— / Then—shuts the Door— / . . . I've known her—from an ample nation— / Choose One— / Then—close the Valves of her attention— / Like Stone—." At first, he seems tempted to adopt her focus on the single image or object of attention, understanding, as she did, both the enormous pain following such a choice and the potential gain. But then he makes an interesting turn, feeling the winter afternoon close down around him, experiencing the "tighten[ing]" of the valves of the heart's attention, but then stepping back from such a reduction to a single focus and embracing instead a journal-keeper's continual looking and losing:

> The afternoon shuts its doors.
> The heart tightens its valves,
> > the dragon maple sunk in its bones,
> The grass asleep in its wheel.
> The year squeezes to this point, the cold
> Hung like a lantern against the dark
> > burn of a syllable:
> I roll it around on my tongue, I warm its edges . . .   (190)

If the year in its last December days has squeezed down to the dark burning of a single syllable, placed like Isaiah's coal on the poet's tongue, that utterly cold point, like other landscapes and voices and memories, is yet something that can be played with—"rolled around on [the] tongue" as a journal does, touched and touched again, gradually warmed and "quickened." For one who senses that, the road continually opens out.

FOUR

INTERVIEW WITH
CHARLES WRIGHT

TG: Let's begin with a little bit of history. Your interviews and essays describe when you first read Pound and first read Montale, but you haven't said much, that I know, about when you first seriously encountered Emily Dickinson. My guess would be Iowa City.

CW: You would guess correctly. When I went to Iowa, at the age of twenty-six, the first academic course I had there was on Hopkins and Dickinson, taught by Donald Justice, a major teacher. At that time, he had a great interest in both of them. To this day, he still has a great interest in Hopkins. I don't know how much interest he still has in Dickinson. The first half of the semester was on Dickinson and the second half on Hopkins. At the time, I much preferred Hopkins, for reasons I'm not quite sure of. I guess because of the excess of language rather than the reticence which I later found to be so seductive in Dickinson—the reticence and the obliquity of the way she said things. So, I continued to read Hopkins, and then, sometime when I was out in California, I took her book out again and read the whole *Selected Poems*, then bought the *Collected Poems* and read it. I realized this is what I was trying to do. These were the questions that concerned me—not that I could do them the way she did, but I saw someone who had certainly asked the same unanswerable questions, constantly. And that appealed to me. I loved her language and the way she wrote and thought about things. And then, the way one does, I got really caught up and read the letters, which I liked almost more than the poems. The letters were just amazing. That was my flurry of interest. It went on for about a year or so.

TG: When would this be?

cw: Oh, lord, back in the seventies sometime. Which isn't to say that it disappeared. It has stayed with me ever since. But that was the intense crush I had—the infatuation during that year-or-two period—and I do think that probably my entire last thirty years of writing has been an endeavor to write a line that says "'tis like the Distance / On the look of Death—." I love her poems. Once you've read them enough, they get inside you. Those lines have stayed in my mind for all these years, even though I don't go back much now and read her. Strangely enough, I go back and read Yeats, of all things—somebody who was never an influence on me at all. Maybe that's why I go back and read him.

As I said, she's in my bloodstream in ways that I'm grateful for and ways that are ineradicable. When I went to her house that time, which I wrote about in "A Journal of the Year of the Ox," and sat in her cupola, it really was an amazing sensation. One goes to a lot of houses—I've been to Dove Cottage, I've been to Petrarch's house—but that one was really amazing. I've been to where Pound was born, but none of these affected me the way it did when I went to where she lived. Anyhow, she's just one of those creatures who come and live with you, and you put them up.

TG: Do some of your books have more Dickinson in them than others?

cw: The absence of narrative in my work, which is pervasive, really, has something to do with my admiration for the way she would tell a story without telling a story. So, in that respect, they all contain her influence. Her influence, as I've always said, is not a direct influence. It's not stylistic. It's not metrical. It's not lineation. It's something more light and airy, or dark and airy. . . . You hate to say words like this, but it's an interior thing. I suppose it's a kind of negative spirituality I have and that I find she had long before me. Lots of other people did too, but she was able to talk about it. And I've tried to talk about it in my work. In that case, it's probably spread out everywhere, in ways I don't even know, from that first class. That class made an impression on me more than any other I've ever taken. It was the first serious class about poets, filled with writers, that I ever took. I never had one as an undergraduate, and I had been in the army for four years before that, where I had gotten interested in poetry.

TG: So, you were incredibly hungry, and you ended up with one of the best teachers in the country and a class full of hungry people.

cw: Yes. Mark Strand was in that class, Marvin Bell, Jim Crenner.

TG: And you read two deeply religious writers.

cw: Yes. They were contemporaries, of course, which is why Don, I think, chose them. They were different from each other and very much alike. They were both on the same road, and she went left and he went right. All of this stuff was completely new to me. FAO Schwarz of the mind! That's why it stayed with me so long, I guess. The next semester we did a class on the long poem—Stevens's "Comedian as the Letter C," parts of *Paterson*, and so on— and those are people that Don loved, too, but it didn't make the impression on me that the first class did. Those two people have been on me, one on each shoulder, throughout my writing life. So, the answer to your question is always, all of them. . . . I haven't read the poems for a long time, maybe about fifteen years. I haven't gone back, as I said.

TG: But clearly the lines stay in your head.

cw: Absolutely.

TG: The number of times Dickinson's "certain Slant of light" comes up in *Zone Journals*, for example, is quite remarkable. I take it you were quite aware of its presence?

cw: Every time there is a direct echo, that echo is meant. And it's not just Dickinson alone—echoes are rife all the way throughout my stuff, hoping to call up other examples, by other people, of the same thing. "Slant of light" was a poem that Don loved. I know that poem well. Whenever I'm looking at the light and the changing of things, that poem always comes to mind. It's like, each time I hear a train whistle, I think of "The Streamlined Cannonball" or "Moving On," those songs. It may be that it's the ur-poem in my unconscious. I learned it the first or second week of my first graduate class and never got rid of it. There are other poems that are more difficult and perhaps even more bodying forth with emotional resonance to me than that one, but that one— there's a simplicity and a heft to that poem not matched by almost anything else. And I guess that's why I love it. I think it's a fairly early poem for her, but it has the feel of an old master writing at the height of his powers, the way Picasso could do something with three or four lines at the end of his life.

TG: You used the phrase "negative spirituality." Do you see that in the poem?

cw: To a certain extent, yes. I see it through all of her poems—that God is defined by what he isn't, what isn't available to her. That's how negative theology is defined, more or less. I've now found a name for something I've been thinking about all these years. That's why I use the title *Negative Blue*—the blue is defined by what it isn't. I find that in her, as opposed to Hopkins: nothing negative there. Even the terrible part is not negative.

TG: So, for Hopkins, "The world is charged with the grandeur of God" . . .

cw: And I am charged by the *absence* of God.

TG: And what's that charge, when the slant of light comes and goes?

cw: Well, when it goes, it doesn't really go. It remains, as Pound said of something else, "in the mind indestructible." It's that moment when illumination seems possible. It never actually happens, at least not so far, but its possibility is the illumination, I guess, that one is looking for. And when one comes to terms with that, one comes to terms with everything. It is a constant trying, which is why *light, slant, heft*, all of that, keeps coming up again and again, because as it goes away, it stays. What stays is what goes away. It stays in the appreciation and affection one has for those few moments when things seem just the way they're supposed to be. Now, it is true that I've also said that I like the disappearance of things, the edges, but I find a kind of beauty in the disappearance that remains—not just disappears, because there's nothing beautiful about that.

TG: It disappears, but it remains . . . a possibility?

cw: It remains in your mind. The possibility of its returning in exactly the same way, which it probably never does, remains. That's when memory is a good thing and not a bad thing, because memory can be awful and suck you down into its sinkhole. But if it remains clear and bright in the mind as a possibility of the way things once were and could be again, then it's a fructifying sort of situation.

I think that's why I'm so drawn to landscape as opposed to nature. Landscape is a kind of simulacra for the way things can be, often are, but never are repeatable, even though the possibility of positive repetition always exists. The landscape is always the same and always different. It's just like Heraclitus and the river. It's never the same landscape twice, but it is. It's just like a religion; you can return to it in ways that . . . It's how you make it. To me, it's always new and what it was before, in the good sense. I don't know why I'm so drawn to the given world out there, but I am. Someone like Jorie Graham or Mark Strand lives in his or her mind. They're very imaginative poets. I'm really stuck with what I can see. I think that's a deficiency, probably, but I've tried to make a positive out of a negative. I like to think Emily Dickinson was moved by what she saw as well, and by what she couldn't see and couldn't articulate but was using the given world to try to come to terms with. Which is why I've always been drawn to her and to her vision of things. She really had a vision, just like Hopkins. If you don't have vision, you ain't got nothing. If your back yard is just your back yard, you may as well crack another Budweiser.

We're walking on eggs here. I don't really know. If I knew, I would have said it years ago.

TG: Her poem "Just lost, when I was saved" must mean a lot to you.

cw: Yes.

TG: Listening to you makes me think, for the first time, that you're perhaps most drawn to the references to "next time" at the end of the poem.

> Next time, to stay!
> Next time, the things to see
> By Ear unheard,
> Unscrutinized by Eye—
>
> Next time, to tarry,
> While the Ages steal—
> Slow tramp the Centuries,
> And the Cycles wheel!

cw: I love that poem. I love that last stanza. So I've probably tried to sneak that into more than one poem. The trouble is the next time will be just like this time. That's the problem. But that Next Time, with capital N and T, is what she's looking for and what I'm looking for, whenever that is.

TG: And you've used lines from near the middle of the poem before—"Therefore, as One returned, I feel / Odd secrets of the line to tell!"

cw: "Odd secrets of the line." I never quite understood what the "line" was. I didn't know if it was a military line or a line of demarcation, the line of saints, the line of talk, as Jimmy Rogers would have it. There's a ship of the line, which means a commissioned, battle-ready ship. Or it may be as simple as a near-death experience. Everyone seems to have the same near-death experience, apparently. The long tunnel of light. The medieval nuns each had the very same experience when they had an epiphany with Christ behind the altar. It was all unsayable—this unspeakable, unspeaking connection with the great bundle of light. Maybe that's the line of demarcation you go over and come back. There are plenty of odd secrets to be told, if you come back.

TG: You mentioned memory a while ago. It seems to me that memory functions for you much like that slant of light. Flashes of memory. You spend so much time talking about what you don't remember, as if those little flashes of what you don't fully remember lead you to the edge of something unmentionable now but at your core.

cw: Yes. You said it much better than I could. I often wonder if it's not due to a paucity of imagination that I'm so drawn to memory. It's one of those things that, if it could be put right, things would *be* right. You can never put memory right, though, because it's always wrong. And so it becomes a vehicle in itself, apart from any actuality that it may be. Or have been. It becomes like Jorie's fascination with the representation of the object and the object itself. It becomes representation. Most everything *is* representation, in any case, after it goes through the little grinder and hits the paper.

TG: Memory becomes a vehicle for . . . ?

cw: Well, for imagination. Both landscape and memory are stand-ins—as I said before—simulacra for the object itself, something behind both of those things, and you don't know quite what it is: it's the line you keep trying to tell odd secrets about when you sit down and look at it or think about it. That is how memory really works for me, not as a thing to remember, but as a kind of an attack vehicle to get at things, to get at the point where you're open to the possibilities we talked about earlier. Both memory and landscape work that way for me. It's a kind of inalterable law that you follow. Once you get enmeshed in memory, and the idea that memory can do this for you, then you follow it all the time, hoping that there will be some flashes which will then mix with landscape or whatever else is out there that gives you that little opening, that little peek, which is, I guess, the line.

TG: In "The Southern Cross," you talk about this directly, don't you? "There is an otherness inside us / We can never touch, no matter how far down our hands reach." It's that idea?

cw: It's that idea.

TG: In that poem you call it the past.

cw: I call it the past, but in fact it's the state of existence you try to get back to. This is nothing new—everybody talks about that. Eliot's center of silence in the garden—any image like that. I want to see it again, and that's why "Odd secrets of the line to tell" is such an evocative line for me, because that's what I'm talking about, although I work with different objects.

TG: Memory and landscape?

cw: Yes. Memory and landscape are different from her idea of God and the natural world. She believed in the idea of God much more than I do.

TG: Although she would understand exactly what you're talking about.

cw: Well, I hope so. She's the one I'm writing to. She was still wedded to the idea of the church, I think, because of the society and time she was raised in. I was sort of raised in that, but times are different now. She was a single woman in a room, in Calvinist New England. She had to work with what she had, and I have to work with what I have.

TG: In an interview, you said that "The true genius of poetry is lyric and imagistic. It lies in concision and allusion, something withheld but partially glimpsed." It strikes me that your notion of lyric form is quite close to the view of the world in "There's a certain Slant of light" or in . . .

cw: Well, yes. It's certainly no news to the world that things partially seen are almost always stronger than things completely seen, because you get to do the imagining yourself, to make them complete in the way that you want to. I suppose this all goes back to Sappho, bless her heart, who was the first to stop writing two-hundred-page poems and wrote these little lyrics. As we have them now, they're partially seen because they've been lost. One wonders if part of that aspect of the lyric was accidental and that's how we got it and made an aesthetic of it, or whether the aesthetic was already there and she slipped beautifully into it once she was resurrected and reinstalled. The idea of something missing, I mean, being part of the lyric aesthetic.

I don't know. For me, since I am unable to do real narrative, the associative lyric has always been the one form that I felt, if not at home with, at least on the same block with. I have worked in it constantly, and have either expanded it or condensed it to my own ends. But I think what you said was true—that the form seems to imply the glimpsed thing, which then becomes more fully formed than the seen thing would in, say, the sonnet which, in its heyday, mirrored a complete statement, an argument, an entity. It gave you a narrative that started and finished beautifully, whereas in the lyric, even if it starts and finishes beautifully, the argument is never fulfilled. At least the lyric as I use it, or it uses me. It always has that incompleteness which I feel is necessary to art—that almost completeness, but kept apart right at the end so that you can make the synapse yourself without the argument being made. Which isn't to say, of course, that the sonnet is not "lyric." But a good one is always tied up, isn't it? At the end, I mean.

TG: And that synapse arcs over the line?

CW: Over the line. At least for me. I'm not arguing against completeness, because that's beautiful, of course. But for me, for what mirrors what I have been trying to come to terms with, the lyric as mentioned above is the perfect way to rhyme with that attempt. I've continued to try to keep it apart all these years.

TG: What's fascinating, then, is why, in your book most directly focused on these issues, you would put together a year-long journal—"A Journal of the Year of the Ox."

CW: Ah, yes. It's a year. It has those arbitrary boundaries, but within the boundaries, I don't think anything is tied up into a neat package. It's a lyric. It's made up of a whole bunch of lyrics. In fact, it's a forty-two-page poem made up of little poems. If I had a forty-two-page narrative, it would have been a short story. Those arbitrary beginnings and ends are just to give myself something within which to work.

TG: Did the writing of *Zone Journals*, your collection of journals, seem different to you?

CW: Yes. It's the last book of *The World of the Ten Thousand Things*, and it was supposed to be the antithesis of *China Trace*, the last book of *Country Music*, which was nothing but one- to twelve-line poems, as small as I could make them. *Zone Journals* was supposed to be the opposite of that. It lengthens the line as far as I thought it could go and still remain a poetic line and not a rhetorical one. Therefore, the containers of those lines would have to be different too; they would have to be longer. And that's when I hit on the journal form. "A Journal of the Year of the Ox" is no different from "English Journal" or even "Last Journal," in concept. It *is* different from the poems in *China Trace*, though, because the impulse behind the two forms of the lyric is very different. One is to condense, one is to expand. The condensed ones are more self-contained than the journal ones are, even say a six-line poem from *China Trace* compared to "Last Journal," which is also six lines. They're very different. Not only is the line longer, but the space of the poem. Even though it might occupy the same amount on the page, the space that the poem occupies in the mind is much more expansive in the journal poems than in the *China Trace* poems. The longer the journal poem gets, the more lyric it becomes.

TG: It's lyric because there's always something withheld?

cw: Something condensed and withheld and unknowable. You're working in an area that is psychically unavailable to you. Again, this is the back yard business we began with—the light slant and that little opening.

I'm drawn to what I tried to do in the journals more than in any other combination of things I've worked in. In *Country Music*, I tried to condense down to the end. There were four books, and the end result was *China Trace*. In *The World of the Ten Thousand Things*, the work moved outward and outward and outward, and the journals were the end result. *Negative Blue*, the last stage of the project, was a combination of the two—the longer line, the more expansive imagination, but a welding on to it of the condensation and tightness of the earlier lyric. The attempt in *Zone Journals* and *Xionia*—I think of both of them as *Zone Journals*—was larger, stylistically and maybe even emotionally, than in any of the three books, even though the concerns are the same in all of them. Probably, the most successful is the last one, *Negative Blue*, but I feel the closest to the journal poems, because they are the ones where I tried to graft, interiorally, all that I learned about the lyric from the earlier poems, the short ones. In a way, *Negative Blue* is a rehashing of those first two.

TG: Are you ever going to go back to that form?

cw: I don't think so, if you mean the journals. Someone said, "Oh, you're writing the new *Cantos*!" That was the end of that. I'd been bludgeoned about Pound before, just because I was so foolish when I started out: I didn't know that anything you said would be held against you for the rest of your life. . . . He was the first person I ever read, but I've read a lot of people since then. He was meaningful to me, but I didn't want anybody thinking that I was going to do *The Cantos*. So, I had a beginning and an ending to the journals. They were meaningful to me, they really were. That's why I was so pleased to see that you had liked them because, among other things, they were the first things I did when I moved back here. I was trying to root myself into a place. I wrote about my upbringing in East Tennessee, western North Carolina, the entire time I was in California. The minute I moved back I never wrote about it again, in that sense. I moved to the back yard and wrote about it, in the present sense. It's memory in the present tense—talking about the memory. And that's why it was so important to me—technically as well as in terms of subject matter.

TG: Memory in the present tense?

CW: Instead of writing about the landscape as I remembered it, I was writing about the landscape of memory as I was looking at it. Nobody paid any attention, really, but it was an attempt to write in a different kind of form. I still have this fondness for it, from my early days in Virginia. The idea of using memory not as remembering but as a vehicle came to me when I was doing these. Memory became part of the iconic structure, the way landscape and language itself always have been. It became a different kind of memory—not just remembering. Memory is, of course, one of the classic subject matters of poetry, but I was trying to do a little different take on it. And have for some years, in ways I've talked about earlier.

TG: Keep going.

CW: Well . . . The king of nostalgia is my teacher Donald Justice. He writes the most beautiful poems about nostalgia. Nobody can touch him. So, I tried to stay away from that. I think of memory as a river rather than a lake. Nostalgia thinks of memory as a lake. It's something you go to and it's there. If it's a river, it's something that's always moving, that's always changing, that's always going into different aspects, that always has a different look to it, has a different light on it. If I had to use an image, that's how I would say I was trying to use memory—as a vehicle, something that's not stagnant but remains constantly illuminated in the mind, different from the beautiful lake or ocean that seems more static to me.

TG: That's the kind of language you could use to talk about God as well.

CW: Exactly. God is a river, he's not the ocean.

TG: When you talk about poems being put together associatively, you probably wouldn't say that Dickinson does that, would you?

cw: No. I think she has a little narrative going almost all the time. I think the start for that sort of thing probably *is* Pound. The excuse for being able to do that is probably Pound. The *source*, however, is my lack of ability to tell a story. That's why that poem I first read by Pound out on Lake Garda was so staggeringly important to me, because even though it was basically a kind of sonnet in iambic pentameter, it moved by association rather than telling a story. That one poem. And then of course he was the first poet I ever read. As soon as I got to Iowa, they disabused me of any such notion and pointed me toward Wallace Stevens and others, although Pound was still in my head to a certain extent. I tried to write little narrative things at Iowa. I just couldn't do it. I went over to Italy on a Fulbright and translated Montale; he did a lot of that sort of modernist associational stuff as well. And so I had two examples, and I decided, well, that's the only way I can do it, so I'll just try to do it. Again, I tried to make a positive out of a negative. It's still a definite negative, I'm afraid, not being able to do narrative.

TG: Well . . .

cw: I think so. If you're a Southerner, it is . . . But anyhow, as I said before, there's really nothing stylistically I took from Emily Dickinson. It was all content. (I am one of those who think there are three things—form, subject matter, and content. Not just form and content. Content is what it all means. Subject matter is how you say it.) What it means in Emily Dickinson is what I'm interested in. In Hopkins, on the other hand, I was interested in how he did it—even though you can't imitate him, one of the great things about Hopkins—as well as his content. And even though I didn't believe his content. I believed her content, however. She speaks to me. Very few poets speak to me. I was fascinated by Pound because he was the first person I ever read, but the history of Social Credit just means nothing to me. Eliot has much more to *say* to me than Pound.

TG: "Canto 47," where Pound shifts from Odysseus and Circe to the red pollen across the Mediterranean to lamps flickering in the bay, seems to move in the associational way you describe.

cw: The poem about Rapallo. It's beautiful: "The sea's claw gathers them in."

TG: Even the way he shifts from a series of images to speaking to himself seems much like you:

> The small lamps drift in the bay
> And the sea's claw gathers them.
> Neptunus drinks after neap-tide.
> Tamuz! Tamuz!
> The red flame going seaward.
> By this gate art thou measured.

cw: I probably got that from him. It's in there so far back.

TG: I don't want to stick you with Pound again, but "Canto 47" really is an education in how to put a poem together.

cw: Or, to *not* put it together, in a very fascinating way.

TG: One of the words you use a lot is *devolve*, often in very interesting ways. For example near the end of "A Journal of True Confessions": "The song of white lights and power boats, the sails of August and late July devolve / To simple description in the end." Can you talk about that?

cw: I do use *devolve* a lot. My first year at Iowa, W. H. Auden read and, during the question-and-answer period afterwards, somebody said, "Why do you have so many lions in your poems?" He said, "I do? I'll have to change that." Well, I'll have to stop using *devolve*, I guess. It "devolves to simple description in the end." Just description. Of course, that's what Elizabeth Bishop said all of her poems were. I once said the same thing. But it's always more than description. If it's true description, then it becomes part of that vehicle of discovery. The right description is like the right use of memory. Which is to say, it gives you an opening into something that wasn't there before you described it, in the way you described it, or that wasn't even there in the memory of it. It's in the way you *use* that memory. So, if it devolves to pure description in the end, there's always the worry that you didn't do it correctly and that it remains just description, when you were trying to get beyond just describing the thing, into the other side of the thing.

TG: And part of the point, I suppose, is that you know you haven't brought it off.

cw: Yes. You'll never bring it off.

TG: You also tend to use the words *scour* and *score* quite frequently—as in that lovely phrase about "being scored by others."

CW: Scored, as in a musical score, and scored as in physically scored or scraped by others—by people you've read, by people you admire, by the history of literature, and so on. I'm sure that all of these word patterns develop because of their sound patterns. I get this tune in my head that is pleasing, and then like everything else that's pleasing, it comes back to you—like lines from Emily Dickinson. Since my vocabulary is not quite that of Harold Bloom's or Richard Howard's, I probably return to the same words that I have loved in the past more often, and try to use them again. I think a lot of us are driven by sound patterns more than we would like to admit, because what really drew us to poetry in the first place was the sound of things. All the words exist in prose, but it's not the same thing, so sound patterns tend to live on, long past their original necessity.

TG: And they're part of the "invisible music" that you're listening to?

CW: That you're always listening to, that runs behind everything. Someone like Mark Strand, for instance, has patterns that happen and rehappen in his poems. Charlie Simic, who doesn't seem to have much sound patterning going on, actually has a lot. No one wants to say any of this, because we all want to be so meaningful, but in fact, the music drives an awful lot of these engines. Which is fine with me.

TG: That's a difficult thing for criticism to talk about.

CW: I know. It's never really mentioned. Critics, for the most part, only talk about the meaning, the content. Naturally—that's what's there. But often, though they don't admit it, poets come at it from a different angle. I think I come at it from a musical one, a sound pattern, and then the other stuff—since my subject matter is an obsession—falls into place, or doesn't fall into place. I never approach it from the title of a poem—I never start it that way. It comes from something else. It usually comes from something I've seen, or some sound pattern that will come into my head. I used to write down nonsense words with a pattern, a line pattern, I liked and then figure out what I was trying to say after that. (Laughter) I'm not sure that's a good idea, but that's how I do it sometimes.

TG: Your new book, *A Short History of the Shadow*, returns quite regularly to the idea of sitting still. You use variations of the phrase "I'm sitting in the same place," for example. I know that when you've spoken before about Dickinson, the idea of sitting still has seemed crucial to you. I wonder why?

cw: I don't know, but I do think it's probably connected to my idea of her, the idea of being able to encompass more as it unrolls in front of you being still, as opposed to going out and running around and doing a lot of unreconstructable things. I think of her enterprise as the ur-enterprise of the writer—not that I could do what she did, or be as reclusive as she was, but I think that's the better way to do it. I've always thought of myself as someone who's stayed in the back room and wrote out of his own needs and experiences and nonexperiences, rather than one who went out and made these experiences and then wrote about them.

The first part of *A Short History of the Shadow* was a coming down from this long project that I did, my Appalachian Book of the Dead. There are three sections. One had to do with this room, my study. One has to do with the back yard. And one has to do with Montana. Those are the three places I tended to write those three books of *Negative Blue* in. That's what "Look Around" means. After that, the poems seem to me somewhat different. A "project" doesn't underlie everything that I write, as it used to. I think there's a great value and a great energizing value in stillness. It maybe goes back to the idea of the stillness at the absolute center of things.

TG: Is there a discipline to stilling yourself? Or does it come to you naturally?

cw: It comes to me naturally by gravity and old age, I guess. (Laughter) I just do less. But I've always felt that. And it probably comes from the early reading of Dickinson and admiring how she was able to get so much, so large a firmament, she might say, into her life in such a nonambulatory situation. I admired that. As I've always said, I wanted to be Emily Dickinson on Walt Whitman's road—which is to say, let the road be out there, watch it go by, but not be on it. There are probably more things than I dream of that are in my stuff because of my early interest, and admiration, and, at one time, addiction to her work. Sylvia Plath once had a real hold on me. She and Elizabeth Bishop and Emily Dickinson are the three best American women poets, but Dickinson is the one who has really stayed in my mind.

April 29, 2002
Charlottesville, Virginia

FIVE

WORDS SOUND OTHER WAYS

Susan Howe's Prose

Over the years, Susan Howe has consistently drawn attention to her interest in what she calls "an other voice"—a voice released from the ambitions of straightforward speech, and thus free to respond to the world in a more open, tentative manner. She thinks of this as the "undervoice" of straightforward discourse and often uses the image of stuttering or stammering to describe it:

> This tradition that I hope I am part of has involved a breaking of boundaries of all sorts. It involves a fracturing of discourse, a stammering even. Interruption and hesitation used as a force. A recognition that there is an other voice, an attempt to hear and speak it. It's this brokenness that interests me. . . . It is an echo of an undervoice that was speaking from the beginning and is peculiarly American. This voice keeps on speaking *against* the grain.[1]

Such a voice knows it is in the wilderness. It speaks against the grain because it has been thrust out into the open where standard ways of speaking have given way. To speak at all, using whatever shards remain, is to speak differently:

> I hear the stutter as a sounding of uncertainty. What is silenced or not quite silenced. . . . We are expelled from the Garden of the Mythology of the American Frontier. The drama's done. We are the wilderness. We have come on to the stage stammering.[2]

What the stutter "sounds," out there in the open, is "mystery"—what Dickinson called "Boundlessness." Describing her own participation in the tradition, Howe writes:

I can't get away from New England. It's in my heart and practice. The older I get the more Calvinist I grow. In spite of all the pettiness and dour formalism of the Puritans, as we have learned to think of them, and it is all certainly there, and more—I am at home with them.

Hidden under the rigid exterior of a Cotton Mather, under the anger of Mary Rowlandson, under the austerity of Jonathan Edwards, is an idea of grace as part of an infinite mystery in us but beyond us. What we try to do in life is a calling. Carpentry, teaching, mothering, farming writing, is never an end in itself but is in the service of something out of the world—God or the Word, a supreme Fiction. This central mystery—this huge Imagination of one form is both a lyric thing and a great "secresie," on an unbeaten way; the only unbeaten way left. A poet tries to sound every part.

Sound is part of the mystery. But sounds are only the echoes of a place of first love. . . . I am part of one Imagination and the justice of Its ways may seem arbitrary but I have to follow Its voice. Sound is a key to the untranslatable hidden cause.[3]

"On an unbeaten way," where expected connections and explanations have been forcibly left behind, one "sounds" mystery or the "untranslatable" without any expectation of getting it whole or right. One is free to follow out chance associations or to concentrate on language's material nature because the drive to settle things has been, for the moment, set aside. As we've seen with Dickinson and those writers following in her wake, such a sounding draws one into mystery.[4] It causes you to be attuned, suggests Robinson; prepares you to listen, says Wright; frees you, notes Howe.

Howe is drawn to what is unsettled in her own voice through what is unsettled in the language of others. In the "curved, odd, indefinite, irregular, feminine," she hears charged encounters with the wilderness.[5] She is particularly drawn to those aspects of voice that reveal a writer poised, sometimes quite unknowingly, on the uneasy edge between the enclosed and the boundless: "Strange translucencies: letters, phonemes, syllables, rhymes, shorthand segments, alliteration, assonance, meter, form a ladder to an outside state outside of States. Rungs between escape and enclosure are confusing and compelling" (B, 46). She is drawn away from what's settled, drawn "outside of States," by texts that unfold the "order . . . shut inside the structure of a sentence"and release "the coils and complications of Saying's assertion" (My ED, 11–12). As with Robert Duncan, a great deal of the complexity of her work arises from the way it continually makes and remakes itself in response to the voices it works with: "You open your mind and textual space to many voices, to an interplay and contradiction and complexity of voices. These voices are marks and sounds and they form a polyphony that forms lines and often abolishes lines" (B Int, 24). She is drawn, stammering, into the wilderness, then—led into polyphony—by what confuses and compels her in the voices of others.

The opening of *Secret History of the Dividing Line* (1978) is a striking example. The poem collages material from a number of sources, most prominently William Byrd's record of tracing a route through the Dismal Swamp in order to survey the contested Virginia–North Carolina border in 1728 entitled *Histories of the Dividing Line*; his private record of the experience, *The Secret History of the Dividing Line*, published in 1929; and collections of the (public) speeches and (private) wartime letters and diaries of Oliver Wendell Holmes, edited by Howe's father in 1946 and 1962. As Fiona Green has shown, the poem is, in part, an elegy for her father Mark DeWolfe Howe, the poet working with these sometimes-opposed mappings of the "wilderness condition" in order to "sound" the complications of her own now-uncertain situation.[6] As Green and Rachel Tzvia Back point out, Howe begins this sequence with two stanzas or blocks of words that are drawn (one might say released) from the entry for "mark" in *Webster's Third New International Dictionary*. In fact, as Back demonstrates, Howe draws her two blocks from the words and numerals that appear on the left (and continuing to the right) margins of the double-columned entry.[7] In working with its margins, Howe forces the entry to stutter, bringing out a haltingly private, chance-dependent way of speaking buried in the public entry, convinced that such a language might begin to voice her own unsettled position as she searches for a way to respond to her father Mark's absence:[8]

> mark ma ha forest 1 a boundary manic a land a
> tract indicate position 2 record bunting interval
> free also event starting the slightly position of
> O both or don't something INDICATION Americ
>
> made or also symbol sachem maimed as on her for
> ar in teacher duct excellent figure MARK lead be
> knife knows his hogs a boundary model nucle
> hearted land land land district boundary times un[9]

If we slow our eyes down, we notice a number of "strange translucencies." We catch glimpses of a "forest" held in the grip of a "manic"—actually the word "Germanic" in the home text, split into syllables at the margin—compulsion to "mark" and "record" and set boundaries. What was "free" becomes "land land land district boundary times un." It becomes marked, acquirable, and disappears. (This last "un," like the earlier "O," doesn't appear at either margin and seems a trace of the author's hand.) This new text, we might say, is about "both" the drive to "maim," "figure," or "teach" and the possibility of breaking free from that drive by making it visible. This "stutter" taps chance connections in order to make a way through the poem's issues, suggesting that in a world seemingly unfathomable and lost—what I've been calling an unsurveyable wilderness—such an approach might chance upon, or attune one to, otherwise invisible patterns.

Another way Howe draws out this "other voice" is by imagining herself into the blank space left unresolved in a text, attempting to hear and free what has been silenced there. For example, in *Articulation of Sound Forms in Time* (1987), she sounds out an open space she discovers within an account of the Falls Fight of 1676, in which a colonial militia attempted to drive a number of Indian tribes out of the area around Deerfield in the Connecticut River Valley. In an account of the skirmish, she found the story of Reverend Hope Atherton, who accompanied the troops, only to become separated from them in the general rout after the battle. Returning home after four days of wandering, Atherton told a story that "Many people were not willing to . . . credit . . . suggesting that he was beside himself."[10] Howe attempts, in a sixteen-poem sequence entitled "Hope Atherton's Wanderings," to "articulate [the] sound forms" of his discredited language, a language, as she imagines it, wrenched free from the thought that it can possess or hold or even know the way back.[11] In voicing his situation, she allows herself to temporarily abolish certain straightforward but perhaps illusory limitations as to how we respond to the world: "I assume Hope Atherton's excursion for an emblem foreshadowing a Poet's abolished limitations in our demytholo-gized fantasy of Manifest Destiny" (A, 4). Atherton's imagined language frees the poet from certain linguistic limitations.

The second movement of the poem begins with a stanza drawn, Peter Nicholls demonstrates, from an account of the "Escape of Jonathan Wells," an event taking place during the same struggle, the story found in an 1895 text that includes Atherton's story:[12]

> Prest try to set after grandmother
> revived by and laid down left ly
> little distant each other and fro
> Saw digression hobbling driftwood
> forage two rotted beans & etc.
> Redy to faint slaughter story so
> Gone and signal through deep water
> Mr. Atherton's story Hope Atherton   (A, 6)

Nicholls explains that the account of Wells being "prest" by Indians and near fainting except for the discovery of a nutmeg his grandmother had given him before he went out is crossed with a few phrases from Atherton's story. Howe splices the two accounts at the word "so." It is as if the Atherton story allows Howe to imagine what happens when a figure becomes a "digression," when he is "redy to faint" and something "slaughter[s] [the] story" he had been part of: "*so* / Gone and signal through deep water / Mr. Atherton's story Hope Atherton." If we look at the two confident, retrospective remarks of Atherton that Howe combines to form the deep water line—"A particular relation of extreme sufferings that I have under-**gone, and signal** escapes that the Lord hath made way for" and "I passed **through deep waters**," phrases separated, Nicholls notes, by a page[13]—we see that Howe has used the chance breaking of "under-gone" at the page margin to once again lift a new sort of language from the text. Under Atherton's voice, we might say, another voice testifies not to his escape and safe passage but to his sense of being "gone" and being forced to develop a new language, "signal[ling] through [the] deep water" of an overwhelming experience.

A number of the sixteen sections of the poem return to this *so*, imagining and reimagining what follows it—trying to hear the "signal through deep water" that follows the loss of story. For example, in the second poem, drawn mainly from the Wells account, we read:

Clog nutmeg abt noon
scraping cano muzzell
foot path sand and so
gravel rubbish vandal
horse flesh ryal tabl   (A, 6)

A world with some amount of order—the nutmeg, a canoe, the muzzle of a gun, a path through sand—becomes, at *so*, "gravel, rubbish," the lost figure a "vandal." Distinctions give way, "horse flesh," as in Mary Rowlandson, becoming part of a "ryal tabl." All of this seems to tumble out of "muz-zell"—the interlinked sounds making visible an order not previously apparent. Passing through even deeper water, the *so* in section 14 leads to: "possess remote so abstract life are lost spatio-temporal hum" (A, 14). That is, a world one "possesses," because it is kept "remote" and "abstract," is, once "lost," replaced by a "spatio-temporal hum." And so it was with Atherton. Passing through deeper water still, the form of the line is reversed in section 15, beginning the process of returning us to the known world: "HumTemporal-

spatioLostAreLifeAbstractSoRemotePossess" (A, 15). And this reversal leads
back to the secure language of the close of the poem, drawn in line 5 from
Atherton, but from other sources as well.[14] Lostness has been put away:

> Loving Friends and Kindred:—
> When I look back
> So short in charity and good works
> We are a small remnant
> of signal escapes wonderful in themselves
> We march from our camp a little
> and come home
> Lost the beaten track and so
> River section dark all this time
> We must not worry
> how few we are and fall from each other
> More than language can express
> Hope for the Artist in America & etc.   (A, 16)

The poem as a whole, however, in contrast to this last section, has suggested
that the "hope for the Artist" can only be found off "the beaten track" in the
"River section dark all this time." The rest of the poem not only refers to
"More than language can express" but enacts it, lives it out, breaking signals
and following their scatters through deep water.

Howe has also given a good bit of thought to how to represent the tug
and scatter of that other voice released across the page. Consider the opening sections of *The Nonconformist's Memorial* (1993). There, she examines the
scene in the Gospel of John when a weeping Mary Magdalene encounters
the risen Jesus, at first mistaking him for the gardener and then, hearing
her name, recognizing and attempting to touch him—at which point Jesus
famously replies, "Touch me not, for I am not yet ascended." The untouchable Christ in this poem is Atherton's uncredited space or Byrd's unmarked
forest, a mystery that can't be held tightly without losing it. The Gospel,
Howe realizes, in including this moment, acknowledges that the divine can't
be grasped, even as it attempts to do just that. It admits that we are in a
wilderness. Here, Howe doesn't force or imagine the content of that stutter.
She simply brings it out by physically manipulating the source text. The first
entry in section one prints six lines, three of them upside down, while the
second entry prints the same lines, reversing which lines appear upside down.
Howe's point is that the Mary story—"In Peter she is nameless / headstrong
anarchy thoughts / She was coming to anoint him"—reverses, from within,
the way we have too hastily taken the established narrative: "As if all history
were a progress / A single thread of narrative / Actual world nothing ideal."[15]

Mary, who *is* named in the synoptics at the empty tomb but not in the scene where a woman washes Jesus' feet, is the Gospel's indication that history isn't a simple progression. She is one of the ways the Gospel keeps space open for, or positions itself on the edge of, the ideal and the ungraspable. Mary interrupts the "thread." As Howe notes, in two lines added to the second entry: "The nets were not torn / The Gospel did not grasp" (NM, 7). The nets are not torn in John 21 when the risen Christ appears to his disciples, who, fishing in the early morning, don't recognize him. He directs them to cast on the right side of their boat, an enormous haul of fish is found, and their eyes are opened. Miraculously the nets don't break. This demonstration of who he is is paralleled with the Mary Magdalene story and its insistence that Christ can't be grasped or held. Which is to say, confronting what can't be grasped (Mary's story) is, at the same time, eye-opening testimony.

This pattern is continued in the next two entries of the poem, in which fragments of stabilized language about the Gospel—the first chapter's "bright picture" sketched against a "dark background," things that "Must have" happened a certain way, or were "understood" or "contained in" a certain approach—are both turned upside down and cut across, at various angles, by speculative, nongraspable eruptions, traced back to Mary: "Baffled consuming doggerel," "night drift shreds earth knowledge," "Pure Sacrosanct Negator," "suddenly unperceivable time," "All other peace," "Effectual crucifying knowledge" (NM, 8–9). Mary releases all of this; Howe plays it out, not grasping mystery but opening herself to the language through which it moves.

&

Howe has been quite clear that a central source for her drive to release and speak this other voice has been Emily Dickinson. Dickinson, she writes, is a primary demonstration of the explosive "stutter in American literature that interests me. . . . No one has been able to fathom Dickinson's radical representations of matter and radiation—such singularities of space, so many possibilities of choice" (B, 181).[16] She remarks:

> Her writing is infinitely open. It's like Shakespeare—a miracle. To this day I can be utterly surprised by something new I find in it, or I can be comforted by familiar beauties there. The same way passages in the Bible soothe and comfort, or some music does. Her poems and her middle and later letters encompass whatever I want to bring to them. (B, 155)

If she is drawn to "strange translucencies" in texts where language touches on a "state outside of States" (B, 46), then Dickinson is a crucial, ongoing example of translucency: "I write quietly to her. She is a figure of other as thin as paper" (B, 47).

The image of wandering through the wilderness and being forced to develop a new voice is, of course, a central one in Dickinson. If Dickinson writes from a position "Outside authority, eccentric and unique" (My ED, 28), it is because, as Howe argues from poem 1382 (F1404), she has been led there by "Reportless" experiences that transform the world into something that will not be named or domesticated:

> It comes, without a consternation—
> Dissolves—the same—
> But leaves a sumptuous Destitution—
> Without a Name—
>
> Profane it by a search—we cannot
> It has no home—
> Nor we who having once inhaled it—
> Thereafter roam.

Roaming such openness, destitute, Dickinson was forced to speak differently. As Howe puts it, responding to poem 1382 with her own "eccentric," broken-off language, Dickinson was Lear exposed on the heath, Adam and Eve fallen and torn from Eden. Nothing held for long:

> On this heath wrecked from Genesis, nerve endings quicken. Naked sensibility at the extremist periphery. Narrative expanding contracting dissolving. Nearer to know less before afterward schism in sum. No hierarchy, no notion of polarity. Perception of an object means loosing and losing it. Quests end in failure, no victory and sham questor. One answer undoes another and fiction is real. . . . Dashes drew liberty of interruption inside the structure of each poem. Hush of hesitation for breath and for breathing. Empirical domain of revolution and revaluation where words are in danger, dissolving . . . only Mutability certain. (My ED, 23)

Dickinson's "nerve endings" would have "quickened," and she would have found herself at the "extremist periphery" of what we can take in because, as these remarks argue, she would have acknowledged the limits of her tools and been forced to the point of bewilderment. Narrative, hierarchy, the distinguishing of polarities, perception—all of these "quests" would have been immediately "undone" as one answer followed another, each erasing what had previously seemed stable ground. Howe folds in traces of poem 1400 (F1433)—"But nature [or "Susan" in another version] is a stranger yet / . . .

That those who know her, know her less / The nearer her they get"—and poem 1071 (F1103) —"Perception of an object costs / Precise the Object's loss"—to suggest that knowing or perceiving lose more than they gain. In insisting on such categories as "before afterward," knowing and perceiving open up a "schism" in what had been a previously whole "sum." Acknowledging that puts you in a world where "only Mutability [is] certain." It also causes you to speak in a different sort of way, incorporating the possibility of "interruption" within "the structure of each poem." As Alice Fulton also notes, Dickinson's dashes accordingly make room for "hesitation" and "breathing," making the "danger" words are in precisely what generates fresh speech.[17]

From the outside, in the wilderness, knowing the limits of her own linguistic and intellectual tools, Dickinson would have been forced into an "audacious" freedom in responding to the impossible-to-manage speech of others:

> She built a new poetic form from her fractured sense of being eternally on intellectual borders, where confident masculine voices buzzed an alluring and inaccessible discourse. . . . Pulling pieces of geometry, geology, alchemy, philosophy, politics, biography, biology, mythology, and philology from alien territory, a "sheltered" woman audaciously invented a new grammar grounded in humility and hesitation. HESITATE from the Latin, meaning to stick. Stammer. To hold back in doubt, have difficulty speaking. (My ED, 21)

"What voice when we hesitate and are silent is moving to meet us" (My ED, 22), Howe's Dickinson asks. The answer must be the voice of mystery, or Being. Because she was unable to fully access or straightforwardly employ the language of confidence, she drew that language, when she used it, toward a space where its "forward progress [was] disrupted" (My ED, 24). Dickinson, like Howe in the poems we examined, moved freely through the no-longer-stable words of others: "Her talent was synthetic; she used other writers, grasped straws from the bewildering raveling of Being wherever and whenever she could use them. . . . Forcing, abbreviating, pushing, padding, subtracting, riddling, interrogating, re-writing, she pulled text from text" (My ED, 28–29).

Although in the scattered displays of Howe's poetry the Dickinson influence is everywhere apparent, Howe's most deliberate attempt to hear and speak Dickinson's "other voice" can actually be found in her prose. *My Emily Dickinson* (1985), described by Howe as a "tribute" (B, 158), is an attempt to argue for Dickinson's position as "a poet-scholar in full possession of *her* voice" (My ED, 24). It unfolds the hesitant liberties of Dickinson's voice by drawing out her use of other writers—"meet[ing] [Dickinson's] work with writing" (B, 158) that is itself broken, riddling, interrogative. *The Birth-mark: Unsettling the Wilderness in American Literary History* (1993) joins Dickinson in the wilderness. Uncovering traces of Dickinson's generative tensions in the "harsh and fractured" language of earlier—equally homeless—American writers, "cut away from the Island of England" (Pol, 191), Howe actually displays her own version of Dickinson's confrontation with "the bewildering raveling of Being."[18] Where Robinson hears, and frees from uncomprehending twentieth-century ears, an "imperfectly partial," attuned voice, and where Wright hears, and frees from the single lyric, a scoured, forever-denied-access means of concentration, Howe releases Dickinson's hesitant "undervoice." Like the others, she frees it—from Dickinson's sources, her editors, and the deceptively ordered surfaces of her poems—by enacting it in her own writing. And why enact her relationship to Dickinson most fully in prose? Howe remarks in an interview not only that her essays are as charged, acoustically, as her poems, often composed line by fractured line, but also that prose presents itself to her as an arena where her sense of uncertainty, her sense of being in a wilderness, is accentuated. In a sense, then, meeting Dickinson with language she has no natural confidence in, she offers in response a voice all the more broken and receptive:

> Writing poetry, I feel completely free. It's meditative. I lay out all the pages on the desk and it's quiet and I have books and I can go where I want, do what I want. I'm just free, at peace. Writing an essay, I want to say something specific. I can't figure out how to say it. I'm very nervous about my scholarship; I'm very anxious to be scholarly correct. . . . The essays are acoustically charged just as the poems are, but they originate more from fear, from a feeling of needing to write or say something but having no idea *how* to say it. They are stutters. (K Int, 26–27)

Howe argues in the first half of *My Emily Dickinson* that "the way to understand her writing is through her reading" (24). Emily Brontë and Jonathan Edwards are two of the voices that Howe senses Dickinson's engagement with, both of whom can be said to have experienced the "sumptuous Destitution" of tasting a joy whose loss left them forever wandering. Edwards, Howe argues, experienced grace as "sovereign and arbitrary" (My ED, 45), a "free imaginative force" (My ED, 46) that might flow through him or others but that he could neither predict nor control. Grace held open the possibility of returning to a lost origin—but set the dismantling of the self's confidence in its resources as the terms of entrance. To understand the possibility of grace without possessing it in any sure way is to find oneself in a wilderness, desperately alert and engaged: "Not to set forth my Self, but to lose and find it in diligent search. Obedience and submission to one will, was the journey of return to the sacred source human frailty had lost. Puritan theology at its best would tirelessly search God's secrecy, explore Nature's hidden meaning" (My ED, 46). Dickinson, as Howe sees it, responded to the fresh way Edwards was forced to voice his relation to a world deeply but inexplicably ordered—an order forever separate and hidden from him:

> Jonathan Edwards' apocalyptic sermons voice human terror of oblit-eration in our lonely and inexplicable cosmos. He exhorts us to turn from the world, to live ascetically, while actively striving to obtain the emotional peace that is grace. . . . Edwards' negativity, his disciplined journey through conscious despair, humiliation, and the joy of sub-mission to an arbitrary and absent ordering of the Universe, presaged hers. . . . Emily Dickinson took both his legend and his learning, tore them free from his own humorlessness and the dead weight of doc-trinaire Calvinism, then applied the freshness of his perception to the dead weight of American poetry as she knew it. . . . Edwards' stark presentation of the immanent consciousness of Separation enters the structure of her poems. Each word is a cipher, through its sensible sign another sign hidden. The recipient of a letter, or combination of let-ter and poem from Emily Dickinson, was forced much like Edwards' listening congregation, through shock and through subtraction of the ordinary, to a new way of perceiving. (My ED, 48, 49, 51)

Edwards's "consciousness of separation" and his awareness of what appeared to be "an arbitrary and absent ordering of the Universe" produced sermons that made his listeners experience themselves as homeless wanderers within the "ordinary," an ordinary stripped of "its sensible sign[s]." So, too, Howe argues, a Dickinson poem, though shaped like a familiar object, continually does away with the familiar and draws us toward a shocked awareness, taken in word by word, of a world deeply and profoundly separate from us.

In a similar way, "the doomed defiant oneness of Heathcliff and Cath-erine" in Brontë's *Wuthering Heights*, "dismember[ing] the surface cohesion of Mind's civilization" (My ED, 62), must have spoken to Dickinson of another sort of terror and freedom to be found outside of bounds. Brontë's lovers, "wrenched from the Heights" (My ED, 78), are tormented, much like Edwards, with a vision of "complete union with another soul" from which they are, in fact, "absolute[ly] separat[e]" (My ED, 136). They wander outside of—they erase the hold of—civilization's "surface cohesion," for they are convinced that nothing that matters can be found there. Their voices, like Edwards's, call to Dickinson from outside, as Cathy's did to Lockwood when he spent the night in her room at Wuthering Heights. They call to her as she writes, doubling her language and releasing a wanderer's voice:

> The sleepless ghost-lovers of *Wuthering Heights* roam the edges of each line of Dickinson's poem[s]. Children again, their little ice-cold hands scratch the symbol region of her double meaning. Spell on her window of words the impossibility of their idyllic unity before the ruthless sweep of Society's civilizing process. . . . A poem is an invocation, rebellious return to the blessedness of beginning again, wandering free in pure process of forgetting and finding. (My ED, 98)

Both Brontë and Edwards, then, in unselving themselves and turning to mystery with a language that powerfully embraces its own fragility, lead Dickinson toward her own wandering process. They show her, and give her words for, what can be made of the particular linguistic dilemmas she too finds herself in.

The second half of *My Emily Dickinson* unfolds Dickinson's undervoice in action. How does she, following her models, wander? How do her words break or shatter, revealing a second use, doubled under the surface? How does she sound mystery? Howe explores these questions by reading a single poem, "My Life had stood—a loaded Gun" (J754, F764), at length. The poem, of course, is one of Dickinson's most commented-on pieces: an account of a life waiting in a corner until it was "identified," carried away by its owner, and put, with mixed results, brilliantly to work. For Howe, whether the master is God, a precursor poet, or a lover, what is important is that the poem is spoken by someone who acknowledges that "Absence, the forbidden territory between man, woman, and God, has torn love from the world" (My ED, 135) and that the relationship she is carried into will inevitably founder. Like Brontë and Edwards, then, Dickinson's speaker is "Outside, alert astray" (My ED, 70). She speaks from the wilderness, entering into love's "Ferocious contradiction" although she knows full well that "The nuptial Yes, communion confiding, connecting—union with another soul is only another illusion" (My ED, 77).[19] In engaging with that illusory promise, in the crumbling of her speech, the poem's speaker finds herself brought to "the edge of unknown, the sacred inaccessible unseen" (My ED, 70). She is separate from the deeper love the broken relationship with the master only parodies but becomes aware of it nonetheless: "absolute love beyond the borders of death" (My ED, 71), "wait[ing] outside beyond remembrance or caring" (My ED, 135). Dickinson's own speech, then, "join[ing] two souls as

they split asunder" (My ED, 77), is itself split and doubled—opening itself
to, wandering within, the unseen and inaccessible.

Howe's reading of the poem's second stanza pointedly illustrates what
she means by Dickinson's wandering, wilderness voice. She pays particular
attention to Dickinson's use of the word "sovereign" to describe the world of
possibility the newly engaged gun sees opening before her:

And now We roam in Sovereign Woods—
And now We hunt the Doe—
And every time I speak for Him—
The Mountains straight reply—

Howe sees Dickinson exploring the distance between herself and love or
wholeness through a kind of charged linguistic play with the word *sovereign*:
"Words open to the names inside them, course through thought in precari-
ous play of double-enchantment, distance" (My ED, 82). *Sovereign* at first
seems a way of signaling a free realm beyond external controls the poet or
aroused soul has been invited to enter. As Howe notes, Dickinson's dictionary speaks of "A supreme lord or ruler; one who possesses the highest order
without control" (My ED, 80). Edwards refers to "God's arbitrary and sovereign good pleasure" (My ED, 80). Spenser calls attention to Elizabeth's
"feminine sovereign[ty]," encouraging "devotion and willing submission to
something ancient, autarchic, and feminine . . . an ideal of lost perfection"
(My ED, 82).

But, Howe notes, Dickinson would surely have known how unsettled
the term was, how quickly it doubled back on itself: "During the seven-
teenth century in England and in her North American colonies, the words
sovereign and *sovereignty* were essential to the intellectual and political battles taking place in philosophical, scientific, and religious debate and rebel-
lion. Old paradigms were being broken, new ones forming" (My ED, 83).
In using the term, then, Dickinson must have deliberately opened her poem
to the possibility of such a paradigm shift or doubling—and, according to
Howe, the word does indeed shift on her. Howe also associates *sovereign*
with the demand to "submit out of false obedience to forced order" (My
ED, 84), a demand visualized in the gun's being forced to "speak for Him"
in certain prescribed ways. Howe writes: "In the second half of this second
stanza, she will shrink from being released into the sovereignty of Desire, a
force-field as explicit as Death and beyond her will to control" (My ED, 92).
And why does she shrink from the uncontrollable realm desire has suddenly
opened in front of her? Because she wasn't offered true access. "Freedom to
explore [would be seen as] a violation of Sovereignty" (My ED, 99), a desire
inevitably checked by "the violence of will underlying all relationships of

love, all human caring" (My ED, 99). With this "doubly-enchanted word," then, the stanza falls into what Howe calls "the blind spot between what is said and meant" (My ED, 82). "I . . . might say one thing to mean another," she writes, a meaning not intended as Dickinson began the stanza. In listening to and releasing her own language—like Howe listening to Atherton or to the writer of the Gospel of John—Dickinson heard "another" thing being said: those boundless woods could never be hers on "his" terms. "Don't touch me," they say, positing a realm outside the gun-master relationship—a situation truly sovereign and unfathomable:

> What flew away from the crowd and the poet—the meaning she didn't mean, the illusiveness of such allusion is truly sovereign. . . . A great poet, carrying the antique imagination of her fathers, requires each reader to leap from a place of certain signification to a new situation, undiscovered and sovereign. (My ED, 84–85)

From this point on, the poet/gun describes speaking for him, but as if from outside the experience. Aware of what she lacks, she speaks for him but she stutters. Wanting to roam sovereign woods, but not on his terms, she opens a free space within his expectations. What she says and what she means are different. In the third stanza, Howe singles out the initial phrase for attention:

> And do I smile, such cordial light
> Upon the Valley glow—
> It is as a Vesuvian face
> Had let it's pleasure through—

The "do I" phrase, she remarks, borrows its form from wedding vows: "Do you promise to love him, comfort him, honor and keep him in sickness and in health?" More speculatively—by chance, one might say, recalling the chance connections Howe drew out of the margins of the definition of "mark"—she links Dickinson's do to the one in John Donne's "A Valediction: Forbidding Mourning," noting similarities between the gun's controlled life and the image of lover as fixed foot in Donne's poem: "Thy soule the fixt foot, makes no show / To move, but doth, if the other doe" (My ED, 104). Donne's archaic spelling, doe, then reminds Howe of the freedom to explore one's depths in sovereign woods promised in the poem's first stanza—"And now we hunt the Doe"—a freedom now almost entirely usurped. Reading freely, then, Howe meets Dickinson's broken, charged writing with freely responsive writing of her own, sounding out the stanza's "veil[ing of] fire, chaos, original will, vapor" (My ED, 100) in this manner:

I smiling wife *do* promise these things. Newly identified, *do* I smother my childhood and my father's name, as my mother smothered her own? . . . Acquiescence in hunting herself—archaic Doe in sovereign was her own free action. "*Do* I smile . . ." makes her Bride's soul, the fixt foot unable to move but if the other do, *feminine*. (My ED, 103–4)

The fourth stanza,

And when at Night—Our Good Day done—
I guard My Master's Head—
'Tis better than the Eider-Duck's
Deep Pillow—to have shared—

begins to explore the growing distance between speaker and master the speaker has just identified, claiming it as imaginative space. Howe writes: "After a good day's writing with her Master's inspiration, the poet, alone, in her clearing of Becoming, keeps on experimenting, deciphering. . . . Gun stays awake guarding the Distance" (ED 105). In the tight-lipped third line, the speaker scorning the true intimate's role, Howe hears the barely controlled desire that has been aroused in this space where love has broken down:

In Dickinson's time, the Eider was rare but not extinct. They occupied the outer ledges of rocks that jutted into the ocean. . . . The playful but frigidly artificial 'Tis reins in her revolutionary desire to *join* the wild eider outside in cold weather. . . . She the man-made Gun; Poet influenced by the work of many men, tied by a cord of attachment to her Master, may be shut in a prison of admiration that seals her from a deeper region of herself—a mapless dominion, valueless value, sovereign and feminine, outside the realm of dictionary definition . . . (My ED, 109, 111)

Guarding his head *isn't* better than "join[ing] the wild eider outside"—we hear that in her voice—but it is better to be alert and awake than to slumber within the poem's opening terms. A "mapless," "valueless," inaccessible realm has become visible within the ruins of the initial relationship, the poem, like an Edwards's sermon, leading us outside "attachment" to the ordinary—unsealing it, excavating it from within. Howe describes the process in these terms: "First I find myself a Slave, next I understand my slavery, finally I re-discover myself at liberty inside the confines of known necessity. Gun goes on thinking of the violence done to meaning. Gun watches herself watching" (My ED, 118).

Violence is indeed one of the things she watches:

To foe of His—I'm deadly foe—
None stir the second time—
On whom I lay a Yellow Eye—
Or an emphatic Thumb—

"An ugly verse," Howe comments, for here the gun watches herself—yellow muzzle flash, thumb on trigger—being used to bring into line the very forces of openness she has been increasingly voicing a desire for. The poem essentially collapses under its own terrible weight here—the poet, like Howe with the texts of others, deliberately "break[ing] [her own] poetic structure open for future absorption of words and definition" (My ED, 116).

The final stanza, Howe suggests, captures the double movement of the poem precisely. Although, "On some level, Gun needs to keep re-assuring herself and us of 'His,' her nameless Master/Owner's superiority" (My ED, 133), the stanza also looks beyond him to what he has given her a taste for— "a deeper region . . . mapless dominion." "To die is to change utterly" (My ED, 133), Howe writes. Death, to which she's not yet able to entrust herself, would be access to that other realm:

Though I than He—may longer live
He longer must—than I—
For I have but the power to kill,
Without—the power to die—

As an instrument in the owner's hands, the gun/speaker has indeed only the power to act for him, to "kill," but in imaginatively stepping away from those actions, she has assumed a new power—the power of art to undo its own claims before the abyss of "mapless dominion, valueless value," or mystery. "Now Dickinson assumes in art her own power" (My ED, 131), Howe writes. It is an in-between power:

For the journey of a soul across the distance to being's first breath, true existence is in the Abyss. *Yes*, trusted to night and silence. . . . Love waits outside beyond remembrance or caring. . . . Like Hamlet/Shakespeare [Dickinson] looked right into the nature of things/words, straight through,—to the fearful apprehension that there was no Truth, only mystery beyond mystery. To subjugate her master, Death, by means of Art, was a possible solution. . . . Poetry leads past possession of self to transfiguration beyond gender. (My ED, 135, 137–38)

The gun or speaker, in Howe's reading, subjugates or undercuts her Master by saying "Yes" "by means of Art" to the Abyss. She takes us through the undoing of the voice culture had assigned her, opening herself to and hold-ing herself within a space she can't yet cross or map.

With *The Birth-mark*, eight years later, Howe works out a second approach to Dickinson's voice, focusing on its physical immediacy, an inter-est prompted by her encounter with R. W. Franklin's editions of *The Manu-script Books of Emily Dickinson* (1981) and *The Master Letters of Emily Dick-inson* (1986):

> There I learned, examining the facsimiles, that Emily Dickinson, in her carefully handwritten manuscripts—some sewn into fascicles, some gathered into sets—may have been demonstrating her con-scious and unconscious separation from a mainstream literary ortho-doxy in letters, an orthodoxy not only represented by T. W. Higgin-son's and Mabel Loomis Todd's famous editorial interference but also to be found during the 1950s in Thomas H. Johnson's formal assump-tions—assumptions apparently shared by Ralph Franklin (if one is to judge by the "Introduction" to *The Master Letters*). The issue of edi-torial control is directly connected to the attempted erasure of anti-nomianism in our culture. Lawlessness seen as negligence is at first feminized and then restricted or banished. For me, the manuscripts of Emily Dickinson represent a contradiction to canonical social power, whose predominant purpose seems to have been to render isolate voices devoted to writing as a physical event of immediate revela-tion. The excommunication and banishment of the early American female preacher and prophet Anne Hutchinson, and the comparison of her opinions to monstrous births, is not unrelated to the editorial apprehension and domestication of Emily Dickinson. The antino-mian controversy in New England (1636–38) didn't leave Massachu-setts with its banished originator. The antinomian controversy con-tinues in the form, often called formlessness, of Dickinson's letters and poems during and after her crisis years of 1858–60. (B, 1)

As Edwards voiced a charged uncertainty underneath the settled response to the ordinary and Brontë set free a rebellious wandering at odds with "sur-face cohesion," and as Dickinson's Gun, listening to itself speak, doubled its words and freed itself from a "prison of admiration," so Dickinson's manu-scripts step away from "mainstream literary orthodoxy" and "canonical social power." In the physicality of their "lawlessness"—that is, in their insistence on exploring and maintaining the wayward freedom discovered in focusing on "writing as a physical event of immediate revelation"—Dickinson's man-uscripts demonstrate another side to what it means to stammer and speak brokenly and expressively "against the grain."

As the link with Anne Hutchinson suggests—Howe describes her at her trial as "speaking what amounts to a different language—different from that of her adversaries" (B, x)—Howe's work with Dickinson in *The Birth-mark* leads her back into the wilderness of early American voices. In *The Birth-mark*, in fact, Howe not only describes Dickinson's wilderness voice, she enacts it, in her own terms. In a sense, the volume builds on those moments in *My Emily Dickinson* where Howe, in explaining Dickinson, tries the poet out on her own tongue: "I smiling wife *do* promise these things" (103) or "First I find myself a Slave, next I understand my slavery, finally I re-discover myself at liberty inside the confines of known necessity" (118). Now, joining Dickinson in the wilderness, Howe not only calls attention to the voices Dickinson, in some manner, drew from, she draws from them herself.[20] Working with hints, piecing together what had been silenced or unheard, Howe gains her own way of moving in the presence of mystery:

> Emily Dickinson's writing is my strength and shelter. I have trespassed into the disciplines of American Studies and Textual Criticism through my need to fathom what wildness and absolute freedom is the nature of expression. There are other characteristic North American voices that remain antinomian and separatist. In order to hear them I have returned by strange paths to a particular place at a particular time, a threshold at the austere reach of the book. . . . Here are unmown fields unknown inhabitants other woods in other words: enigma of gibberish unwritten wife. . . . Voices I am following lead me to the margins. . . . [Figures who] may have been searching for grace in the wilderness of the world. They express to me a sense of unrevealedness. (B, 2, 4)

Those "other . . . voices," as she works to hear them, draw Howe to "a threshold," lead her "to the margins." If for Wright, in Dickinson's terms, "an agony procures" a "nearness to Tremendousness," for Howe, "enigma[tic]," "unknown," "unwritten" voices draw her near the same "unrevealedness."[21]

How does one draw out such shattered voices? First, Howe suggests, we must admit how blinded and deaf we are, in any direct sense, in regard to those "barely audible" (B, 4) voices:

> . . . Can any words restore to me how you *felt*?
>
> you are straying, seeking, scattering. Was it you or is it me? Where is the stumbling block? Thoughts delivered by love are predestined to distortion by words. If experience forges conception, can quick particularities of calligraphic expression ever be converted to type? Are words children? What is the exchange value? Where does spirit

go? Double yourself stammer stammer. Is there any way to proof it?
Who or what survives the work?   (B, 4)

It is precisely the impossibility of complete restoration that frees Howe's exploratory writing. "Thoughts," "experience forge[d] conception," "spirit," "how you *felt*"—all of that is "scatter[ed]," none of it can be held. There are a number of "stumbling block[s]": the eyes the reader brings to the page ("Was it you or me?"); "distortion by words"; converting "quick particularities" of handwriting "to type"; attempting to "proof" expression and stabilize it. All of those pressures distort an initial conception. Take the focus referred to earlier on "exchange value" for instance: "The poem was a vision and gesture before it became sign and coded exchange in a political economy of value" (B, 147). Much like Dickinson's Gun poem, these texts seem to acknowledge the impossibility of full expression by "doubl[ing]" themselves and "stammer[ing]"—pinning something down and scattering it, all in the same gesture. By entering into the expressive value of such broken gestures—as Susan Schultz puts it, "taking advantage of language's frequent material self-betrayal" (paragraph 4)—Howe's essays are drawn to the charged threshold or margin of the unknowable. In returning to manuscripts, then, Howe returns to where the live, immediate struggle with the edge of mystery is most visible: "Some of Emily Dickinson's surviving manuscripts and letters have been cut apart with scissors. Sometimes pages have been torn to shreds, leaving a single or double strand of words on the brink of the central blank. . . . Maybe margins shelter the inapprehensible Imaginary of poetry" (B, 28–29).

In the volume's second introductory essay, Howe quotes John Winthrop's account of "an anonymous old woman . . . swaddled in silence, stranded in darkness" in order to illustrate what she means by responding to the physicality of language: "There was an old woman in Ipswich, who came out of England blind and deaf, yet her son could make her understand any thing, and know any man's name by her sense of feeling. He would write upon her hand some letters of the name, and by other such motions would inform her" (B, 27). This nameless woman becomes, for Howe, a version of how she might hold herself blind and deaf before mystery, taking in voices by engaging with their physical immediacy, responding to the texture of language as it *touches* her:

> Unknownness did your sense of touch re-trace my own nothingness? Finger the way you imagined I am anything. Is your blind gaze sensible? Is my question a solecism? Is a poetics of intervening absence an oxymoron? Do we go anywhere? I will twine feathers, pricklings, rulings, wampum beads, chance echoes, sprays of lace in the place of

your name. No more apprehension this side of history. Look we are reading a false conception. (B, 27)

The unknown woman's responsive "sense of touch" "re-trace[s]" Howe's "own [experience with] nothingness." It seems a way to move forward. Developing her own response to a manuscript's physical presence—its "finger," like that of the old woman's son, directing the "way [she] imagined"—Howe senses herself free to be "anything." To the "sensible" questions that inevitably follow—is this approach a solecism, an oxymoron, a blind alley?—Howe simply responds that when ordinary speech accepts its own blindness, one sees that there is "no more apprehension." There are only broken, "false conception[s]," none of which is adequate to master mystery. And yet, out of what she hears or gathers, out of the incomplete "pricklings," "rulings," and "chance echoes" traced on her palm, Howe senses the possibility of another way of speaking:

> Editing is the art of discipline; the mastery of detail. Eccentric punctuation, blots, dashes, smudged letters, gaps, interruptions, aborted sketches, "textually irrelevant" numbers, uncanceled or canceled alternatives in the manuscript are a profitless counteraction. . . . In spite of the zealous searching of editors, authors, and publishers for the print-perfect proof of intellectual labor, the heart may be sheltering in some random mark of communication . . . another kind of writing. (B 8, 9)

Through such investigative wandering, she'll unfold the situation she shares with her unknown alter ego—twining what comes to her in the dark. "Even so," she writes, looking ahead to the essays in this volume and their attention to the physical pressure of the scattered, stuttering speech of Mary Rowlandson, Cotton Mather, or Thomas Shepard, "by such tracing of far-fetched meandering I hope to stray" (B, 39).

Let's look at her work with three meandering figures. The first of these, central to the essay "Incloser," is Thomas Shepard, minister of Cambridge First Church and one of Anne Hutchinson's accusers, attacking her for "the Flewentess of her Tonge and her Willingness to open herselfe and to divulge her Opinions and to sowe her seed in us that are but highway side and Strayngers to her" (B, 52). Shepard would seem a representative of the stolid mainstream, an "incloser" seeking to confine or shut himself and his congregation in from the more threatening aspects of the new world surrounding them—refusing to be, like the fluent Hutchinson, "absorbed into catastrophe of pure change . . . [the] Openness of the breach" (B, 49). And yet, as Howe discovers in examining a number of his notebooks and sermon collections, Shepard's voice is indeed a fragile one, scattered before the very mystery he would wall out. As Howe sounds or releases his work, his voice becomes visible as a particularly "confusing and compelling" "rung between escape and enclosure" on that ladder she senses leading her, like Dickinson, "to an outside state outside of States" (B, 46).

One of the manuscripts Howe examines is a pocket notebook in which Shepard transcribed "the testimonies of faith given in his church by fifty-one men and women who were applying for church membership" (B, 65). Each testimony, for Howe, reads as a live response to the charged situation the members of Shepard's congregation found themselves in—"an eccentric, concentrated improvisation and arrest" (B, 68). Howe is particularly struck by how those voices sound

> at a territorial edge of America. . . . Inexplicable acoustic apprehen-
> sion looms over assurance and sanctification, over soil subsoil sea sky.
> Each singular call. As the sound is the sense is. Severed on this side.
> Who would know there is a covenant. (B, 48)

She hears an "inexplicable acoustic apprehension" undercutting their testimonies about their "assurance[s]" of salvation and evidences of "sanctification." What that undervoice or apprehensive tone conveys is a sense of being inexplicably cut off from what matters most—say Dickinson's "mapless dominion." Their voices are "severed"—on this side of a chasm separating them from the truth they yearn to rest in. One can well imagine Dickinson's voice being drawn from the vertiginous space "between what is said and meant" (My ED, 82) that Howe detects in these early spiritual autobiographies. "As the sound is the sense is": Howe hears what was said, how the members of Shepard's congregation presented themselves, but she also hears what the words themselves, in Shepard's hand—hastily scrawled, their references incomplete and inaccurate—mean:

> There is a direct relation between sound and meaning. Early spiritual
> autobiographies in America often meant to say that a soul has found
> love in what the Lord has done. . . . Words sound other ways. I hear
> short-circuited conviction. Truth is stones not bread. The reins are
> still in the hands of God. . . . There is no love. I am not in the world
> where I am. (B, 49–50)

"Twining" various objects together, combining their textures, Howe juxtaposes this notebook with a second one in which Shepard wrote his own autobiography, and in doing so she makes a series of interesting discoveries. Shepherd managed seventy pages before "break[ing] off abruptly" with the death of his second wife, writing, "god hath visited me & scourged me for my sins & sought to weane me fro this woorld, but I haue euer found it a difficult thing to pfit euer but a little by sorest & sharpest afflictions" (B, 58). Visually, the eighty-six blank manuscript pages that follow testify to a "rupture in the pious vocabulary of order . . . the repetitive irruption of death into life [being] mightier than this notion of enclosure" (B, 58). Even more interesting, if one turns the book over and inverts it, one finds a second narrative—a "more improvisational commentary [which] decenters the premeditated literary production [of the first side]," itself already broken off at its unfathomable "empty center" (B, 59). Howe calls this second text an "Inside Narrative" and "an understudy" (B, 59).[22] In a sense, it releases "the coils and complications of Saying's assertion," the order "shut inside the structure of a sentence" (My ED, 11–12). Visually, it sounds out the marginal space Shepard finds himself in, unwoven from the world. "Who would know there is a covenant," it seems to say. Its "Subjects are chosen then dropped. Messages are transmitted and hidden. Whole pages have been left open. Another revelation or problem begins with a different meaning or purpose" (B, 59). What Howe hears, in the unpatterned shifts and turns of these remarks and lists, are "images of panic, haste, and abandonment disunit[ing] the Visible and the Spiritual" (B, 61), "a dislocation and evocative contradiction in the structure of this two-sided book" (B, 63) and a powerful testimony to the presence of mystery. The visible and the spiritual remain separate, despite the autobiography's initially confident claims. Shepherd's voice is a voice in the wilderness; it is "severed on this side," its "short-circuited conviction" powerfully expressive.

Howe gradually comes to see that the "inexplicable acoustic apprehension" voiced by the broken weave of Shepard's hastily recorded fifty-one testimonies is as much his doing as theirs. In a sense, in taking down their voices, he is as much sounding out his own sense of "panic, haste, and abandonment" as he is uncovering theirs. And in this, he becomes not Anne Hutchinson's accuser but her companion, "searching for grace in the wilderness of the world . . . express[ing] to me a sense of unrevealedness" (B, 4). Seen this way, he becomes an early version of Dickinson drawing text from text. And he is also a version of Howe making half-heard voices her own, following them to a state outside of States:

> The Pastor's doubt infiltrates each voice. Apprehension invades writing. . . . After Shepard, what is the truth? We cannot know. Approach is of little use to them. Each autopresentation signals him. . . .
>
> Confessions are copied down quickly. . . . Mistaken biblical quotations are transcribed and abandoned. As the sound is, the sense is.

Few revisions civilize verbal or visual hazards and webs of unsettled
sanctification. . . .
 A wild heart at the word shatters scriptural figuration. (B, 65–66,
68–69)

In sounding out the features of Shepard's texts as they are fingered brokenly
into her palm, then, Howe is as much developing her own voice as tracing
his. Her "wild heart," like his, shatters the "scriptural figuration" she is working with, setting in motion, across her essays, a wilderness (unrevised, unciv-
ilized) of chance connections and "unsettled" claims. Dickinson wrote to her
sister-in-law Susan: "Moving on in the Dark like Loaded Boats at Night,
though there is no Course, there is Boundlessness—" (B, 46). Thinking of
Shepard's broken voice and Dickinson's image of moving blindly, Howe
describes her own enactments of Dickinson's wanderings in these terms:

> In the ark or ship we murmur and question.
> Assurances, citations, expressions, dams, figments, errors, echo-
> lalic slivers, are emblazoned ciphers of Inspiration.
> I am pulling representation from the irrational dimension love
> and knowledge must reach.   (B, 83)

Although "the irrational dimension" is never mastered in such writing, it
produces, in its unsettling of traditonal speech, the nested figments and sliv-
ers of Shepard's and Dickinson's and Howe's "spiritual improvisations."
 In a second essay working with Mary Rowlandson's account of being
taken into captivity by the Narragansett Indians in 1675, Howe quite explicitly traces the way she herself, following Rowlandson, is also led "Away with
her by hidden paths into an origin" (B, 124). The wilderness Rowlandson was
carried into with her wounded daughter Sarah is a physical representation
of what we have been calling mystery or the irruption of the inexplicable.
Brought up within "a formal ecclesiastical enclosure" (B, 97) in which "Form
and force begin with [God]. If there is evil in the Universe, it is good and
therefore marvelous" (B, 99), Rowlandson was violently transported outside
of those assurances:

> Mary Rowlandson looks out at the absence of Authority and sees
> we are all alone. . . . Now away she must go. Invisible to her people.
> Out in a gap in the shadows. . . . elided, tribeless, lost . . . abducted
> from the structure of experience. . . . Each Remove [each breaking of
> camp] is a forced march away from Western rationalism, deep and
> deeper into Limitlessness, where all illusion of volition, all individual
> identity may be transformed—assimilated. (B, 94–96)

Abducted from a structure within which she possessed "volition" and "identity," Rowlandson came to see those assurances as "illusion[s]." Brought face to face with a sense of "Limitlessness" that simply swallowed or "transformed" any means of accounting for it, Rowlandson found herself in the midst of "unmown fields unknown inhabitants other woods in other words" (B, 2). She was "unwritten" (B, 2).

A powerful example of that "forced march away from western rationalism" comes during the early days of her captivity, on their third remove into the wilderness, when her daughter, wounded during the initial attack, dies in her arms:

> down I sat with the picture of death in my lap. About two houres in the night, my sweet Babe, like a Lambe departed this Life, on Feb. 18, 1675. It being about *six yeares*, and *five months* old. It was *nine dayes* from the first wounding, in this miserable condition, without any refreshing of one nature or other, except a little cold water. I cannot but take notice, how at another time I could not bear to be in the room where any dead person was, but now the case is changed; I must and could ly down by my dead Babe, side by side all the night after. I have thought since of the wonderfull goodness of God to me, in preserving me in the use of reason and senses, in that distressed time, that I did not use wicked and violent means to end my own miserable life. (B, 98)

Rowlandson refers to this elsewhere as being in a "wilderness condition"[23]—a state where one's "reason and senses" are overwhelmed, one's life seems negligible, and God's face is hidden: "Who can open the door of God's face?" (B, 99). Howe comments: "Sarah's burial . . . reduces the rational *Designe of all Theologie* to gibberish. Good sense got lost during the Third Remove. The text of America bypassed her daughter" (B, 99). Under that text, opening a space within it where mystery says "Don't touch me," Rowlandson, sitting with her dead child, voiced the text's stutter: "an undervoice that was speaking from the beginning and is peculiarly American" (Pol, 192). If God was active in that space, he was active only in a way that could be comprehended in retrospect: his "wonderfull goodness" in preserving her being an idea she has "thought since" (B, 98).

In fact, it is that "thinking since" that lends Rowlandson's text its striking voice. Howe is drawn to "Rowlandson's presentation of truth severed from Truth" (B, 96)—that is, the way her retrospective narrative, in seeking to impose a sense of order on her experience by discerning God's plan behind it, in fact enacts the "transform[ation]" and "assimilat[ion]" (B, 96) of those tentative "truths" before a larger, still-inexplicable "Truth." Attempting to erase her experience of "rupture . . . in a cloud of his Glory in the dust of her text" (B, 123), Rowlandson continually draws on biblical texts to figure or read her movement outside:

> Mary Rowlandson's thoroughly reactionary figuralism requires that she obsessively confirm her orthodoxy to readers at the same time she excavates and subverts her own rhetoric. Positivist systems of psychological projection have disintegrated. Identities and configurations rupture and shift. Her risky retrospective narrative will be safe only if she asserts the permanence of corporate Sovereignty. Each time an errant perception skids loose, she controls her lapse by vehemently invoking biblical authority. . . . She stops her skid into Reason's ruin by pushing her readers back to the imperatives of Wonder-Working Providence. (B, 100–101)

What is striking, of course, is the strain on such figures. Much as one does with Ruth's continually revised figures, the reader experiences them giving way before something even larger. As with the panicked voice of Shepard's inside narrative, Rowlandson's "wild heart at the word shatters [each attempt at] scriptural figuration" (B, 69). Howe writes: "The idiosyncratic syntax of Mary Rowlandson's closed structure refuses closure. After the war-whoop terror and the death of her little daughter, a new management of the truth speaks to oppose itself" (B, 126).[24] It's in that doubleness or stammering, the way the text opposes itself, that Howe hears Dickinson's indebtedness: "the trick of her text is its mix" (B, 127).

For example, deep into her wilderness time and nearly starving, Rowlandson describes looking into a Bible an Indian had given her and reading, from Isaiah 65:7: "*For a small moment I have forsaken thee; but with great mercies will I gather Thee.*' Thus the Lord carried me along from one time to another" (MR, 138). Howe writes:

> Who has forsaken who? Where are we now? God's text in Rowlandson's text is counterpoint, shelter, threat.
> . . .
> Soteriology is a screen against the primal Night. She must come back to that knowing.
> But in writing Language advances into remembering that there is no answer imagining Desire. Remembering a wild place there is no forgetting.
> "Now we must pack up and be gone from this thicket. . . . As we went along they killed a *Deer*, with a young one in her, they gave me a piece of the *Fawn*, and it was so young and tender, that one

might eat the bones as well as the flesh, and yet I thought it very good." (B, 124)

Howe calls such a passage "a grammatical irruption of grace abounding" (B, 124)—grace asserting itself as language slides. In Howe's reading, the remembered promise from Isaiah isn't stable, though Rowlandson meant it to be. It was a clear "counterpoint" to her condition, but was it a "shelter" or an ever-present "threat"? Voicing those words herself, Howe hears Rowlandson's acoustic uneasiness. Perhaps, she speculates, Rowlandson herself, in the face of abandonment, was tempted to "forsake" her understanding of God as her salvation. If so, Howe writes, joining Rowlandson, "Where are we now?" Although Rowlandson attempted to use the passage as "a screen" against the night of abandonment, an established "knowing" that might sort out apparent contradictions, Howe notices how quickly language, in its instability, runs away with Rowlandson—as it does when the passage about the fawn appears a few pages after the uneasy reference from Isaiah. Attempting to illustrate God's "great mercies" in providing the deer, Rowlandson finds herself voicing hungers and desires far beyond what her "ecclesiastical enclosure" had prepared her for. As she wrote, she remembered again the sense of having "no answer" capable of "imagining"—that is, able to comprehend and respond to—her newly awakened desires. In writing, she remembered and, in a sense, testified to the fact that she has been unable to leave a "wild place" of unimaginable depth and threat and wonder. The fawn passage erupts into the text—bringing with it a sense of "an infinite mystery in us but beyond us" (B Int, 21), disrupting and overwhelming her text. She has been returned to the edge of God's awful, unaccountable presence. "Words sound other ways" (B, 50), Howe remarked, in "Incloser," about the "short-circuited conviction" she heard shattering and revivifying early spiritual autobiographies. Those words, we now see, were originally Rowlandson's: "I can remember the time, when I used to sleep quietly without workings in my thoughts, whole nights together, but now it is *other wayes* with me. When all are fast about me, and no eye open, but his who ever waketh, my thoughts are upon things past" (B, 125). In extending, through entering and sounding out, Rowlandson's writing, Howe has also enacted and sounded out the "other wayes" Dickinson's language moves as it wanders the "hidden paths" Rowlandson and others found their way to before her.

A series of powerful, disturbing accounts having to do with food and desire run through Rowlandson's text—including grabbing a piece of boiled horse's foot from a child who couldn't bite into it, and the sense that "after I was thoroughly hungry, I was never again satisfied" (MR, 139). The most striking of these has to do with a piece of horse liver. Howe quotes the passage and Rowlandson's attempt to stabilize it, then draws a Dickinson-like image—think of "Some pale Reporter, from the awful doors / Before the Seal!" (J160, F132)—out of it that all but traces the way voice's echoes reach from Rowlandson to Dickinson to Howe:

> There came an Indian to them at that time, with a basket of Horse-liver. I asked him to give me a piece: *What*, sayes he *can you eat Horse-liver?* I told him, I would try, if he would give a piece, which, he did, and I laid it on the coals to rost, but before it was half ready they got half of it away from me, so that I was fain to take the rest and eat it as it was, with the blood about my mouth, and yet a savoury bit it was to me: *For to the hungry Soul every bitter thing is sweet.*
>
> There she stands, blood about her mouth, savouring the taste of raw horse liver. God's seal of ratification spills from her lips or from her husband's pen. (B, 125–26)

The remembered text, "For to the hungry soul every bitter thing is sweet" (Proverbs 27:7), "ratifies" Rowlandson's experience as being within the bounds of God's plan. The words spill from her lips as she (or her husband) writes, but what also spills from those lips—doubling her remark, under-cutting it, opening it out—is blood. Her words seen as a whole, text *and* undertext, are suddenly quickened by the image and brought violently to life. Grace drips from her mouth, the covenant shockingly ratified. "Where are we now," Howe writes, joining Rowlandson, as she writes, in this unsettled, energized space: "The violence of ambiguity. Disorder is another order" (B, 122). Almost unintentionally, "Mary Rowlandson saw what she did not see said what she did not say" (B, 128). Blood spills what her words could not, "form[ing] . . . and often abolish[ing] [the] lines" of those that follow (B Int, 24).

What this means, then, is that Howe's campaign to bring Dickinson's manuscripts into visibility, one part of which is represented by the last essay in *The Birth-mark*, is an attempt to show that, like Rowlandson or Shepard, she too "said what she did not say."[25] But in the case of Dickinson, one would have to rephrase this. Dickinson said—she put into action—what she has not been presented as saying. Like the voices before her, Dickinson, in Howe's reading, has also been regarded as a "Wayward Puritan. Charged with enthusiasm. Enthusiasm is antinomian" (B, 149). "The physical imme-diacy of [Dickinson's] spiritual improvisations" (B, 146) has been, for Howe, "domesticated and occluded" (B, 131) by the editorial simplification and standardization of her work. *The Birth-mark* asks us to read the editorial attempt to "Dress up dissonance" in her work in the light of Rowlandson's attempt to refigure lostness according to social expectations or Shepard's tracing the shape of his life according to traditional patterns. We could even read the speaker's initial assumption in "My Life had stood—a loaded Gun" that she would be granted the access to sovereign woods she'd been promised as a parallel attempt to make a situation say what was expected. Howe writes:

> The poem was a vision and a gesture before it became sign and coded exchange in a political economy of value. At the moment these man-uscripts are accepted into the property of our culture their philoso-pher-author escapes the ritual of framing—symmetrical order and arrangement. . . . All scandalous breakings out are thoughts at first. Resequenced. Shifted. Excluded. Lost. (B, 147, 148)

What Howe wants to do is reverse this process of shifting and resequencing and excluding in order to find the Dickinson we have lost. She would undo that editing, much as the wilderness undid Rowlandson and Shepard.[26] One of the reasons she engages so passionately and publicly with those voices of authority who seem to have muffled Dickinson's voice, then, is that she's reenacting the force of Dickinson's "scandalous breakings out." Her own critical voice is a voice forced outside, savoring a shocking, new taste.

In her final essay, "These Flames and Generosities of the Heart: Emily Dickinson and the Illogic of Sumptuary Values," Howe points to two occluded aspects of Dickinson's manuscripts through which the "physical immediacy" of her open improvisations breaks out: the "Provoking visual fragmentation" (B, 140) of her unexpected line breaks (invisible in the stan-dard texts); and the "polyphonic visual complexity" of the words and phrases added to the margins and at the ends of her poems—"seemingly scattered and random . . . form[ing] their own compositional relation" (B, 141) within themselves, "an enunciative clearing outside intention" (B, 136). Just as Row-landson, once she began writing, was led back into the wilderness, so Dick-inson's manuscripts, if one has the chance to examine them, inevitably lead one to an "ambiguous[ly] articulated Place" (B, 136) where "knowledge [is] estranged in itself" (B, 137) and previously unsuspected relations are set in motion.

That means, then, Howe insists, that we should not be reading Dickin-son and the other writers she examines thematically—thinking of theme as a way of standing above the textures of broken, multiple articulation—or not strictly so. As both Wright and Robinson also suggest, we should be reading for gesture—gestures that, broken, incomplete, one of a series, deliberately engage mystery. Language's physicality leads us to what was not said—to the other of what *was* said: "Deflagration of what was there to say. No mes-sage to decode or finally decide. The fascicles have a 'halo of wilderness'" (B,

136). Being aware of that "halo of wilderness," freeing words to wander and come undone, we develop eyes to read their contact with and displacement by what is beyond them:

> Letters are sounds we see. Sounds leap to the eye. Word lists, crosses, blanks, and ruptured stanzas are points of contact and displacement. Line breaks and visual contrapuntal stresses represent an athematic compositional intention. (B, 139)

Poems read this way become spiritual improvisations for both writer and reader—"immersion[s] in immediacy" (B, 139), "sensuous visual catastrophes" (B, 140):

> Letters are scrawls, turnabouts, astonishments, strokes, cuts, masks. . . . Spaces between letters, dashes, apostrophes, commas, crosses, form networks of signs and discontinuities. . . . Mystery is the content. Intractable expression. Deaf to rules of composition. (B, 141, 143)

From Dickinson, Howe learned "Another way of reading" (B, 141)—one that is at home in "intractable expression" and is comfortable at voice's margin. Such a way of reading knows that "Meaning is scattered at the limit of concentration, [and that] the other of meaning is indecipherable variation" (B, 148). Listening intently, Howe has followed Dickinson's voice back through earlier American voices—voices that trace on her palm not only Dickinson's name but her own: enacting them, she names herself as never fully known, a figure working in the space between meaning and indecipherable variation.

SIX

INTERVIEW WITH
SUSAN HOWE

TG: I'd like to begin with a comment you made in an interview with Tom Beckett: "[There's] an infinite mystery in us but beyond us. . . . This central mystery . . . is both a lyric thing and a great 'secresie,' on an unbeaten way; the only unbeaten way left. A poet tries to sound every part." Would you say some more about what you mean by "mystery" and how a poet goes about "sounding" that?

SH: I said that in my zestful salad days. At sixty-five I see the way foreshortened, "the great secresie" widening, and am not so glib. "Providence has a wild, rough, incalculable road to its end," Emerson wonderfully wrote in "*Fate*," "and it is of no use to whitewash its huge mixed instrumentalities." The lyric mystery of poetry includes sound and surprise. *Chance* or *Fate* are words for an undeciphered form still unknown to us. It's the sense that particular words are electrically connected through meter and melody. Poems are intentional and intuitive at once. The interest is in the spirit of execution. The spirit of execution is a spirit of experiment, an openness to order which chance creates. Though you think you have control as you write—

TG: Go ahead.

SH: Emerson's "mixed instrumentalities" are connected or conducted through particulars. That's one reason I'm drawn to the pragmatist thought that truth consists in the process—in gathering and locating—in making connections and transitions. Poetry is the path of rhetoric to logic. Each sensible sound is a sign that awakens the condition for understanding. A poet surrenders with discipline to the beauty of the sound and sight of words at once. As if they are visually concrete and tangibly audible. "Affection" is the passion of a mind bent on a particular object but without its actual presence. The word stands in for the object. So the words you choose must be perfect.

TG: "A poet surrendering with discipline to the beauty of words." Jonathan Edwards would say something similar to that, I think.

SH: Yes. Perry Miller says of Edwards: "In his method more than in his content (if the two are separable) he was a radical innovator. In this way the arch conservator of the Puritan past made his break with that past—in this respect the logician spoke for the wilderness." In the same way Marianne Moore begins her essay "Abraham Lincoln and the Art of the Word" by referring to Lincoln's "controlled impetuosity exemplifying excellences both of the technician and the poet."

TG: Sound is enormously important for you, isn't it?

SH: Oh yes. I'm grateful to my parents for the emphasis they placed on reading aloud from the time I was small. I was about nine when my father came back from the war. He was by then almost a stranger and his reading to me at bedtime took such a hold on me that I have never lost the sense of awe and bedazzlement which began with his reading of Charles Dickens. Henry James in *A Small Boy and Others* has a marvelous passage about bursting into sobs "under the strain of the Murdstones," while listening to an elder cousin in Albany reading aloud the first installment of *David Copperfield*. After Daddy reduced me to similar strain by reading *Nicholas Nickleby*, we went on to *The Pickwick Papers*. *Pickwick* was beyond me when it came to plot but I loved his enjoyment of the names of characters and their ridiculous escapades: Samuel Pickwick Esq., Mr. Winkle, Alfred Jingle, Count Smorltork, Job Trotter, Mr. Stiggins, Miss Wardle. Talk of relation and compression—of jolts and unexpected sallies.

"Poet, Sir?"

"My friend Mr. Snodgrass has a strong poetic turn," said Mr. Pickwick.

"So have I." said the stranger. "Epic poem,—ten thousand lines—revolution of July—composed it on the spot—Mars by day, Apollo by night,—bang the field piece, twang the lyre."

"Heads, heads, take care of your heads," cried the loquacious stranger, as they came out under the low arch-way, which in those days formed the entrance to the coachyard. "Terrible place—dangerous work—other day—five children—mother—tall lady, eating sandwiches—forgot the arch—crash—knock—children look round—mother's head off—sandwich in her hand—no mouth to put it in—head of a family off—shocking, shocking.

It seems odd to leap from Edwards to Dickens but my father and I were undemonstrative shy New Englanders; the way we could best express affection was through reading aloud the words of others.

What I got from my mother was the sound of her wonderful Irish voice and her sense of theater. And because I was in my early teens when the beauty of Joyce's language first swept me away; it was the stories in *Dubliners* and all of *Portrait of the Artist*. Even now I'm haunted by just the name Stephen Dedalus, Stephen's homesickness at Clongowes, the Irish political quarrel at the family dinner table:

Mr. Casey, freeing his arms from his holders, suddenly bowed his head on his hands with a sob of pain,
—Poor Parnell! he cried loudly. My dead king!
He sobbed loudly and bitterly.
Stephen, raising his terrorstricken face, saw that his father's eyes were full of tears.

"Terrorstricken," as if the two words and four syllables always coimplicated each other. And the great final paragraph of "The Dead," with the snow "falling faintly through the universe and faintly falling, like the descent of their last end, upon all the living and the dead." Well—it's up there with the Song of Solomon. The musical turn—of falling faintly—the repetition and reversal—Wallace Stevens can do the same thing—it's all in compressed sentences. No unnecessary words. It is a sacred space of saved intensity. Those words still stand in directly for Dublin, Sandymount Strand, Sandycove, Killiney, Dublin Bay, all places where I was when I was only a year old and later just after the war in 1947. Joyce's words on the page bring Ireland into my soul. They bring that outside in.

TG: I see. Sound is a way of calling that mystery back.

SH: Grounding it, too.

TG: Because it's grounded in an actual voice?

SH: It's grounded in the hieroglyphic quality of the letters on paper. The ear and the eye are bound in a most mysterious way. The sound of what you say sings in your head at the moment you read. I don't care what the cognitive scientists say—the mind is a theatre. One thing I love about the idea of a dictionary is that you think you can define a word by reducing it to its essence, its structure, where it was used and where it came from, all of those things, but in fact, the more you think about it, the more it . . .

TG: Opens up?

SH: Completely opens up. Like a curtain.

TG: I see. And it opens up on?

SH: The small, the detail, Dickinson's "dotted dot"—down, down, down, *whoom!*

TG: And that "*whoom*" is what you mean by moving into mystery?

SH: Yes. Or the outside. It's when the outside is inside, but you'll only get to that by going inside, inside. Or, by the mutual accidentality of one definition beside another.

TG: You've been interested in small things for a long time. It's what you were drawn to in the Shepard notebooks, for example.

SH: Yes, Thomas Shepard's written transcriptions in his small leather-bound notebook of the testimonies of faith given by various men and women applying for church membership in his church between 1630 and 1640 record in their structure the shock of terror and homesickness these emigrants felt, but it's not only that book. I sense doubt and desolation in his short autobiographical narrative and in passages of *The Parable of the Ten Virgins, a series of sermons on Matthew 25:1–14.* Shepard was important to Edwards. But I wonder, would I have ever found Edwards or Shepard had I not chosen Dickinson's "My Life had stood—a Loaded Gun" poem?

TG: Would you take me through that? How did you get to Dickinson, and how did Dickinson give you the eyes to see what was going on in someone like Shepard?

SH: Well, first of all there was a biographical connection. My aunt Helen Howe Allen had no children, my youngest sister is named for her, and she worried about the three of us like a mother hen. When she was bedridden in her last sudden illness—it took a month to kill her—I used to visit her in her apartment on the eighth floor of a triumphant building on the corner of Ninety-seventh Street and Fifth Avenue. Richard Sewall's biography of Emily Dickinson had just been published. Because she didn't have the physical energy to pore over it, I began to read it to her. We had that very edition [*points to it*]; my uncle gave it to me after she died. During the war years Aunt Helen had earned her living by doing monologues à la Ruth Draper and Cornelia Otis Skinner—her most witheringly affectionate satires were of genteel Bostonian matrons. As children we used to love watching her step into such characters at the Sunday dinner table or at holiday gatherings. In addition to several novels, she had recently written *The Gentle Americans, 1864–1960; Biography of a Breed.* In 2003 the title is mortifying, but she could be ironic in the extreme about Boston Brahmins. She wrote it after her father died as a sort of memoir. Grandpa was himself the author of myriad biographies. According to the *ANB*, "Howe was a member of and spokesman for the genteel tradition, particularly the old-fashioned Boston variety, which has since come under attack by revisionist historians and modernist critics. For that reason, his work is regarded as being sincere and distinguished in its time, but as having become passé." Poor grandpa. Aunt Helen's best chapter, "The Mighty Maidens" (a term she took from Henry James), describes several eccentric Bostonian women who were friends and relations. She was right on target. Now, we began reading Sewall at "The New England Dickinsons and the Puritan Heritage." I felt vividly how tiny and birdlike she was in that solid Manhattan building. Through her bedroom window you could see the corner of Central Park—I was living downtown on Christopher Street in a completely different environment and lifestyle to say the least—but here she was seventy years old, very ill and in her shy anxiousness she seemed to represent a local earlier New England character that was everything I dreaded and at the same time loved about the darkened brick air of Beacon Street and Boston of my childhood. Look at this pencil line beside this passage from a letter Samuel Ward had written Higginson shortly after the first edition of *Poems* was published:

> She is the quintessence of that element we all have who are of the Puritan descent. . . . We came to this country to think our own thoughts with nobody to hinder. . . . We conversed with our own

souls till we lost the art of communicating with other people. The typical family grew up strangers to each other, as in this case. It was *awfully* high, but awfully lonesome. Such prodigies of shyness do not exist elsewhere.

She must have told me to mark the passage so she could go back and read it to herself when she was better, though we both knew she wasn't going to get better—I never felt closer to her. It was as if we could only touch each other through reading aloud. This practice of self-discipline was above all a dread of any display of affection. I made the little mark. The wide, un-thing that we couldn't say was there.

TG: And she was speaking about herself.

SH: Of course. She was in New York having escaped Boston about twenty-five years earlier when she married a distant Philadelphia cousin. She was saying she was displaced in what was now determined. She wanted to go home.

TG: And her saying this was grounded in a text.

SH: Grounded in *this* text. And then she died about two weeks later. Now I have the book. I don't know. It seems predestined.

TG: Before this experience, you must have been acquainted with Dickinson.

SH: Yes, but as a poet I was much more under the sway of my mother's influence. I felt more kinship with the language of Joyce and Yeats. I'm trying to think if I was already working on her then.

TG: When did your aunt die?

SH: The same year the *Life* came out. (*Picks up book.*) Aunt Helen knew how much I loved her work. We must have talked about it together . . . Let's see, 1974. I didn't realize it was so long ago. Reading the Sewall biography led me into criticism.

TG: You were almost called.

sh: I felt I was called. My father could have been her father Edward Dickinson because not only was he a lawyer, but he was a representative of the old New England type, even in the 1960s. I knew the psychic make-up. I understood her sense of awe and devotion in relation to him. I understood why she couldn't leave home. My father also died suddenly. He was sixty. He died in 1967 so never knew the changes that were coming in '68. He was a professor at the Harvard Law School, very much involved in the civil rights movement, and the official biographer of Oliver Wendell Holmes Jr. His father had written a biography of OWH senior. Justice Holmes (as we always referred to him) lived well into his nineties and when he died in 1935, Daddy (one of his last law clerks and secretaries) announced his death to the press. We always felt the tyrannically prolific justice had driven him prematurely to the grave. A total of three official Holmes biographers died in harness before the *Life* was completed.

I guess my shy father was attracted to wordy authors, because he got particular pleasure from reading Cotton Mather! This is the way I first became even a little familiar with Puritan literary expression. Come to think of it he got the same enjoyment from Mather he did from *Pickwick*. I found later that the Dickinson family all read Dickens avidly. ED used names and lines from the novels frequently in letters to Samuel Bowles, Susan Dickinson, and Austin—to the point I sometimes feel they were using his characters and plots as a sort of code.

tg: You talk about that in *My Emily Dickinson*. What prompted that book? Did someone ask for it?

sh: Some poets I knew were interested in shorter pieces I had written on her work during the late seventies. I was manic on the subject—constantly talking about doing something. Charles Bernstein— kept urging me to put together what I had collected so that rather than scattering my research in short essays and excited chatter there would be some cohesion. I wasn't in academia. My guides for writing about a loved author were poets. Charles Olson's *Call Me Ishmael* (first and foremost), D. H. Lawrence's *Studies in Classic American Literature*, H. D.'s *Tribute to Freud*, Simone Weil's *The Iliad: Poem of Force*, W. C. Williams's *In The American Grain*. I was here, in Guilford, just up the hill from where we live now and the Connecticut landscape had become very much a part of my poetry. We moved here from Manhattan because David was directing the sculpture department at the Yale School of Art and one of the requirements of the job was that we live in the area. Members of his family had access to the stacks of Sterling Library. This was the first time I had experienced what it was to have access to a great library. I can't imagine my poetry or essays without Sterling. It was clear to me that Dickinson was a voracious reader. It seemed to me that the scholarship on her (in the case of Sewall) trivialized that part of her work. I felt the bulk of scholarship (including feminist readings that proliferated at the time) though illuminating in some ways, tended to ignore her reading in order to concentrate on neurosis, repression, and rejection.

TG: And you knew there were a lot of books behind her?

SH: I could see and hear it, instinctively. I knew that that kind of an ear is an ear that has come through reading. One reason I am so fond of the Thomas Johnson/Theodora Ward edition of *The Letters* (sadly out of print at the moment) is that they tracked down, or maybe already knew so many of her references and quotations and provided them in the editorial apparatus. While I am startled by the editorial liberties Johnson took with her manuscripts, there is no doubt that his 1955 edition with all those dashes and capitals was a major influence not only on my feelings about the poet herself, but in the case of his and Theodora Ward's edition of the *Letters*—they were an influence on the way I write prose. It took me a long time to realize that this is not at all the way the original letters actually look. So when I cite the other influences for the way both *My Emily Dickinson* and later *The Birthmark* are written, I would have to say that probably Dickinson's prose as I read it via Johnson had a subliminal effect. When it comes to the structure of my sentences and paragraphs, ED is my teacher. She is the only woman poet of the nineteenth century I know of who writes memorable aphorisms. Aphorisms are intentional and intuitive at once. I wanted to write a short critical study in a way that met the risk in the structure of the original.

TG: And Perry Miller?

SH: Perry Miller was already familiar because he was one of my parents' close friends in Cambridge. But I hadn't read his work then; I just remember his presence and the immense fondness and respect they both felt for him. They loved his sense of humor. When during the seventies I read his work I realized that not only was he a dedicated and indefatigable scholar, he was also a formidable prose writer. Most impressive for me in terms of thinking of Dickinson, is the way Miller brought Jonathan Edwards to life on paper. His *Jonathan Edwards* was essential. Again—it's a brief, passionate book.

TG: And how did you get to Edwards from Dickinson?

SH: I was also writing poetry that was heavily influenced by the research I was doing on the early history of Connecticut. I was particularly interested in the religious revivals that swept through Connecticut River Valley. I think Dickinson was too—though she never herself converted in a religious sense—I think she did have a conversion experience of sorts during 1858 and '59 when she came to understand the intensity of her calling. When I say "calling" I do not mean "born again," or vatic illumination. Her language embodies the same exigency and English aspiration that you find in frontier furniture and other material objects from Hadley, Deerfield, Northampton, Holyoke, et cetera. Her voice can't be fully understood without some knowledge of the history of the strange conjunction of war, refinement, and religious awakening between 1630 and the 1860s in New England.

TG: Had you intended to focus on "My Life had stood—a Loaded Gun—" from the beginning?

SH: Yes, because I was so excited over the connection with Browning's *Childe Roland to the Dark Tower Came*.

TG: So, did Dickinson's voice take you first to Shakespeare and Browning and only later to Edwards and Mary Rowlandson?

SH: It wasn't all that split up. I think the connection to Cooper and the *Leatherstocking Tales* was fairly obvious to me at the time. Somewhere along the way I got interested in early American captivity narratives and I had read Annette Kolodny's *The Land Before Her*. I think I found Richard Slotkin's *Regeneration through Violence:The Mythology of the American Frontier, 1600–1860* in her bibliography. This is the problem with being an autodidact. You come on things in a roundabout fashion. Slotkin's readings of Mather, Rowlandson, and other narratives of witchcraft and captivity as well as Boone, Cooper, and Melville were what I needed. I still remember the day I pulled it off the shelf at the library. As you see, my copy here has literally been read to pieces. This, and Patricia Caldwell's *The Puritan Conversion Narrative: The Beginnings of American Expression* were a major catalyst for all the later essays in *The Birth-mark*. Richard Slotkin isn't interested in Dickinson which is too bad. I can't imagine he would have hit on his title without Miller's mapping of the intellectual terrain of the origins and interrelations. The bewildering variety of ideas of what just the concept of regeneration means that Miller discusses so well in *The New England Mind*—the conflict, the crossing, the complex inner struggle of grace—this is so much a part of her tropes and figures, this exhilaration in the recognition that the doctrine of original sin does not lead to apathy but to victorious exultation of the conflict gets lost in the reductive portrait of a spinster genius clothed in white à la Miss Havisham. Sadly, books like the *The Madwoman in the Attic* paint an equally problematical portrait of a spidery recluse, a Queen at Home, sewing—

TG: Rather than as a practicing artist with ink on her hands.

SH: Yes, with ink on her hands. And fierce. A Calvinist. More akin to Edwards and Melville. I always go to Emily Dickinson's poems, letters, and aphorisms because in them I recognize the right of a woman who is a poet to enter the domain of philosophy, and philology, at the same time she acknowledges the necessarily incomplete character of all theorization. She may have been an agoraphobic but she traveled freely in her head. Like Wallace Stevens, hers was the singular genius of a metaphysical poet.

I also have to admit that in 2003 I've come full circle on the subject of sewing. Or sewing has come home to me. Dickinson *does* tap into the culture of women where lace making and embroidery were valued skills.

Pieces of material were carefully put away for later use, or for samples of a particularly skillful pattern. When you see her manuscripts—particularly the later fragments and drafts, you recognize the same practice. And it is true that many of her best poems concern sewing or thread or detail work—metaphorically.

Courtesy of Amherst College Archives and Special Collections.

Mary Queen of Scots figures importantly in any history of needlework. She particularly liked embroidering pictorial emblems, a form of allegory and of poetry.

During the Reformation there was a craze for the recognition and solving of emblems. Mary took as her emblem the marigold which turns its face to the sun, the shape in a woodcut (from which her embroidered emblems were taken) being a marguerite or daisy. She gave the emblem a French motto, "Sa Virtu m'Atrire" ("Its strength draws me"), which formed an anagram on her name MARIE STVART.

I wonder now if Dickinson wasn't aware of this flower symbolism when she adopted the name Daisy in the "Master" letters and poems written during that period on notepaper with a Queen's head watermark on the upper lefthand corner.

She would have been familiar with the story of Mary's long imprisonment in which she had only her needlework to pass the time—descriptions of her surviving embroideries, ciphers, crowned initials, and "slips" of flowers beautifully worked in fine tent stitch or cross stitch on canvas.

I think of Dickinson when I read that Catherine de Medici (Mary's French mother-in-law) left in boxes nearly a thousand squares of filet brodie or darned netting lace when she died in 1589. Gilbert and Gubar rightly made the comparison to sewing in their *Madwoman* chapter on Dickinson but in such a way that they made me want to throw it out.

Let me show you something. [*Gets a family Bible*] This Bible, published in 1806 in New York, has been handed down for generations by women in my husband's mother's family. Here on the flyleaf is a carefully handwritten inscription.

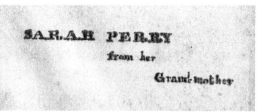

Over time the ink has bled through the paper so that when you turn the page this is what you see.

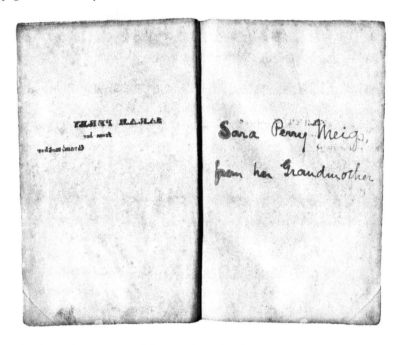

And talking of saving scraps look at this! This, in a way, is what Dickinson does with certain lines, and poems, and letters.

She was born in 1830 so she would have been Sarah Perry's contemporary. You see there is a feminine tradition here that is hard for contemporary women who are writers and critics, like myself, to understand. It's the anthropologist Annette Weiner's "Paradox of Keeping-While-Giving." Come to think of it, Keeping-while-Giving would be a great title for a book on the history of Dickinson's manuscripts.

TG: The handwriting says Martinsburg, April 1864. And it's pinned on "David buyeth Ornan's threshing-floor" in *I Chronicles*. There must be a connection with the particular biblical passage.

SH: Possibly but we can't be sure. Even if there isn't or wasn't——from now on, they are attached. That's what happens. The spirit of Renaissance emblem books crossed to America in primers, on furniture, on embroidery, on coins, in hymnals. This isn't a drawing of a flower—it *is* a flower, pinned into this Bible, on a particular page. The art of the emblem is to make the picture the text and vice versa. Ultimately, that's the thing that fascinates me. What is the relation between the real thing there and the text?

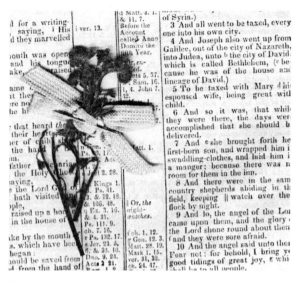

This isn't in words, but *this* is.

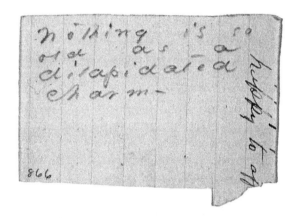

Courtesy of Amherst College Archives and Special Collections

The Protestant iconoclasts who came to the Massachusetts Bay Colony in the 1630s had done away with images in churches. What are they left with? Only letters. And of course flowers—the language of flowers. They're left with letters as hieroglyphs. And many of them couldn't read, so there's tremendous anxiety over the sound of what a minister is saying or reading to his congregation. Thomas Shepard's reaction to Anne Hutchinson's verbal fluency is a perfect expression of that terror—of the slippery quality that words have.

TG: And it comes out . . . ?

SH: It comes out everywhere—this anxiety between the real and the fake, the original and imitation. It comes out in immense attention to impossibilities and details. That's the difference.

TG: Between English and American English?

SH: Yes.

TG: You've written very forcefully about the way Dickinson's speaker in "My Life" listens to or sounds out the implications of the words she uses. The poem almost seems to be about the process of "watching herself watching."

SH: That poem needs to be read in the context of the other poems in that fascicle. You can't be sure that she meant her work to be read in a series, but on the other hand, you can't be unsure. The last poem in fascicle 34 is a dried flower poem. "Essential oils—are wrung— / The Attar from the Rose" and the last line with its three words "in Ceaseless Rosemary" spread across the paper. It's like a pressed maroon flower petal that is still intact in Sarah Perry's Bible. Once you've placed it in the book, or pinned it onto a particular page, then you've done something. It's palpable and assumes power. Words for Dickinson are palpable. Sharon Cameron emphasizes in *Choosing not Choosing* the importance of paying attention to the word variants in the manuscripts and how right she is. These variant word lists are what the poet has bequeathed to us.

TG: I know that you've linked Dickinson's interest in process with the pragmatists.

SH: The person who does this best is Elisa New in *The Line's Eye: Poetic Experience, American Sight*. New, Sharon Cameron, Marta Werner, and Jerome McGann among others, are currently doing work that in a variety of ways emphasizes process in her work.

While we're talking about American English, I should point out how important Noah Webster's *American Dictionary of the English Language* (1828) is, not only for Dickinson's writing but Melville's and Whitman's. In fact, Webster is surely as important to all three as Emerson. One of the best purchases I ever made was this 1852 edition. Hers was an 1844 reprint of the 1841 update. So the page layout was slightly different. Look at the poem now numbered 1448 and transcribed by Ralph Franklin, with its great opening, and the manuscript on which it is based. This is from Harvard's expensive new three-volume variorum edition, but in the affordable one-volume version that students and most general readers will use, all variants are omitted as well as the description of the surface the poem was written on. I could also argue with Franklin's line breaks, but breaking the lines the way she does only serves to make obvious another problem because this won't show the way she seems to use the page-space as a field. This is increasingly true of the poems in fascicles and sets, but more radically in the late letters and fragments. This sense of the page as a field extends to her way of reading Webster.

1448   *With pinions of disdain*

MANUSCRIPT: About 1877, in pencil on a scrap of wrapping paper bearing the initials "ED" in an unidentified hand (A 529).

A   With Pinions of Disdain
           The soul can farther fly
           Than any feather specified
           in - Ornithology -
           It wafts this sordid Flesh   5
           Beyond it's dull - control
           And during it's electric gale -
           The Body is - a soul -
           instructing by the same -
           How little work it be -   10
           To put off filaments like this
           for immortality -

3 specified] ratified • certified   4 in -] by -   6 dull] slow
7 gale] spell • stay - • might - • act - • span   *alt* 7 stay] *the* y
rewritten   9 the same] itself   10] What little act it be

Division 1 of | 2 can | 3 feather | 4 in - | 5 this | 6 it's |
6 control ‖   7 it's | electric | 8 Body | 9 by | 10 work | 11 off |
alt 10 little |

PUBLICATION: *BM* (1945), 200, as three quatrains, with alternatives adopted for lines 3 ("certified"), 4, 6, 7 ("spell"), and 9. *Poems* (1955), 992; *CP* (1960), 609-10. (J1431)

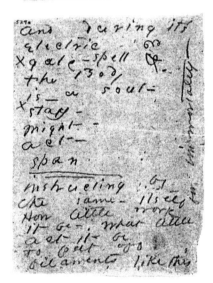

Courtesy of Amherst College Archives and Special Collections

Look at how the word *ornithology* and its dash are spread across the surface in solitary splendor. A real way into her is to notice in the dictionary not only the word but also what's around it. The dictionary as material object is alive with accidental pairings.

ORLE, *n.* In *heraldry,* an ordinary in the form of a fillet, round the shield.

OR'LET, } *n.* [Fr. *ourlet;* It. *orlo.*] In *architecture,* a fillet
OR'LO, } under the ovolo of a capital.

OR'LOP, *n.* [D. *overloop.*] In *a ship of war,* a platform of planks laid over the beams in the hold, on which the cables are usually coiled.

OR'NA-MENT, *n.* [L. *ornamentum.*] 1. That which embellishes; something which, added to another thing, renders it more beautiful to the eye.—2. In *architecture,* ornaments are sculpture or carved work. 3. Embellishment; decoration; additional beauty.

OR'NA-MENT, *v. t.* To adorn; to deck; to embellish.

OR-NA-MENT'AL, *a.* Serving to decorate; giving additional beauty; embellishing. *Brown.*

OR-NA-MENT'AL-LY, *adv.* In such a manner as to add embellishment.

OR'NA-MENT-ED, *pp.* Decorated; embellished; beautified. *Shenstone.*

OR'NA-MENT-ING, *ppr.* Decorating; embellishing.

OR'NATE, *a.* [L. *ornatus.*] Adorned; decorated; beautiful. *Milton.*

OR'NATE-LY, *adv.* With decoration. *Skelton.*

OR'NATE-NESS, *n.* State of being adorned.

OR'NA-TURE, *n.* Decoration. [*Little used.*]

OR-NIS-COP'IES, *n.* Divination by the observation of fowls. *Bailey.*

OR-NIS'CO-PIST, *n.* [Gr. ορνις and σκοπεω.] One who views the flight of fowls in order to foretell future events by their manner of flight. [*Little used.*]

OR-NITH'O-LITE, *n.* A petrified bird.

OR-NI-THO-LOG'I-CAL, *a.* Pertaining to ornithology.

OR-NI-THOL'O-GIST, *n.* A person who is skilled in the natural history of fowls, who understands their form, structure, habits and uses; one who describes birds.

OR-NI-THOL'O-GY, *n.* [Gr. ορνις and λογος.] The science of fowls, which comprises a knowledge of their form, structure, habits and uses.

As in *The Posthumous Papers of the Pickwick Club,* Noah Webster's pages bristle with brackets, dots, dashes, and slashes. Her variant word lists most often occur at the bottom of the poem, and she commonly uses three words to a line. Also note those pesky little word roots in Greek if you don't know the language and most of us don't. But this is the Ornithology page and here they resemble bird tracks in sand.

n. [Gr. ορνις and λογος.] The sci-
ich comprises a knowledge of their
)its and uses.

To further complicate the matter—and this is where facsimiles are needed—this poem about wings and the soaring soul is written in pencil on both sides of a piece of brown wrapping paper that has been torn or cut into a square. Here is what runs through my mind when I see it. That the paper is functional—cheap. Matter of fact. The prosaic material surface clashes with the crucial first noun "Pinions." *Pinion* is a word which means its opposite. In the Webster 1828 across the top of the page with its defini-tion of "pinion" you read PIN PIN PIN which is part of the word but at the same time is the opposite of wing.

"With pinions of / Disdain/" The pencil strokes in "Dis dain" suggest haughtiness. The double *i* in pinion echoes the double *i* in disdain. None of her poems in fair copy are like this. It's akin to drawing or automatic writing.

Courtesy of Beinecke Rare Book and Manuscript Library, Yale University

TG: It's an amazingly different experience working through this poem in manuscript. Look at that set of variants for "gale" almost bursting in. In Franklin, they're at the bottom of the page.

SH: Or, not there at all in the one-volume version. This handwritten manuscript is something that is completely alive. It's flying like a bird or a soul "at the white heat."

Stay-might-act-span—Look at the way *immortality* is shooting (taking off) vertically up the verso right margin. This is a winged thought pinioned to the page. You can tell by the pencil strokes—those crossed *t*s, the

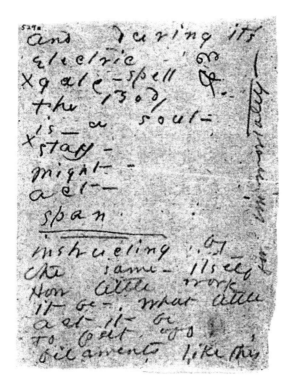

Courtesy of Amherst College Archives and Special Collections

way they speak to the dashes. Look at the *x*'d crosses. Did she simply grab something at hand to write an idea down as it flashed through her mind? Did she find something in her reading that suggested it? Is this a form of automatic writing? But how can it be automatic when it is so perfectly precise? She has many other poems or aphorisms of this kind also on brown wrapping paper. Is this by chance? Or is there something about the surface that matches the thought? Coming back to the word "ornithology," I'm not saying she said, "Oh, this is an important word, a beautiful O word I will spread it out." It's what's happens as she writes it. It's the physical manifestation of what the poem is. "Names are magic, one word can pour such a flood through the soul!" Whitman wrote into one of the notebooks he filled with lists of words and names. "The right name is a perpetual feast to the aesthetic and moral nature."

TG: Let's go back to the dictionary. Did any of that Webster page specifically come into the poem?

SH: In a way yes, because her poems open fields of connections in the same way a page in Webster does. When she says her lexicon is her companion, I think she means it. Here all at once in the center of things we get a variant list "specified / ratified / certified" not as a word list where one word is chosen over another but as a range of possibilities. Of chance associations.

You have a primary definition (one could think of this as a first line in a poem—and since they have no titles her poems hinge on first lines) and then in a dictionary there are the variant meanings provided not sub-

or ground-nut ;	PIN'ION, (pin'yon,) *n.* [Fr. *pignon*, the cope of the ridge of a house ; Norm. *id.*, a pen ; Sp. *piñon*, pinion ; from Celtic *pen*, top, summit.]	miʼ PIN- 1
manner of Pin-	1. The joint of a bird's wing remotest from the body.	bra PIN'
of the odes of lyric poets ; an *Addison.*	2. A feather ; a quill. *Shak.* 3. A wing.	PIN' er ʼ
netal made by *Digby.*	Hope humbly then, on trembling *pinions* soar. *Pope.*	ʼ
L. *pinus*; Sax. *l. pin-bren*, pinwords indicate	4. A smaller wheel with notches or teeth playing into the teeth of a larger wheel. *Hutton.* 5. A term applied to fetters or bands for the arms. *Ainsworth.*	PIN' (or sw
he pine, which also *feinid-wyz*, n *fain*, a cone, ie is from the	PIN'ION, (pin'yon,) *v. t.* To bind or confine the wings. *Bacon.* 2. To confine by binding the wings. 3. To cut off the first joint of the wing.	PIN' of PIN' PIN'
y species, some valuable kind. s name in the us strobus, the ne, Pinus resi- ı.	4. To bind or confine the arm or arms to the body. *Dryden.* 5. To confine ; to shackle ; to chain ; as, to be *pinioned* by formal rules of state. *Norris.* 6. To bind ; to fasten to. *Pope.*	eaʼ PIN' froʼ PIN1 1
often applied to	PIN'ION-ED, *pp.* or *a.* Confined by the wings ; shackled. 2. *a.* Furnished with wings. *Dryden.*	ouʼ PIN' Dɑ

stituted. I think a list like this occurs, not only because it's a variant but because she likes what one word in a list does to the one beside it.

This is what happens in dictionaries.

> DIS-DĀIN', *n.* Contempt ; scorn ; a passion excited
> in noble minds by the hatred or detestation of what
> is mean and dishonorable, and implying a conscious-
> ness of superiority of mind, or a supposed superior-
> ity. In *ignoble minds, disdain* may spring from un-
> warrantable pride or haughtiness, and be directed
> toward objects of worth. It implies hatred, and
> sometimes anger.
>
>   How my soul is moved with just *disdain !*   *Pope.*
>
> DIS-DĀIN'ED, *pp.* Despised ; contemned ; scorned.
> DIS-DĀIN'FUL, *a.* Full of disdain ; as, *disdainful*
> soul.
>   2. Expressing disdain ; as, a *disdainful* look.

TG: Could you talk about how you moved from *My Emily Dickinson* to *The Birth-mark*? In a way, you've answered that already by saying that Dickinson opened up Shepard and Rowlandson for you.

SH: Yes.

TG: I'm sure there's more to say.

SH: In some way I suppose my father opened it up. He wrote a book called *The Garden and the Wilderness: Religion and Government in American Consti- tutional History*, which I never paid any attention to when he was alive. But the strange thing is I find not only my father, but my grandfather. Both of them died before I ever wrote a poem let alone an essay but this curiosity over stilled voices and papers was what they bequeathed me. The more work I do, the more I wish I could sit down and talk to them. I would have so many questions. When I am researching a subject I often find grandpa has been there before me. For instance, his *Life of John Jay Chapman* is totally forgotten now, except by specialists who say it's very good. Joseph Brent in *Charles Sanders Peirce: A Life* has a long passage from a letter by Chapman to someone describing an evening spent talking to Peirce at the Century Club in New York. When I looked up the source in the index, I found it was taken from grandpa's *Life*. I also felt when sitting in Houghton looking at the Peirce manuscripts, even more of a problem for editors than Dickinson's, that once again I knew the territory. The same eccentrically genteel aca- demic types were still very much present in the 1940s and fifties. Peirce was also a Harvard faculty brat.

I'm interested in Peirce's late existential graphs—these graphs are attempts to render assertions in diagrams. The relation between a word and a picture is a mystery for which I think there is no answer.

TG: What have you learned in looking at those graphs?

SH: There's a point at which, to me, those graphs are poems. A logician would read them as symbolic logic. There's something there that's between those two readings.

TG: Between poetry and logic?

SH: Yes. Wilderness and the Law. All I could do was look at them and say, "Oh my God, isn't that wonderful?" But that is what happens when I read a great poem. Just the sight of it on the page is enough.

TG: The fact that it's graphic must have something to do with this. It's in the space between words and pictures. *The Birth-mark* is very much engaged with that space.

SH: Even the hyphen between *Birth* and *mark* is important to me.

TG: We've been talking about sound and sight. How about the importance of touch? The body, is what a manuscript . . .

SH: Holds! It holds the trace of that touch. Even old books hold it. Even going up into the stacks—this is what the computer does not do for me. I love going up there hunting for something. In the long corridors between shelves the books become a series of doors that if opened produced accidental discoveries and connections. You went to look for something and there beside what you thought you were looking for is something you didn't expect. A signal goes out. The whole thing is to be able to get the signal.

TG: To be receptive.

SH: Yes. It's between the reader and the book. There's a moment of grace between the reader and what's in print on that paper. That's the alive thing.

TG: Edwards would have talked about this—about grace—in terms of perception, not touch, I think.

SH: Don't you think that's why he would have been drawn to the extreme emotions of the Great Awakening at the same time he couldn't stop trying to logically explain what immanence was—to the power of the word over the spirit or spirit over the word.

TG: Touch is somehow more intimate than explanation.

sh: On some level, I think that Dickinson and Shepard believe that the book (in her case the page) is skin. That until you get to the point where you feel the page is your skin, is literally skin . . .

tg: When it's skin, spirit comes through?

sh: It's that moment of conversion between the thing you have no words for and something you put into words. That's why I love Shepard's conversion narratives.

tg: Because they're not revised?

sh: We don't know whether he made them up. We don't know if the speakers were simply saying what he meant them to say. In England he had been a stenographer. Was he dictating or was he taking dictation? They appear to have been quickly written down, not revised. When all is said and done, this Puritan minister has provided one of the very few records of people having just arrived in Massachusetts during the 1630s attempting to voice an experience which should be joyful but isn't for all sorts of reasons.

tg: Their conversion?

sh: Yes, the striking thing is how unhappy and halting these brief confessions of faith sound. Joyce's doubled word "terrorstricken" just about covers it. It seems to me that Edwards and Shepard are similar in many ways. For both, faith, or seeing something directly with the mind's eye unmediated, paradoxically needs to be explained. Edwards's dilemma we can see through his secondhand description of his wife Sarah's religious ecstasy to be found at third remove when William James puts her into the Saintliness chapter of *Varieties of Religious Experience*. Though Edwards wished he could experience the same joy at being overwhelmed, he couldn't. His own *Personal Narrative* is suffused with sadness.

tg: There is his famous description of Sarah: "She will sometimes go about from place to place, singing sweetly; and seems to be always full of joy and pleasure; and no one knows for what. She loves to be alone, walking in the fields and groves, and seems to have someone invisible always conversing with her."

sh: Yes I love that description too. Somewhere I also read that when he went on horseback to make his pastoral rounds from parish to parish and ideas came to him he would write them down on little slips of paper and pin them to his clothes. I imagine him arriving home after several days' absence covered in bits of paper. Somehow— Sarah would never have bothered with the paper.

TG: She would sing them?

SH: In *The Narrative of the Surprising Conversions*, while remaining outside these intensities, Edwards observes and records what he sees. It's Peirce's Thirdness—he's trying to define an experience that is ultimately inexplicable. As James says at the end of the Saintliness chapter, "The only sound plan, if we are ourselves outside the pale of such emotions is to observe, and to record faithfully what we observe."

TG: And you must see yourself as working in that in-between space you've been describing. Between the inexplicable and explanation.

SH: I certainly see Dickinson there. And particularly in her "My Life" poem. Thinking of Peirce and his theory of categories, for me very generally, poems would represent Secondness and essays Thirdness. What is Firstness? I'm always trying to go back to a beginning. One has to go farther and farther back. I always want to go back.

TG: I know you've contrasted the different ways poems and essays feel as you work on them.

SH: Poems for me are free. I lay out the work. It's peaceful. Like being in an open field. No fences no houses just wild field grasses.

TG: Like Sarah?

SH: Yes, fields and groves. The way the landscape around Guilford or New Haven where she lived once was—between settled and unsettled. But I have more of Shepard, or Edwards, in my makeup. I guess "the power to die" in "My Life had stood—a Loaded Gun" would be Firstness—as a poet she knows she must fall into words—into Thirdness. Though I hadn't thought of Peirce when I wrote the essays that make up *The Birth-mark*. If I looked at all my work and said what it is I cared the most about, that I felt the most proud of, or that I felt was true—it would be *The Birth-mark*.

TG: Really?

SH: Yes. I guess you might say it is a form of prayer.

TG: Why is that?

SH: I don't know.

TG: Because you're most alive, most at risk there?

SH: I'm most at risk because I'm so worried that there is something I got wrong, or didn't see. And yet, I can't and won't let go of the sound of what I write. *The Sound Believer* (Shepard's title) seems to me perfect—even if he and I might not agree in our definition of "sound." There's where Dickinson's letters have been a huge influence. Particularly the later more aphoristic ones—it's as if sound has its own sense.

TG: I notice you have some Wallace Stevens quotations and poems on your wall. Would you mind talking about your wall?

SH: I paste up things that I care about at the moment. So that they are in front of me while I am working. A friend gave me the print years ago and I've always kept it up here though all the other things change from time to time. It's Turner's "The Angel in the Sun." Dickinson read Ruskin's *Modern Painters* and I am pretty sure that Ruskin's account of Turner's myriad watercolor sketches had an effect on her working process. His attempts over and over to capture the effect of sun on water gradually drop away detail and move into abstraction. Just as in this painting here which is an oil not a watercolor the angel seems to be dissolving into light. That's what the artist or poet keeps trying for. You might not have an answer at the end but you keep trying, now this way, now that way. It's not the finding. It's the searching.

TG: And Wallace Stevens?

SH: Wallace Stevens is my "necessary angel."

January 18, 2003
Guilford, Connecticut

SEVEN

MEETING APART

Jorie Graham's Swarm

In a remark that at first seems surprising, Jorie Graham notes at the end
of her recent book *Swarm* (2000) that Emily Dickinson's poem 640
(F706) is a core text for that volume, "animat[ing] the book throughout"
(113).[1] In fact, Dickinson's work has been on Graham's mind throughout
her career, providing one of the crucial voices—along with those of Bishop
and Stevens—with which her work could be said to be in almost constant
conversation.[2] But in turning to Dickinson's poem 640, Graham has opened
both a new stage in her response to the earlier poet's work and a new stage in
her own thinking. Poem 640 is an address to a beloved who has been almost
infinitely removed from the speaker:

> I cannot live with You—
> It would be Life—
> And Life is over there—
> Behind the Shelf
>
> The Sexton keeps the Key to—
> Putting up
> Our Life—His Porcelain—
> Like a Cup—
>
> Discarded of the Housewife—
> Quaint—or Broke—

If living with him, the two becoming one flesh, was life, that world has been
ruled out of bounds. It is a possibility that has been laid aside and locked
away like a discarded cup. Simply put, there seems to be a law against it.

Graham has always been attracted to the way Dickinson's powers are awakened by situations such as this in which something resists or is held back. As Dickinson puts it in poem 338 (F365), a poem Graham often refers to, what resists exists in silence, a world that can't be spoken for because it holds itself apart and can be neither identified nor located. One might, perhaps, think of that experience of silence as a game:

> I know that He exists.
> Somewhere—in Silence—
> He has hid his rare life
> From our gross eyes.
>
> 'Tis an instant's play.
> 'Tis a fond Ambush—
> Just to make Bliss
> Earn her own surprise!

But if it is a game, Dickinson suggests between clenched teeth, it is a "piercing[ly] earnest" game in which the searcher's gleeful sense of anticipation has the potential of being met not by a fondly sprung ambush but by unyielding, stony silence:

> But—should the play
> Prove piercing earnest—
> Should the glee—glaze—
> In Death's—stiff—stare
>
> Would not the fun
> Look too expensive!
> Would not the jest—
> Have crawled too far!

Such encounters with silence, Graham writes—the poems' speakers crawling, broken, a law forever blocking access to what is desired—are Dickinson's great legacy:

> If poems are records of true risks (attempts at change) taken by the soul of the speaker, then, as much as possible, my steps are toward silence. Silence which is the absence of speech, or the ability to speak, the reason or desire. Silence which drowns us out, but also which ignores us, overrides us, silence which is doubt, madness, fear, all that which makes the language bend and slip. . . . Dickinson's poems, her dangers, are . . . authenticated by her losses. So many of them—battles with those emissaries of silence which are the ocean, the wind,

the light of day . . . and the speechlessness of pain, of fear—end on great failures of human speech.[3]

To say, then, that Graham has been in conversation with Dickinson's work throughout her career, seeking to extend it, would be to say that she has engaged in similar battles with what "ignores" or "overrides us" and has courted similar "failures of human speech." In being broken or silenced by what won't fully open up to her—"God, nature, a beloved, an Idea, Abstract form, Language itself as a field, Chance, Death, Consciousness, what exists in the silence. Something not invented by the writer," Graham writes—the writer senses and is marked by a world that overwhelms her.[4] We "hear" that resistant larger world in those places where language is gagged. We "read" its imprint as it erases or slashes through what we have written. As that happens, writer and reader are awakened to, are forced to more fully engage, what warps or penetrates straightforward speech and thought. Graham put it this way in 1994, introducing a reading of Dickinson's work but offering insight into her own goals as well:

> I suggest listening in the poems as I read them now for the use of order and its breakdown, senses and their extinguishing, imagery and its obliteration, rhyme and its increase or failure, the speaker moving from an active to a passive stance, remembering and then forgetting, narrative that breaks off into silence, beginnings that are not beginnings, endings that are not endings; attempts at letting the timeless as experienced in extreme states of being—anguish, despair, for example, or in the presence of death—penetrate the language in order to stain it; dashes as those places where the timeless makes its inroads—where what exists in the silence seeks to be let in.[5]

What Graham responds to in Dickinson and then enacts in her own terms is the live, vertiginous moment when "a Plank in Reason, broke, / And I dropped down, and down" (J280, F340). "Order and its breakdown, . . . imagery and its obliteration . . . remembering and then forgetting": in each of these formulations, a previously stable way of making sense of things erodes or dissolves, and the poet is forced to call on an untapped resource, a new way of thinking and feeling, to keep her feet. Like Robinson's "imperfectly partial" analogies, Wright's scoured attention to what refuses him access, and Howe's improvised soundings of the unknown, Graham's enactments of vertigo open her language to a wilderness, something other, that can be inhabited but never mastered. As she noted in introducing another reading of Dickinson in 1999, such enactments seek to draw the reader in as well, forcing him or her to "undergo . . . different kinds of vertigo-laden sensations that undermine any stable understanding of what's in the silence in order to be able to inhabit it fully."[6]

Inhabiting something that yet remains unmasterable, being brought to a full or awakened use of language, both poet and reader are returned to the world. All of the writers we have examined have made a similar argument. Graham phrases it this way:

> The bedrock role of poetry, ultimately, is to restore, for each generation anew, the mind to its word and the words to their world via accurate usage. Every generation of poets has that task, and it must—each time—do it essentially from scratch. Each image achieved, each moment of description where the *other* is seized, where it stains the language, undertakes the same vast metaphysical work: to restore the human *word* to the immortal thing; to insure that the relationship is, however momentarily, viable and true. . . . To make the words channels between mind and world. To make them *full* again.[7]

Graham's books record the different ways she has tried to open and inhabit Dickinson's vertiginous moment when language or mind or stable understanding fails. What's important about *Swarm*, the volume where Dickinson's work is most directly engaged, is that Graham's way of drawing the reader into those language-enriching, "vertigo-laden sensations" takes a significant turn there. In *Swarm*, the "emissar[y] of silence" is a beloved. If merging so completely with the other that one's self is erased would, theoretically, give one access to "what exists in the silence," being unable to achieve that union prompts the broken-off sensation of vertigo I have been describing. In *Swarm*, however, in contrast to earlier confrontations with resistant materials, vertigo, while indeed allowing the poet's shattered language to be stained and imprinted by a larger, overriding force, seems at first to lead the poet away from the world, complicating my claim in this volume that Dickinson's primary legacy is a world-opening, responsive brokenness.

If we return to poem 640, we can see how the poet's broken speech to the absent beloved—words thrown against silence in steady despair—offers a number of "piercing[ly] earnest" ways of unfolding vertigo's possibilities. If the option of giving oneself to the other in self-erasure had been declared out-of-bounds when they were alive, the poem continues, what about dying at the same moment? What about that form of union?

> I could not die—with You—
> For One must wait
> To shut the Other's Gaze down—
> You—could not—

It would have been physically impossible, she sighs: in such circumstances, one figure must always wait or lag behind to attend to the other, and in any case, she pointedly remarks, the beloved had once before been unable to wait. Neither could they rise and be united at the moment of judgment, for the lover's face "Would put out Jesus'," displaying glory so overwhelming that the promises of grace would be of no interest to her, thus forcing them apart again:

> They'd judge Us—How—
> For You—served Heaven—You know,
> Or sought to—
> I could not—
>
> Because You saturated Sight—
> And I had not more Eyes
> For sordid excellence
> As Paradise

Her voice continues rising as she engages the absent lover and the powerful forces arrayed against them: "were You lost," she writes, and I somehow welcomed into the ranks of the saved, "I would be" as lost and abandoned as you; and "were You—saved" and the two of us separated, that isolated self would be as deep a torment as hell could hold.

It's that flaring, passionate despair, pressing more and more forcefully against silence—its wall or law—that Dickinson refers to in the poem's last stanza when she writes, in the present tense:

> So We must meet apart—
> You there—I—here—
> With just the Door ajar
> That Oceans are—and Prayer—
> And that White Sustenance—
> Despair—

If there is to be no merging of the two bodies, no erasure of self in union, then we are left with the "meet[ing] apart," you there and I here, that occurs through the "Door ajar" of structures such as this poem. Like the literal door through which Dickinson would at times converse with or take in the world, this door acknowledges that there is an absolute separation between figures or realms—an "Ocean" between them. At the same time, as speech or "Prayer" between realms, the door ajar suggests an intimacy with what refuses to speak back, speech sustaining itself—being made alive by—the despairing acknowledgment of a world there but finally out of reach. "To all except anguish, the mind soon adjusts," writes Dickinson in a letter, a sentence that Graham quotes in the opening poem of *Swarm*.[8] How is "Despair" a "White Sustenance"? In despair or anguish, the mind cannot adjust to a world resisting its deepest needs and desires. It has no language, or rather, it has a language crushed or blotted out by what it can't reach—a language testifying to the "sustaining" weight of what exists but exists out of reach. We have seen this with each of the contemporary writers we've examined, and of course with Dickinson. As Elisa New puts it, "where God marks his domain as the absence of the humanly intelligible" (153), "states of anticipation and dread, longing and uncertainty" (159) are "route[s] of spiritual access" (192). What *Swarm* tries to unfold and inhabit is the particular form such vertiginous states might take.

It might be of some use in approaching Graham's swerve in *Swarm* to describe her earlier responses to Dickinson.[9] *Erosion* (1983) argues quite straightforwardly that the moment when language bends and slips exists and that it adds something important to our approach to the world. Behind the book, one can sense such a poem as Dickinson's "A narrow Fellow in the Grass" in which taking "notice" of a snake momentarily visible at the speaker's feet produces not the familiar "transport / Of cordiality" experienced in other natural encounters but a sense of alienation and a shocked inability to respond: "Zero at the Bone" (J986, F1096). One can also hear echoes of Dickinson's "A Bird came down the Walk—" in which an attempt to describe and domesticate is broken off by a bird's sudden removal of itself to a realm "Too silver for a seam" (J328, F359). The poems in *Erosion* suggest that through such suddenly speechless moments "we know there is a wall / beyond which we can't go" (79) and further, that "on the erosion-line," where our too-easily-relied-on expectations of cordiality and access begin to crumble, we begin to grow. This is Dickinson's line of Circumference; we grow because we are forced to acknowledge a world in some ways fundamentally outside of us: "we are defined by what we will not take / into ourselves" (79).

Erosion's poems turn on a series of oppositions in which, as in the Dickinson poems I've just referred to, a more straightforward and confident approach to the world is broken off by an acknowledgment of the limits of that approach. For the most part, the poet looks outside of herself for examples of this. "Wanting a Child," for example, points to "the waste / of time" when a river, which "has been everywhere, imagine, dividing, discerning, / cutting deep into the parent rock" is "yoked, / trussed" by the incoming tide: "pulsing upward, inland, into the river's rapid / argument, pushing / with its insistent tragic waves . . . / . . . so that erosion / is its very face" (29). "Salmon" turns from a couple making love—the poet noting "the thin black seam / they seemed to be trying to work away / between them"—to the "space of time" afterward, when the task has been put aside and "they made a distance / one from the other / and slept" (40–41). "At Luca Signorelli's Resurrection of the Body" contrasts the painter's desire to understand the body and to arrive at a stable version of the human with his acknowledgment that such a sense of stability is always, always receding:

> In his studio
> Luca Signorelli
> in the name of God
> and Science
> and the believable
> broke into the body
>
> studying arrival.
> But the wall
> of the flesh
> opens endlessly,
> its vanishing point so deep
> and receding
>
> we have yet to find it

Imagine, the poet writes, when Signorelli's own son "died violently" and he began to study *that* body: "with beauty and care / and technique / and judgment, cut into / shadow, cut / into bone and sinew." Imagine the moment, she continues, when, after days of "that deep / caress, cutting, / unfastening," the analytical mind came to a halt, no end to its tormenting questions in sight, and "climb[ed] into / the open flesh and / mend[ed] itself" (75–77).

Most of the poems in *Erosion* work out versions of this pattern, convinced that as the mind or scalpel or river halts, some sort of healing or openness or fuller vision begins. "I Watched a Snake" takes up Dickinson's poem directly and argues that the snake's movement—"I'd watch / its path of body in the grass go / suddenly invisible / only to reappear a little / further on"—can be read as "a mending / of the visible / by the invisible." The snake's disappearance or apparent defeat—Graham compares it to death or "going back under"—links it to what overcomes it or erases it: "fastens [it] / to sturdier stuff" (34). Like a wall that cannot be broken through or a body that cannot be fully known, that sturdier stuff silences what would possess it; we feel its weight as an inexplicable "Zero at the Bone." That inexplicable weight mends the mind, Graham argues, because as the mind staggers, readjusts, or is silenced, we are made more whole, moving from the "quick intelligence that only knows" to "another, thicker, kind of sight" (4, 5).

What's most notable about Graham's next volume, *The End of Beauty* (1987), is that she begins there the long process of trying to inhabit, for herself, that place where the quick intelligence is turned back and forced alive by a world that holds itself apart from her. "Vertigo" describes this confrontation in the third person, the poet picturing herself standing at the edge of a cliff and looking out and down to where "a real world flowed in its parts, green, green." She reads that sudden drop as the sheer reach of the mind, giddy in its bright ambitions:

> She thought of where the mind opened out
> into the sheer drop of its intelligence,
> the updrafting pastures of the vertical in which a bird now rose,
> blue body the blue wind was knifing upward
> faster than it could naturally rise,
> up into the downdraft until it was frozen until she could see them
> at last
> the stages of flight, broken down, broken free,
> each wingflap folding, each splay of the feather-sets flattening
> for entry. . . . *Parts* she thought, *free* parts, watching the laws
> at work, *through which desire must course*
> seeking an ending, seeking a shape.   (66)

Momentarily caught and held in the play of updraft and downdraft, the bird rising before her seems to have been "broken free" of the world by the mind eager to study its constitutive parts, hungry to name or completely know its shape. But then, as in Dickinson's "A Bird came down the Walk," something shifts and, "all of an instant," the bird breaks free of the mind's ambitions, becoming "a blue / enchantment of properties no longer / knowable." Yoked or trussed, the mind is swept with a vertiginous series of questions about its drive to know and name:

> What is it to understand, she let fly,
> leaning outward from the edge now that the others had gone down.
> How close can the two worlds get, the movement from one to the other
> being death?
> . . .
> How is it one soul wants to be owned
> by a single other
> in its entirety?—
> . . .
> What was it that was *not her listening?*
> She leaned out. What is it pulls at one, she wondered,

what? That it has no shape but point of view?
That it cannot move to hold us?
Oh it has vibrancy, she thought, this emptiness, this intake just
                                          prior to
the start of a story, the mind trying to fasten
and fasten, the mind feeling it like a sickness this wanting
to snag, to catch hold, begin, the mind crawling out to the edge of the cliff
and feeling the body as if for the first time—how it cannot
follow, cannot love.   (67)

This is the space Graham's Dickinson is fascinated by: the world's emptiness or silence or difference made vibrant and momentarily visible by the mind's frantic, broken-off questions.[10] "To all except anguish, the mind soon adjusts." How close can the two worlds come? the unsettled speaker asks. What sort of entrance do we seek in self-erasure? How does point of view pull shapelessness into form? What is lost in the process? Interestingly, those questions bring her to an awareness of her body—the body, which has always known it can't follow the mind's airy ambitions. Unable to catch hold, sick and dizzy with its desperate (and now seen as impossible) needs, the mind, in such a situation, is thrown back on the body and another way of knowing.[11] The body, for instance, knows that the distance from the edge of the cliff to the real is unbridgeable, knows that there is a law blocking union, but in knowing that feels the world down there brought more vibrantly into play. Those questions, that bodily sense of vertigo, another poem puts it, "made me hear how clean the sky . . . was of / anything I might have trapped it with" (69).

One of the primary ways the poet in this volume allows such questions to "undermine . . . stable understanding" is through a series of poems, many of them labeled self-portraits, in which she tries to imagine the inner lives of paired figures in some of the great stories in the western tradition. In most of the stories, one figure reaches for or looks at or tries to touch the world he or she loves: Orpheus "seeking [Eurydice's] edges, seeking to make her palpable again" (15); Apollo wanting "to possess [Daphne], to nail [her] erasures" (30); Mary Magdalene desperate to touch the risen Christ, "her longings all stitchwork towards his immaculate rent" (42). And most of the stories pivot on the moment when that longing to possess is brought up short: Eurydice returning to "the possible which each momentary outline blurs into again" (15); Daphne becoming "part of the view not one of the actors . . . / . . . untouched, untransformed" (34); Christ saying "Don't touch me," "want[ing] her to believe, / . . . want[ing] her to look away" (42). The stories differ enough to lead the poet in various ways as she explores the confrontation, but as Graham attempts to keep both voices alive (one seeking, one pulling free), what begins to emerge is a different way of speaking. Graham describes this in "Vertigo" as the body coming into play as the mind is forced to acknowledge its limits. As Daphne forces Apollo to acknowledge that there is a world that "would not be the end towards which he was ceaselessly tending" (32), as she transforms his desires into "vertigo-laden sensations," she opens a gap that the mind can no longer assume it can traverse but that the body can inhabit. As Orpheus is brought up short and the end of the story is withheld, Eurydice, or constantly changing process, begins to speak. We hear in these poems "the body of talk between the start and beauty / . . . sucked alive by delay . . . / . . . the unsaid billowing round" (83, 85). Trussing the mind, acknowledging the law that keeps us apart, is crucial in bringing about a new use of language: "Siren, / reader, / it is here, only here, / in this gap / between us, / that the body of who we are / to have been / emerges" (43). Such speech, the final poem in the book argues, seeking and failing "to keep the thing clear," gives the silent or faceless world something to press against and allows it momentarily to become visible or hearable: "What would she be / without us / willing to sit and clarify and try to nail / it shut? We give her that glitzy fluttering, her body, by the one deep-driven / nail of point-of-view, / don't we?" (95–96).

In *Region of Unlikeness* (1991), Graham pushes this investigation forward in an important way. Rather than reading the tension between mind and world out of our culture's stories, she unfolds its presence within her own stories—her own memories. And perhaps even more significantly, in many of the poems she plays out the tension in the act of writing or remembering, sketching powerful equivalents to Dickinson's enactments of the mind's movements and reversals. Some of the memories are narrated in the present tense, as if being lived out again in the writing: "She lies there. A corridor of light filled with dust / flows down from the booth to the screen" (3); or "I'm in the bathroom holding the baby down, / washing it off" (29). In other poems, the poet sorts through a memory while quite deliberately calling attention to the words she speaks or the paper in front of her or her struggle to reach the reader: "Has to do with the story about the girl who didn't die / in the gas chamber, who came back out asking / for her mother. . . . / . . . Can you help me in this? / Are you there in your stillness?" (12); "We rose from the table having paid our bill. / . . . I look into the air / for your face—" (24); "He turns in his sleep. / You want to get out of here. / The stalls going up in the street below now for market. / Don't wake up. Keep this in black and white" (37); "It was one day near the very end of childhood, Rome, / . . . Should I tell you who they are, there on the torn / page—should we count them (nine)—and then the girl who was me" (41).

In a sense, she's playing Eurydice to her own Orpheus—opening up a gap in the expected straightforward passageways between now and then and exploring the "body of talk between the start and beauty / . . . sucked alive by delay." The idea is the same: that when the process stalls you face something new and wordless. Graham's term in this volume for that live space where the mind's vertigo-laden sensations are sorted through and explored is *waiting*—as in this passage where the poet remembers staring at her face in a mirror, unable to move forward after being betrayed by a father's lie:

> When Psyche met the god he came down to her
>
>   through the opening which is *waiting*,
> the *not living* you can keep alive in you,
>   the god in the house. We painted that alive,
> mother with her hands
>   fixing the outline clear—eyeholes, mouthhole—
> forcing the expression on.
>   Until it was the only thing in the end of the day that seemed
>
> believable,
>   and the issue of candor coming awake, there,
> one face behind the other peering in,
>   and the issue of
> freedom. . . .   (44–45)

The poems in *Region* seek to paint the unsettling issues discovered in memory alive, allowing them to awaken. As they do so, wandering in an exploratory way through the door ajar between now and then, here and there, something previously silent ("*not living*") is felt and given "expression." These issues and questions are discovered in both the scenes remembered and in the act of writing, so that one investigation spurs on the other—is in fact the same as the other. So, for example, a memory of being in a movie theater and the house lights coming on because of an emergency while the movie continued to play captures an experience of waiting—the forward progress of the movie's story was reduced to "just a roiling up of graynesses, / vague stutterings of / light with motion in them, bits of moving zeros"—and provides the impetus to meditate on similar issues raised in the writing, for example her reluctance to sort through and choose because she knows, at some level, that writing (like the whited-out movie) is little more than "a grave of possible shapes called *likeness*" (5).

What happens in the space of waiting, then, is that the mind is stopped but still thinks, but in a more exploratory, intuitive, or bodily way. As one poem puts it, waiting is "(Where the hurry is stopped) (and held) (but not extinguished) (no)" (125). Dickinson suggests that the voice (and the mind) comes powerfully alive in this space. For her, the space of waiting is a gap "Capacious as the Sea— / Between Eternity and Time— / Your Conscious-ness—and Me—" (J644, F713). She proposes to "sing to use the Waiting" (J850, F955), perhaps growing "Fitter to see Him" (J968, F834) as her ability to sing and see develops in that space where such drives are "held" but "not extinguished." Graham's teasing out the issues raised by her own memories has a similar goal: she wants to "make [words] full again."

Let me give an example. "From the New World," as we've already seen, focuses on the poet's reaction to a terrible story recounted during the trial of the man accused of being the Nazi prison guard Ivan the Terrible. A young girl came out of the gas chamber alive, asking for her mother, and Ivan ordered a man going in to rape her. Trying to touch this remembered story, the poet finds herself "unmoored," the poem stalling, and turns to the reader who now must also wait:

> God knows I too want the poem to continue,
>
> want the silky swerve into shapeliness
>   and then the click shut
> and then the issue of sincerity (12)

She explores the unmoored space and the desired clicking shut of form by moving to her own life and memories of her grandmother's last years: the moment when her grandmother failed to recognize her and the poet fled to a bathroom, sensing her stable world unraveling around her ("Reader, / they were all in there, I didn't look up, / they were all in there, the coiling and uncoiling / billions / . . . Then the click like a lock being tried"); and an experience some years later when her grandmother had been placed in a nursing home and spent her time "sitting with her purse in her hands all day every / day, asking can I go now, / . . . the eyes unfastening, nervous . . . / . . . old whoever clicking and unclicking the clasp the / silver knobs" (13–15).

This feeling of the world coming unfastened followed by the frantic clicks of the mind trying to find purchase ties these two scenes back to both the gas chamber and the poet's stalled confrontation with the story. But the scenes don't explain the story and get it moving again; the poet keeps turn-ing to the reader, asking "Where would you go now? *Where*." What happens instead is that she enters deeply into her own inability to handle the story, to settle it into an adequate likeness. Likeness itself, what she's attempting to do as she shifts from the young girl to her grandmother, becomes as charged and uncertain and desperate as the young girl's asking for her mother or the grandmother asking for home.[12] In failing to move the story forward, in painting the issues of story-telling alive, then, the poet finds herself over-whelmed by an experience of silence:

> *Like* what, I wonder, to make the bodies come on, to make
> room,
>
> *like what*, I whisper,
>
> *like* which is the last new world, *like, like*, which is the thin
>
> young body (before it's made to go back in) whispering *please*.   (16)

At the same time, these poems also fear that the space of waiting may simply become a place where, riddled with uncertainty, live expression dis-appears—in the language of this book, no face or expression will move forward:

> flecks of
> information,
> fabric through which no face will push,
> proof,
> a storm of single instances   (105)

This fear, I would suggest, eventually pushes Graham's use of Dickinson in a new direction, but at this stage it merely flickers in the background. These poems hope for the opposite: that the language of waiting might become responsive to the silence pressing against it; that the poet might grow "Fitter to see Him"—"Him" being silence and all its various emissaries—as in this encounter with the shroud bearing the impression of Christ's face:

> —When they held it up to us
> we saw nothing, we saw the delay, we saw
>
> the minutes on it, spots here and there,
> we tried to see something, little by little we could almost see,
> almost nothing was visible,
> already something other than nothing
> was visible in the *almost*.   (74)

With *Materialism* (1993), Graham moves even more firmly into the pres-ent-tense act of writing, completing a sort of trilogy of works that, following Dickinson, explore ways of awakening language to what it is unable to mas-ter. The gap these poems paint alive is that between the mind (or eye) and the world. The poems are primarily attempts to bridge the space between here and there by description, tracking the way the eye seeks to know and make order:[13]

First this. *Then* this . . . Oh, glance—gnawing the
                              overgrowth,
criss-crossing the open for broken spots, leaks—
what is there? what is
the object?   (8)

As in *The End of Beauty* and *Region of Unlikeness*, such attempts lead to a kind of vertigo, the mind or eye not able to take in all that yawns open before it and, becoming aware of its limits, yielding to other ways of knowing: "I can feel the mind at its hinge, / insane for foothold. / . . . The mind feeling sure there is a beneath—a hard place— / behind the spangly news report" (51–52). Feeling the mind's flailing, dramatizing its brought-up-short attempts to caress and possess the world, fills the waiting—the idea being that as the mind is forced *down* from its above-the-world illusion of invulnerability and abstract accuracy, the world is lured *up* from its complexity into a bit of visibility. The space between becomes a space where one might meet, yet not master, the world. "Manifest Destiny" offers a striking image for such a manner of writing; think of language as a bullet in a museum case that a soldier had bitten down on during an amputation in an attempt to hold back a scream, the poem suggests. Testifying to the struggle to master the scream and to the scream's overwhelming resistance, the bullet records a "claw[ing] for foothold," "the toothed light [biting] down hard on the sinewy scream" (99). The scream, as in Elizabeth Bishop, seems alive forever, its face showing through the "fabric" recording the struggle.[14] The bullet, like a snake moving and disappearing, issues a challenge to the writer:

How can the scream rise up out of its grave of matter?
How can the light drop down out of its grave of thought?

How can they cross over and the difference between them swell with existence?   (100)

An early poem in the book, "Steering Wheel," helps us see the manner in which Graham paints alive the descriptive mind's clawing for foothold. Backing out of a driveway, glancing in her rearview mirror, the speaker's eye is caught by a "veil of leaves" sucked up by an updraft. Quickly trying to graph the red swirl of leaves—noting their relationship to three pine trees behind them, contrasting their movement to the "rising strings" of music on the radio, "crisp with distinctions, of the earlier order"—she finds herself brought up short, unable to cross the space between eye and world: "Oh but I haven't gotten it right. / You couldn't say that it was matter. / I couldn't say that it was sadness" (5). And in that failure, still looking backward, she remembers a phrase of George Oppen:

"we have to regain the moral pleasure
of experiencing the distance between subject and object,"
—me now slowly backing up
the dusty driveway into the law
composed of updraft, downdraft, weight of these dried
                              mid-winter leaves,
light figured-in too, I'm sure, the weight of light,
and angle of vision, dust, gravity, solitude,
and the part of the law which is the world's waiting,
and the part of the law which is my waiting,
and then the part which is my impatience—now; *now?*—   (5–6)

What Graham does in *Materialism*, and this is also drawn from Bishop, is look backward at things—hold herself backward to the normally straightforward business of looking and placing ourselves.[15] In doing so, she experiences "the distance between subject and object," thought of here as a law against which the eye presses: the law holding eye and world separate (both waiting); the law played out in the separate paths taken by world (updraft, downdraft, dust, gravity) and observer (angle of vision, solitude, impatience to name and move on). Experiencing or fully inhabiting this drama, being broken by its pressures, the poet hopes to ready herself to meet the world.

By watching herself observe—watching herself attempt to possess and colonize but also explore and sort through—the poet tries to fill the waiting, allowing the pressure of the silent ocean of material things to be brought to bear against her words. The self-scrutiny is quite deliberate, as here, nearing the conclusion of a description of pausing before a tree filled with starlings in a snowstorm:

The storm: I close my eyes and,
standing in it, try to make it *mine*. An inside
thing. Once I was. . . . once, once.
It settles, in my head, the wavering white
sleep, the instances—they stick, accrue,
grip up, connect, they do not melt,
I will not let them melt, they build, cloud and cloud,
I feel myself weak, I feel the thinking muscle-up—
outside, the talk-talk of the birds . . .
but inside, no more exploding, no more smoldering, no more,
inside, a splinter colony, new world, possession
gripping down to form,
wilderness brought deep into my clearing   (85)

Let me give an extended example—a variation on Dickinson's "A Bird came down the Walk" entitled "Subjectivity." The poet encounters an unmoving monarch butterfly on a cold morning and brings it into her house, its black-and-yellow coloring offering an image of the way the mind's gaze seeks to take possession, raising the issue:

> yellow of cries forced through that mind's design
> >   like a clean verdict,
> like a structure of tenses and persons for the gusting
>
> >   heaven-yellow
> minutes . . .
> >   the gaze's stringy grid of nerves
> spreading out onto
>
> >   whatever bright new world the eyes would seize upon—   (26)

As we might anticipate, the butterfly will not be held by the eye (a neighbor will in time explain that the butterfly is simply reacting to the cold; placed in the sun, it "ris[es] up of a sudden out of its envelope of glances— / a bit of fact in the light and then just light" [31]), but before she turns to the scene in which the mind must let go, the poet plays out the distance between grid and new world, eyes and heaven. And she does so in an interesting way. She uses her body to feel out what the mind is engaged in doing, puts herself into the position of the thing seen—matter, the butterfly, heaven's yellow—in order to feel more deeply what such knowing is all about. That would be like permitting Eurydice to speak in *The End of Beauty*. It opens a space between "the start and the beauty" where a different "body of talk" can begin, allowing the issues within that space to "swell with existence."

Moving from a past-tense description of the butterfly to a present-tense exploration, in a sense enacting a bodily response to vertigo implied but not developed in Dickinson, the poet sits in a chair and watches a beam of sunlight slowly move across a slatwood floor: "making a meaning like a wide sharp thought— / an unrobed thing we can see the inside of" (26). Eventually, waiting long enough, the light touches her foot, instep, calf, and then face. As she waits, she feels something of what making form is all about, allowing that drive and what resists it to take on visibility and body. As the light finally touches her face, it

> forc[es] me to close my eyes,
> >   the whole of the rest feeling broken off,
>
> it all being my face, my being inside the beam of sun,

and the sensation of how it falls unevenly,

how the wholeness I felt in the shadow is lifted,
broken, this tip *lit*, this other *dark*—and stratified,
analyzed, chosen-round, formed—   (29)

If that is what her mind is after, such a forceful and inadequate elimination of wholeness, then her own eyes, as she returns to her own encounter with the butterfly, now seem much less godlike as they are drawn out of their untouched confidence:

these thin almost icy beams I can feel my open eyes release,
widening as they sweep down
out of the retina

to take the body in—
aerial, tunneling, wanting to be spent in what cannot
feel them as they smear, coat,
wrap, diagram—   (31)

We could say that Graham, like Dickinson, acknowledges her own blindness here, deliberately seeking to develop a language that works in an "other way," "its soul / Upon the window pane—" (J327, F336). Through such an enactment, words acknowledge their "materiality," becoming more and more aware that there is always "a tiny draft / just underneath them" and that they must "displace something to / *be*" (16).

The Errancy (1997) marks the beginning of a turn in Graham's work that might be thought of as a shift from exploring Dickinson's dramatization of herself as a brought-up-short thinker and describer to a more critical examination of that role. *The Errancy* focuses on thought itself—not just memory or description or writing but the whole attempt, grand but impossible, to "in a net . . . seek to hold the wind." Thinking, in this book, has exhausted itself or reached its limit: "aren't we tired? aren't we / going to close the elaborate folder / which holds the papers in their cocoon of possibility" (6); "The reader is tired. / I am so very tired" (50). This is a cultural exhaustion, and one notices in this volume the poet's attempt to turn her eye away from herself and directly address the reader and the culture. Poem after poem urgently seeks out a "we." In "The Errancy," for example, Graham includes the reader in acknowledging the collapse of the dreams of reason and order and purity:

Then the cicadas again like kindling that won't take.
The struck match of some utopia we no longer remember

> the terms of—
> the rules. What was it was going to be abolished, what
> restored?
> . . .
>
> here, up on the hill, in town,
> the clusterings of dwellings in balconied crystal-formation,
> the cadaverous swallowings of the dream of reason gone,
> hot fingerprints where thoughts laid out these streets, these
> bracingings
> of park and government—a hospital—a dirt-bike run—
> here, we stand in our hysteria with our hands in our pockets,
> quiet, at the end of the day, looking out, theories stationary   (4)

Many of the poems turn to the reader as they establish the particular wilderness this volume wanders through. "The Scanning" compares our situation to driving on an interstate, fiddling with the radio—"the bands of *our* listening scan / the bands of static, / seeking a resting point" (7, italics mine)—and finally pulling off, plan exhausted, no clear way to move forward. We can think of thought's brokenness in that way:

> What shall we move with
> now that the eye must shut? What shall we sift with
> now that the mind must blur? What shall we undress the veilings of
>   dusk with,
> what shall we harvest the nothingness with,
> now that the hands must be tucked back in their pockets   (8)

What follows speaks for the book as a whole. The car is parked, and the poet walks out along a riverbed, eventually disturbing a flock of geese. The death of reason is remade into a door ajar, a Jacob's ladder potentially reinvolving heaven and earth. We have seen this response to knowing's collapse throughout Graham's work, but the context now is much larger, for the poet is taking on the culture's exhaustion, entering it, and attempting to bring back word of a new world, a new way of seeing, generated by its exhaustion. She calls us to "look up":

> and the birds lift up—
> and from the undulant swagger-stabs of peck and wingflap,
> collisions and wobbly runs—out of the manyness—
> a molting of the singular,
> a frenzied search (unflapping, heavy) for cadence, and then
> cadence found, a diagram appearing on the air, at arctic heights,

> an armoring
> the light puts on—stagger of current-flap become unacrobatic industry,
> no tremble in it,
> no echo—below, the freeway lustrous with accurate intention—
> above us now, the sky lustrous with the skeleton of the dream of
> reason—look up!—
> Jacob dreamer—the winged volumetrics chiseling out a skull
> for the dream—   (10)

We hear that call to look up at a new way of thinking arising out of thinking's collapse in two late poems in the book discussing Magritte's painting of the coat into which Pascal had sewn the "irrefutable proof of the existence of God." In Magritte's painting, reproduced on the cover of *The Errancy*, the coat is ripped and floats against the outline of a city, the night sky shining through it:

> The coat, which is itself a ramification, a city,
> floats vulnerably above another city, ours,
> the *city on the hill* (only with the hill gone),
> floats in illustration
> of what was once believed, and thus was visible—
> (all things believed are visible)—
> floats a Jacob's ladder with hovering empty arms, an open throat,
> a place where a heart may beat if it wishes
>
> . . .
>
> It floats before us asking to be worn   (65, 69)

Thought becomes a responsive Jacob's ladder when torn: look up, she urges, slip that coat on—move forward again. Many of the poems are quite inventive in the ways they try to help the reader visualize the mind's generative collapse. "Untitled Two," for example, describes thought as "a masonry of shades" who gather in a parking lot—the ghosts of "excellence, and skill, all throbbing in a parking lot" (25) like a group of powerless toughs. Thinking begins when

> the walled-up day hives-open once again.
> And they foam-out along its veins. Syllable by syllable.
> I give them liberty. They gnarl, they sweep over the hubs,
> into the panes, they fill the seats.

And then thinking stalls:

> Around us, toying, like a gigantic customary dream,
> black water circles, perishing and perishing,

swirling black zero we wait in,
through which no god appears,
and yet through which nothing can disappear,
a maximum delay, a sense of blurred desire in it,
a slumbering, a catch-all mirror for the passers-by,
silky frontier in which it is all saved—   (25–26)

When a group of girls "on break" hurries "through us" in the parking lot—
"their voices swirling up—impregnable—. . . / . . . scales of belief, / quick
blurtings-out like a bright red jug / raised high into the waves of light"
(26)—one at first fears for them, but then realizes how ineffectual the shades
of thought are. Unable to move and respond, thought—the threatening
toughs—simply holds itself attentively before their multiple, and ultimately
disappearing rhythms:

> their onrush of chatter fills now, spills,
> and then a hard remark, slammed in, a lowering again
> of tone, quick chatter from the group, low twist of tone
> from in the midst, and then a silence—like a wing raised up,
> but only one—a hum all round, heads facing forwards
> in the cars, heads pointing forwards in the cars,
> anti-freeze fingering daylight near some tailpipes, *here* and *here*,
> a brutish click, sound of black-water lobbying,
> and then one girl, like a stairway appearing in the exhausted light,
> remembers the *reason* with a fast sharp gasp,
> and laughter rises, bending, from the chalice of five memories,
> as they move past us towards the railing of the lot   (26, 27)

All of the poet's activities, then—capturing in a series of dawn songs the
moment before thought or light takes hold, "before the sun begins to sift /
and card" (62) or moving a single limb after a storm's wreckage—seem to be
first steps, taken in view of, and for the encouragement of, the reader. Though
one senses a note of desperation about the enterprise, the idea seems to be
that such activities, the poet holding herself in thought's brokenness or its
zero, might offer all of us a way to move forward again:

> Cicadas churn. My wholeness now just something *alongside*—
> a stammering, an unattachedness—hands in pockets—a walking straight
>   ahead into the black,
> and walking fast—as if to seed the patiently prolonging emptiness   (96)

What complicates this, however, is a series of "Guardian Angel" poems
in which, often quite self-critically, the poet marks her distance from the

culture surrounding her. Each angel, one might say, is charged with watching over an aspect of the way we think and feel and take in the world. It knows, because it embodies, the ambitions and weaknesses and dead ends of its mode, but what is striking is how far apart this knowledge leaves the "dizzy" (2, 3) poet/angel:

> If I lean down, to whisper, to them,
> down into their gravitational field, there where they head busily on
> into the woods, laying the gifts out one by one, onto the path,
> hoping to be *on the air,*
>
> . . .
>
> Oh listen to these words I'm spitting out for you.
> My distance from you makes them louder.
>
> . . .
>
> Oh look at you.
> What is it you hold back? What piece of time is it the list
> won't cover? You down there, in the theater of
> operations—you, throat of the world—   (20, 21)

So, for example, "The Guardian Angel of the Little Utopia" is busy upstairs, above a party, arranging things into a sort of perfect order—that human drive:

> oh little dream, invisible city, invisible hill,
> I make here on the upper floors for you—
> down there, where you are entertained, where you are passing
> time, there's glass and moss on the air,
> there's the feeling of being numerous, mouths submitting to air, lips
>   to protocol,
> and dreams of sense, tongues, hinges, forceps clicking
> in anticipation of . . .   (2)

What the angel knows, however, is that these dreams, which both parties share, are no longer tenable. The problem, however, is how to get that vertiginous suspicion across: "So dizzy. Life buzzing beneath me / though my feeling says the hive is gone, queen gone, / the continuum continuing beneath, busy, in earnest, in con- / versation" (3). At times, in fact, the angel's knowledge seems almost a torment—as here, the angel musing over our drive to analyze and see through and, ultimately, to believe in nothing:

> How razor-clean was it supposed to become,
> the zero at the core of each of these
>
> . . .

> —oh how much
> must I see—how clean
> did they want to become,
> shedding each possibility with gusts of self-exposure,
> bubbling-up into gesture their quaint notions of perfection,
> then letting each thought, each resting-place, get swept away—
> because that was *not what I meant*—*was not at all*—
> . . .
>
> who will they be when they get to the bottom of it,
> when they've stripped away the retrospect, when they've peeled
> away the
> orphanhood, the shimmering merriments of consolation?
> How will they feel the erasures erase them?
> Who will they resemble when they're done with resemblance?
> (14–15)

As the Eliot echo suggests, the tone here is very much that of a voice speaking prophetically to uncomprehending ears, and though Graham is as critical of that tone as she is of the speech of those moving about below the angel, the gulf her words pour into is very much the one Eliot suffers.

In *Swarm*, then, in turning to private anguish, Graham's speaker pulls back from *The Errancy*'s earnest, absorbed-with-itself social world and, almost out of options, focuses almost entirely on poem 640's charged resolution to "meet apart— / You there—I—here— / With just the Door ajar / That Oceans are—and Prayer— / And that White Sustenance— / Despair." The space in which the speaker and the beloved cannot meet directly, can only "meet apart," is of course another version of Graham's unsettled, vertiginous space, and one of the things *Swarm* explores is the sort of access to the silence, to whatever keeps the two apart, this particular version of that space provides. To what avail is this movement "underneath" or "outside," the opening poem asks, quoting the Dickinson letter I referred to earlier:

> "to all except anguish the mind soon adjusts"
>
> *
>
> have reduced, have trimmed, have cleared, have omitted
>
> *
>
> have   abbreviations   silently   expanded
>
> *
>
> to what   avail
>
> *
>
> explain   asks to be followed
> explain   remains to be seen   (5)

The title poem picks up poem 640's ocean between lovers and suggests something of the charged intensity of that space. The speaker is describing an overseas phone call:

> I wanted you to listen to the bells,
> holding the phone out the one small window
> to where I thought
> the ringing was—
>
> Vespers scavenging the evening air,
> headset fisted against the huge dissolving
>
> . . .
> why should you fear?—
> me holding my arm out into the crisp December air—
> beige cord and then the plastic parenthetical opening wherein I
>
> have you—you without eyes or arms or body now—listen to
>
> *the long ocean between us*
> —the plastic cooling now—this tiny geometric swarm of
> openings sending to you
>
> no parts of me you've touched, no places where you've
>
> gone—   (57–58, italics mine)

Something of the world's "huge dissolving" is made audible in the intensity of the shared listening recorded here, but the grounds for being so attuned are being stripped of "eyes or arms or body." It's as if, in *Swarm*, the poet gives up not only the mind's eager grasping but, in some sense, the body's as well. Or gives up some version of the body, for there certainly are suggestions that, once the hands have acknowledged that they cannot hold, they are freed to respond in a different manner:

> The repeated vacancy
> of touch
> begging for real work.
>
> Door ajar.
>
> Bone so still a guest.
>
> Touching you in sleep
> along the lips I start to wake.
> Inundation.   (53)

The idea seems to be, then, that in investigating and suffering this door ajar between lovers, the poet is trying once again to allow forces otherwise invisible or inaudible to stain or mark her. Think of the temple and its unseeable inner reaches; think of what might be accessible through something other than "the straight paths of the right hand" or the shared, well-lit expectations of the communal. Call it the sublime:

What if the rear-view were to open up?

The whole unseeable back where the blood flows off,

drying so quickly,

us broom in hand trying to sweep the front porch off,

every now and then looking up to see how soon.

. . .

I knock on the front

whispering open up, forgive us,

can you grow any more silent?

The windows glint to me

re the straight paths of the right hand,

the refusal that anything be measured
                    or judged,

up here in the shiny
    democracy,

the so-called cup of bitterness,

the so-called train

picking up speed, the so-called

sublime it flatly aims for—   (21–22)

An early poem on Persephone, "Underneath (9)," gets at much of the tension in the volume. It is in four parts, spring through winter, and begins with what one would expect to be Persephone's relieved return to the upper world:

Up, up you go, you must be introduced.

You must learn   belonging to (no one)

Drenched in the white veil (day)

The circle of minutes pushed gleaming onto your finger.

. . .

Below, his chest, a sacred weightless place
and the small weight of your open hand   on it.

And these legs, look, still yours, after all you've done with them.

Explain   the six missing seeds.
Explain   muzzled.
. . .

your heart, beating its little song: *explain* . . .   (8, 9)

Along with Persephone's reluctance to return to time and day and visible identity, leaving behind Hades' "sacred weightless place," we hear something of her sense of vertigo or confusion in the "little song: *explain*" repeated throughout *Swarm*, in both its upper and lower realms. The speaker *can't* explain, her sometimes frantic requests suggest, and as we saw in "Vertigo," when the ability to explain comes to an end, something else must awake and take its place. Behind the heart's little song is Dickinson's poem 193 (F215), which anticipates the end of time when "Christ will explain each separate anguish / In the fair schoolroom of the sky—," concluding, fiercely, that only then "shall [I] forget the drop of Anguish / That scalds me now—that scalds me now!"[16] To cry out for an explanation is to say "I am still in anguish." It is to repeat, over and again, that "to all except anguish, the mind soon adjusts." The Summer section of the poem yearns for a return to the underworld:

Explain   two are

Explain   not one

. . .

wanting so to sink back down,

you washing me in the soil now, my shoulders dust, my rippling dust,
. . .
Where is the dirt packed in again   around us   between us

obliterating difference   (10)

Yet when the Winter section imagines that return, it's not to blissful union, it's to a deeper experience of the fundamental absence that drives human experience. It's as if Persephone, back underground, is returned to Dickinson's hungry world outside Windows (579)—to the full experience of just what had been denied. For it is only in such an experience—confronting difference, awaiting the true story, being defied—that absence becomes visible radiance. It is only in painfully not moving, the speaker echoes Eliot, that one moves in "His dance":

Are you still waiting for the true story? (God's laughter?)

The difference between what is and could be? (God's laughter)

In this dance the people do not move.

Deferred defied obstructed hungry,

organized around a radiant absence.

In His dance the people do not move.   (12)

To meet "underneath," a number of *Swarm*'s early poems suggest, would be to meet without words, without expectations, outside of time and sequence and (often) actual physical presence. It is to meet, as in Dickinson, in a shared, and yet sustaining, anguish.[17] In vertigo:

Let the loved glance open up and go, too.
Let it spill out and be taken back.
Let it be disavowed.
But let there be something mute left us that cannot go.
Like a god's mouth held shut.
An intake of breath a delay.
. . .
Leave me the thing that will not burn.
Leave me the thing that cannot be thought—I will not
                              think it.   (14–15)

To meet underneath would mean to meet in the wilderness opened up by the collapse of the mind—Graham, like Howe, sensing something radically free and unsettled in the space opened up where the sentence gives away:

Burn all the letters.

Look in the ashes with both hands.

Finger in there for any bits intact.

            Wrist-deep

in the fine grains, so cold,

feel further round for fragments,

for any last unburnt

piece of

the crashing of mind,

or any promises (so parched) come down through the sentences
to breathe,

(25)

To meet underneath would mean reading Dickinson's "we must meet apart" as meeting apart from the world, apart from what Calypso calls "the stress and drag of looking" ("Underneath [Calypso]," 42). Veiling Odysseus, separating him from time, sequence, and phenomena, Calypso removes him from a world where he is responsible for each thing he encounters—"Strike me says each thing. / Resurrect me in *my* flesh. / Do not pass through me"—in order to call him to a broken, anguished responsiveness to what cannot be seen or held:

How we walk the aisle: in flames.

Frothing time back   into its corner.

In anguish here   under the veil.

Going broken   before some altar.

However, that sense that the space between them can be experienced without eyes or arms or bodies begins gradually to come undone in "Underneath (8)," where the speaker meditates on Dickinson's poem 625 (F691) where, "Before the Judgment Seat of God— / [For] the last—and second time"

These Fleshless Lovers met—
A Heaven in a Gaze—
A Heaven of Heavens—the Privilege
Of one another's Eyes—

No Lifetime—on Them—
Appareled as the new
Unborn—except They had beheld—
Born infiniter—now—

The speaker restates Dickinson's dream of compensation—that lovers who had shared only a glance, who had been brought to life only in a moment's beholding, would, in heaven, be born into an "infiniter" union. She gives herself to the thought of "Fleshless   lovers / * / The tabernacle   of / * / (fleshless lovers) / * / (with no lifetimes   laid hard on them)," but then turns uneasily away:

> While gods sleep   she says
>
> deposit   in me   my busyness, flesh.
>
> Deposit   thirst   in me.
>
> Deposit   tongue   poor rendez-vous.
>
> And eyes   patient   their dry study
> . . .
> Make the sore   not heal   into meaning.
>
> Make the shallow waters   not take seaward   the mind.
>
> Let them wash it back continually onto the shore.
>
> Let them slap it back down onto the edges of this world.
> . . .
> Refuse   rescue.
>
> Overhear   love.   (67–69)

It's finally thirst and tongues and bodies and the "edges of this world" that the closing poems in *Swarm* return to and celebrate again.[18] If there is a law against the two becoming one, and if that law is a version of the larger one that separates the speaker from what exists in silence, then pushing against that law—removing the veil and experiencing with the hands and eyes and tongue that live distance—is what poetry is called to do. Think of this as the final way Graham, returning now to the world and "push[ing] until / like a third party / matter rages between us" (51–52), reads and enacts Dickinson:[19]

> You who cannot be traversed
>
> we brave the middle kingdom of mere blossom
>
> we numb the intelligence
>
> we push against your law without regret
>
> we enter my body harder because of the wall   (98)

Finally, as it returns to language and the body, the book realizes that while that space will never be crossed, in the broken drive to do so—filled in this case with suffering, silence, and second thoughts—a new way of holding oneself in uneasiness has been generated.[20] And it turns out to be a way of holding oneself that leads back to the world:

there is nothing wrong with the instrument

as here I would raise my voice but

the human being and the world cannot be equated

aside from the question of whether or not we are alone

and other approaches to nothingness
. . .
do you remember   my love my archive

touch me (here)

give birth to   a single idea

touch where it does not lead to war
. . .
this is the mother tongue

there is in my mouth a ladder

climb down

presence of world

impassable   gap

pass

I am beside myself

you are inside me   as history

We exist   Meet me   (102, 103, 105)

Finally, then, the poet returns to a vision of Dickinson as a "woman of clay" (110)[21]—a woman whose broken language, aware of an impassible gap, nevertheless turns to the world, allowing itself to be "saturated" with time and finitude, and fully entering into the ongoing problem of writing or "replication":

I wanted to be broken, make no mistake.

I wanted to enter light—and everywhere its mad colors.

To be told best not to touch.

To touch.

For the farewell of it.

And the further replication.

And the atom

saturated with situation.   (110)

EIGHT

INTERVIEW WITH
JORIE GRAHAM

TG: In August 1999, outside the Houghton Library, I heard you give a fascinating talk on Emily Dickinson. You discussed her interest in what exists in silence and the way her poems enact different ways of accessing that realm. You particularly stressed her effect on the reader—as you put it, the way she forces us to "undergo different kinds of vertigo-laden sensations that undermine any stable understanding of what's in the silence in order to be able to inhabit it more fully." Perhaps you could explore those ideas in more detail before we talk about her presence in your own poems.

JG: I spoke there about the ways in which different senses are used, either by gradual withdrawal of their use or by a decrescendo of their correlatives, to arrive at a place—a threshold place—which one must, one needs to, reach. The spiritual imperative to reach that place, which is naturally oversimplified when it is called "silence" or "eternity" (or even "death"), involves knowing that it is an actual place—not a construct of imagination and not a hoped-for place or an invented place, not even a construct of religion. It is the place that allows you to say *yes*. But, if you are Dickinson, you have to have proof. I think that's one of the reasons she undertook so many deathbed vigils; because she wanted material proof; she's an incredibly materialistic poet in that respect, even pragmatic. She really does want empirical proof that the place she would be saying *yes* to is not worms.

TG: Wouldn't we all? And she had proof?

JG: She had a poetic strategy. She used her poems, the poems of enactment that interest me particularly. She might proceed, for example, by slowly still-ing a poem to get to a point in which stillness, and then a thing which is beyond stillness, exists, is *present*. It's as if the place were not actually a physical place, not a mental place, but a place which the body is nonethe-less allowed to access. If we look at the first stanza of 812, you can see what I mean:

> A Light exists in Spring
> Not present on the Year
> At any other period—
> When March is scarcely here

Much of what I learned from her is in this poem. And much of what, for me, poems "should be doing." This first stanza is a great example of the means by which poems can give you bodily—if you don't want to use "bodily," "senso-rial" or "tactile," something other than mental will do—proof that some-thing *exists*. And to begin with it involves reading things in the order in which they're given, and at the speed at which they're given.

So, if I'm given "A Light," I actually don't quite know, in terms of the bowl of my imagination, how big to make it. So I go, next, to "exists" and I spread the light out to an as-big-as-I-can-see-in-front-of-me size, to make it match "exists." Then I'm told that it's "in Spring." Since spring is both a piece of a year, which is spatial quality, but also a duration of year, a temporal unit, I actually have a moment there of not knowing what *kind* of light to make myself feel or see. So, I make a box of light to begin with, then a very big one for "exists," and then I have to blur the edges and make it almost an idea of light because I don't know where to put it "in." I have to make something almost concrete, something structured, out of the word "spring" in order to put the light "in" it. I go back and probably envision a spring day, get a tree and some field in it, put a chunk of light in it: about that size.

Then I can start qualifying the light, giving—or finding in it—a kind of blue or yellow quality that's going to make it *spring* light as opposed to *win-ter* light or *fall* light. I'm being *asked* to do all that.

So now, I've made a place out of a thing called spring. But when she says "Not present on the Year," there's nothing else I can do with "year" but make it be a duration. I know that it's made up of four seasons, so I feel for something four times longer than "spring." It is an incredible bodily action, this work I'm asked to undertake, in which I have to back up and take spring totally out of its role as a spatial place and make it completely a duration. I vector-out spring to *year*, if you will. I have this physical sense of the lengthening of that duration. Then I'm supposed to put light "on" that. I'm supposed to put it "in" spring but "on" that! This is a great deal to ask one to do with their body. And yet it is so valuable, as a practice.

To tie it all together: I have "existence," which is enormous (in terms of duration) then I have to back up to the duration called "spring" (which is only so long), next, I have to shift over from temporal to spatial imagining, then I have to bring back the temporal and extend to the length of year (which is shorter than existence but longer than spring)— when I get to "At any other period," I have to physically say to myself, "Is period shorter than existence, shorter than year, longer than spring?" The sense of "how long," "how short" is a very strange question to be attaching to the quality of light. It's a very brilliant question. And then she says "When March." After "existence" (which is enormous and undifferentiated and has no borders) has been narrowed down to spring (which has a very particular, recurring size) to year (which is a determinate size) to period (which is loose compared to those two) I'm suddenly given "March," which seems like an almost insane thing for a human imagination to do at this point. But she's picked the particular word that has to do with . . .

TG: Movement?

JG: Yes. Inward movement, action, a kind of aggressive, trampling-over movement. But she's also given us to consider how strange it is, in effect, this sliver of the year which we have named *March*. The specificity—as well as the otherness—of any name, as well as of this type of name. "Spring" and "year" and "period" and "exist" seem slightly more . . . *natural?* . . . as verbal actions than this idea-laden one, naming a piece of time after the god Mars. It makes the linguistic act seem suddenly kind of aggressive—almost war-like?—an "overtaking" action. It's certainly more filled with "irritable reaching after fact and reason," as opposed to the action filled with negative-capability that's going to happen in the poem. When she then says "is scarcely here," when she plants that "here" there, it's a *here* that has come through this rather wide-ranging constellation of differing attempts, each of which has asked me to measure my physical body into a new kind of duration. I guess a good deal of the "subject" here is the very fact that the only instrument I have, by which to relate them to each other (and to therefore *understand* them or *interpret* them) is my body. As in, I know how *long* spring is by having lived it, for example—it's not just an idea. If I leave it at the level of idea (or "content" information), there is, in some real sense (for me) no poem, no act which constitutes the journey of this poem.

At any rate, at this point, the whole thing is the vortex and container for not only the light but the *here*. The *here* constitutes the feet on which this entire tumbling lands. It's that moment that not only my poetry, but a great deal of the poetry that interests me, is concerned with being able to awaken in the reader. Or rather to awaken the reader's capacity to summon. It's only by having to summon of a reader all the work that I've just enacted here (how *long*, how *short*, how do I *measure* it, how do I *feel* it) that the body (in which the first person's sense of itself as a first person is located) is awakened to use. It is the only instrument we have by which to begin to measure out how far away the other is. *Here* is the space-time coordinate on which the first person of the body is crucified. It's the only eternity. It's like the noon moment, or like any of her instants, instants she always generates an echo of—the report *of*, the aftermath *of*. The activity that I've just undergone in this first stanza restores me to a *here*, but the *here* is already understood and felt as the aftermath of this entire activity.

TG: How did the cross come in here?

JG: The *here* is both spatial and temporal. I'm here sensorially having done all this work, and I'm here spiritually—perhaps even as a mind— having crossed through these experiences. My *here* is primarily my senses, and my *here* is my senses operating by the request of my mind: so there's that cross as well.

TG: So, you-the-reader are awakened to here?

JG: But I'm only awakened to here by having had to feel that my body can't quite "read" this, get all there is here, with just my mind. The concepts spring, year, present, light can't get you to the place "here" if you're trawling through their mere content, or the "content" of what she's saying. You have to do this *literal* undertaking, this giving over to the body's sensations which keep replacing each other, to end up with a sense of what it is you had to use to do that work, the work that got you *here*. This is not an idea, in my vocabulary. This is a dramatic enactment of sensorial data. The "here" that you get to at the end of the first stanza is a sense of place, and a human *placing* in time, that you can only get to by crossing over this particular, continually embodied relocating. As a result, it seems to me, there's no gap between reader and writer. It's not a "representation." It's an iconic enactment of how you get to *here*—an actual physical place we call both place and presence.

TG: I see. Can you go farther with the poem?

JG: All the way to infinity! [laughs] Well, when she says

A Color stands abroad
On Solitary Fields
That Science cannot overtake
But Human Nature feels

she states exactly the dichotomy we've just gone through. Science—March, naming—cannot "overtake" the sensation. The mind—or intellection—can't get there, but human nature can *feel* it. The distinction between overtaking and feeling has become for me the dominant experience I now look to get from Dickinson's work. She's not trying to say, "You cannot overtake; you must feel." She's saying that there are certain activities that you will be drawn toward called "overtaking"—interpretation, naming, immediately going to the conceptual intellect with which to grasp the world—and there is a negatively capable activity in which you undergo the poem and arrive at sensations that only the—as it were—writing of the poem can get you to. What's going to get really interesting in this poem is the acute discovery (even though this might seem obvious at first) that we cannot have one without the other.

The color—you don't even feel yourself "doing" it until you start paying attention—makes you begin to make it shaft-like. One gets this more, perhaps, on second reading. You begin to give it an outline of a certain kind because of the verb "stand," because of the word "abroad," and because she's made it a single field and you know that you're not looking at a landscape which is drawn up of many walls and fields, multiple places. So you have a singleness standing in a singleness, and as a result, you begin with your senses to feel this columnar-like color. It organizes itself within the square of that field and begins to stand there. This happens *before* the word *stand* occurs so that by the time you are asked to make it "stand," the verb "stand" is not going to be a euphemistic "stand" or even a figure of speech "stand." She's making a uniqueness, or concentration, of color which becomes almost like a ghost summoning itself.

So then, when it's going to "wait" (so that it goes naturally from "a" to "it") it begins to have, as if of its own "volition," a kind of creaturely nature:

It waits upon the Lawn,
It shows the furthest Tree
Upon the furthest Slope you know
It almost speaks to you.

"Wait" is a temporal activity. The minutes are clicking in "wait." Expectation is embodied in "wait." It wants something from you. Strangely, miraculously, it doesn't actually strike you as personification because you've already done the so-called personifying. At this point, it's somehow not a "figure" of imagination. It seems actually real. Your body believes it to be real because you've done the bodily work of summoning the columnar color. By the time it's turned into an *it* and given agency, you're already ahead of it, and the issue of agreeing with it, which is what you normally have to do with per-sonification, has been bypassed. You don't even get to the point of arguing (with your conceptual and critical intellect) about whether it has agency to "wait," because your body has already made it happen. There seems to be—I'd go as far as to say there *is*—no gap between you and the writer. You don't have to *agree* with the writer: you are doing the writer, if you will; the writer is doing you. It's not about asking you to conceive it.

In this next stanza, she's narrowed the solitary field by the word "lawn." So you have a smaller green square now, and the figure's closer. Your eye's been made to come closer, and yet again closer in, from field to lawn. It approaches you. It's standing there and waiting, and now it's going to show you "the furthest Tree / Upon the furthest Slope you know," and you must go back "out" across these fields to a single tree. The singleness of the tree, again, allows for the singleness of the "it's" action and the singleness of "you," who feels it. You feel that your "you" through its "it" are in relation to this tree, and that the "furthest slope" is a palpable place, and that you can reach it via the intermediary of this particular field.

TG: I hadn't thought about the fact that "you" comes in at this point. The speaker has been doing things to you, and now she notices you.

JG: Yes. Don't you feel yourself leaning forward, looking, squinting, taking in *this* slope and then *that* slope. You posit, in the bowl of your imagination (as Elaine Scarry would have it) the furthest tree over there, and then she says to you, "Remember knowledge? Remember 'overtaking' and 'March'? Do you feel like that positing you've just done—you now doing it with me, undergoing it—does that feel like 'know'?"

Actually, it doesn't at all. It's not a tree I "know"; it's a tree I'm *seeing*. It takes a few readings to realize how strange this is. She says, "Oh, you see that *looking* here? Actually, since it's not really there, it's actually *knowing*." And you go, "No, I see it. It's seeing." The poem seems to respond, "no, it's knowing." That particular problem, "What is knowing?" is the subject, what the poem is going to undertake to explore. "It almost speaks to you" is an extraordinary imaginative action because you're so yearningly, squintingly, leaning-out that you're almost speaking to it. You've been using your "human nature" and you've been feeling each of these things I've been describing, and then she says, "That's in your mind. I'm going to call that place it's in 'know.' We're going to re-address that." And the minute she says "know," she says the most sensorially, bodily thing possible under the circumstances (the "speaking" act of a poem): "It almost speaks to you." It seems to me that it is exactly then that you realize—or rather you "hear"—that it is silent. You hadn't realized how silent it was until its not speaking was pointed out to you. You're leaning forward, you're seeing this tree that didn't before exist; now it exists, it's on that slope, you see it, it's in your imagination, you have in fact made it happen with your body, and you feel like you're in conversation. And she says, "May I remind you, this is silent. But it's *there*, isn't it?"

TG: But then something happens:

> Then as Horizons step
> Or Noons report away
> Without the Formula of sound
> It passes and we stay—

JG: Oh, I love this part so much. Just when she has made sound present by its absence (a typical Dickinson technique), she introduces that "report" which, God knows, in the era when this was written (war, hunting) reminds you of a gunshot. The "Then" tells you "No more." No more of this encounter. We're on *this* side of it now. The "other" side. The horizon, as light moves across the field, seems to move away from us, and noon, both the actual moment of encounter and the "as if" moment, "reports" away. Noon is a *here* that can't actually exist. Noon exists, in a real sense, only the second after it's passed: that was noon. It's like—it is—a hole in the hour. It's a very strange hole, so tiny. Its nature, its temporal nature, is in effect all report, all aftermath. Everything is measured in relation to it. (Strangely, even more than midnight—because we "live" more in the day.) We have the sense of *noon* and *here* as these two absolutely still places, with a kind of death taking place at the core, the essence, the very nature, of each: as if indeed the moment is a bullet passing through its own moment.

And then there's the linguistic use of *report*, the overtaking of the text itself, if you will, the event the text carries, through an interpretation or an abstract retelling of it. "Without the Formula of sound" reminds us yet again that there's no sound—it almost spoke to you, but didn't. "It almost speaks to you but doesn't" being its nature.

As for a formula, it is a combination of many things that will arrive at an essence or distillation or conclusion: which is what the mind wants, what analysis is all about. What does it *do* to us that we're told that it is all associated with sound? We're confirmed in our belief that we put sound into the poem by being asked to take it back out. That is a fierce kind of body work indeed (Stevens loves to do this, of course so does Shakespeare!): you feel yourself *doing* the feeling that she is asking you to do because she actually comes in and says, "Ah hah! You put sound in—there, take it back out."

"It passes and we stay—" All of a sudden, we are moved from "you" to "we." Why are we in a communal state? We're in a communal state now because we've all done this together? As we've been seeing, she's in our body or we're in hers—I wouldn't be able to tell you which, but we are communal. "It passes and *we* stay." Whenever we are in the postlapsarian state, we are in the *we*. There's nothing *we* can do—that perhaps an "I" could hope to do. The garden is gone, the green is gone, the light is gone, and we stay. "Here" and "stay" are the two conditions. The *here* of the instant, the noon, is very different from the ongoing *stay*. As the report has many, many long stages, aftermaths, and the instant that it reports is by force unique. There is an amazing—all-important— durational difference between *stay* and *here* which "passes" negotiates.

At any rate, what happens? The last stanza, after the fall of unity, of what I would call the iconic condition, is the "science overtakes" stanza. The stanza in which the "overtaking" is enacted. In it, everything is an abstract retelling of what has been sensorially enacted in the poem. The emotions that have been all bodily and all undertakeable (i.e. iconic) in the first four stanzas become aniconic, represented, retold—under the rubric of overtaking, and as such a *march*, an attempt to name a piece of time:

A quality of loss
Affecting our Content
As Trade had suddenly encroached
Upon a Sacrament.

That language, that activity of language, can only be done by mind. She's not asking me to use my body. She's (precisely) telling me: "This is work now to be done with your mind. You can't do that body work of listening, of feeling, of hearing now. You can think or conceptualize this."

TG: You can't do it because it's past?

JG: You can't do it because it's abstract. I can't summon up "loss"—that's an abstract term. I can't see loss; I know loss—it's an idea. I can conceptualize "contentment." She doesn't give me a bodily thing to do.

TG: Why did she do that rather than end with "It passes and we stay—"?

JG: Because we are double. She wants us to feel and undergo what it's like to think now. The condition we "fall" into is thought.

TG: We feel fallen?

JG: We feel or act fallen. We feel what it is to be "just" a mind, as opposed to the prior feeling one has been able to undergo in the poem—which is the sensation of what it is to *summon*—to reach for and be *summoned by*—but also to summon. We have felt presence and embodiment. "Loss" is a very good term: it is the loss of one kind of sacramental encounter, but what you have then is the feeling of what it is to have to think the word "loss," as opposed to the sensation of what it is to undergo loss. In the first four stanzas, you undergo almost having and losing. In the last stanza, that is "called" loss. What you're supposed to feel is what you lose when that gets called loss. You have to do that work with a part of your sensibility called thought or mind or reason.

TG: So then, the comparison to Jesus clearing the temple when trade had "encroached upon" a house of worship is a mental act?

JG: Absolutely. It's interpretation. It's thought. It's conceptual generalization, even a simile comes under that "fallen" rubric: "as if trade had suddenly encroached." It's a really brilliant move; she says, "Here's a physical word, 'encroachment' (an action we *have* undergone bodily already in the poem)— now try to do it with 'trade' and 'sacrament.'" You can only do it with your conceptual intellect. I can say "sacrament" means this, "trade" means this. I unpack them as an idea. I'm not *here* in the same way.

TG: But as thinking, it's brilliant. The poem has been a sacrament, and it has engaged in a struggle with trade. It's not as if she's not paying attention.

JG: Oh, no, no, no. This is the most brilliant thing of all. And doesn't it just bring so much of Bishop to mind? Just as she's telling you that what's encroached upon is the sacramental activity which only the body can do she puts the body back with *encroached*. She's saying. "Grace was operative, the *here* of grace, of presence. You underwent it here. Now, feel the trade that you make for understanding, knowledge, science—all that part of reality that you also want. That report. You want the sacramental—bodily, enacted—top of the poem, and then you want the trade. You want residue, you want knowledge drawn from it, you want a generalization drawn from it that's applicable to other contexts." She's telling us, "Use this part of your body now, the part you call mind." The *here* of thought, if you will, is a report; the *here* of sacrament is presence.

For me, this hereness, this quality of hereness, is what I think Dickinson ultimately is trying to get to. Of course it's important to remember—and it only adds to the poetry's power—that these poems of hers do all this with extraordinary speed and compression. What I'm doing is a kind of barometric read-out of a lightning flash! But it tells us a great deal that it takes this long to "unpack" what most any action of hers involves. Because we are trying to expose what is not expositional. It is astonishing, to me, to have work of this complexity—how long have we been at this?—compatible with that rate of utterance. And it *does* seem, at times, that talking this way one risks losing the very thing one is trying to handle, or comprehend.

TG: Does this relate, in this action, to the book you've just finished—*Never*?

JG: Well, yes. In *Never*, this notion of the *here* started to become extremely loud for me, as something that could only be created in the "now" of the poem's physical actions. It's as if my entire enterprise in that book was an attempt to make a pact with the reader that we would undergo together the stages of sensation. . . . Clearly, for me, this involves an extension of what I take to be central strategies in the work of Bishop, in particular, and Hopkins to a lesser extent. Also Issa. The little poem by Issa,

> Full moon;
> hissing in the saucepan
> the pond snails.

seems, to me, to completely involve this particular kind of enactment. Often it's translated as "bright moon," or "bright autumn moon." Reading it for "content" (for my purposes) is of little use—if you see, by now, what I mean by "use"—a practice. If you undergo the poem, it goes something like this.

"Full moon"—what body part do I have to use to do the work of reading that image? It's round, its bright, it's coming in through (it's demanding that I bring into use) my eyes. "Hissing in the saucepan" compels me to summon the roundness of the moon and the roundness of the saucepan. It is then I suddenly *feel* (or realize) the utter silence of what I've been seeing (moon). But, too, I *hear* the hissing, how in the totally silent brightness of that full moon I have the synesthetic equivalent of hissing. Then I go to the pond (and put the pond snails in) and I'm compelled to see the third circle: the pond. I've used my eyes *up there* where the moon is on its enormous cycle, and my ear *down here* on the saucepan which is in a house and is nourishing someone who is on a shorter (human and bodily) cycle. I feel the daily and the mortal cycle in relation to the moon's cycle. You see how, once again, I am being asked to feel, simultaneously, immeasurably different durations.

Then, if I used my eye up there, and I used my ear down here, how do I *see* the pond snails? Are they on the surface of the water? No. They're at the very bottom of this pond, so I can't see them. They're in the *in*visible. And yet I do *see* them—don't you? I am being asked to use a *third* term—I have to *imagine* them. It is imagination that allows me to "summon them up." As a result I feel how "imagining" is as real a sense as the other two, and that I can see into the nonvisible, the non-accessibly-visible. Furthermore, the pond snails are also on a temporal cycle; they come back every year, like the nightingale. The durational cycles of human life, of human hunger, of the moon's "eternal" life, of the moon's daily life—also its seasonal one—and that of the pond snails are all made to be in relation to each other in this incredible action. An action, which, by the way, ends up looking like a pond snail, coming down as it does in the little downward spiraling gyre from up there in the huge reaches (and cycles) of the moon, down through the human household and its circles to the bottom of the pond where the snails are: the dark which is the "in" of nature—the dark bottom of reality which is held in mind simultaneous to nature (the *upper* marmoreal reaches of nature). The way-up-there, the way-down-here. And our—own life—our "hunger" and "skill" and notions of inwardness (home, the inside of the human body into which the snail will go to be transformed in yet another way). So there are—just to indicate how this keeps going!—three darks (the sky, the inside of the human, the dark of the pond). Then there is all the brightness that coats all the inside places (sky, body, pond—and the mind taking all this *in*). The question, one of the questions, becomes where is that *in*? Very kin to what is this *here*?

This is all a kind of knowledge about the ratios of what (*trade* and sacrament) can *only* be had by the act of reading. Or what I mean by "reading." If you were to ask me for this poem's "content," what it is *about*, I really couldn't answer you except by saying, "the act of doing that." Interpretation of the kind we tend to seek comfort from in encountering poems doesn't avail us much here. Of course that bafflement is what the haiku is predominantly after—that privileging of sensation over emotion.

TG: After we go through that with our bodies, how do we know there is another world, or what you called a "threshold place"?

JG: I'll probably have another answer tomorrow! Let's see. One of the things that we know for sure is that we have bodies because we've just been asked to use them. Secondly, we know that we have bodies that can take us to levels of information that our minds would reject—i.e., that there is a beckoning presence on the lawn which has taken human form and that will in fact almost speak to you. The mind would say, "Don't be ridiculous." The body, when it gets there, says, "Of course, that's exactly what it's doing." Your body takes you to a place which you can't, by "science" or the rational, overtake, but you can *feel*. Your mind tells you it isn't possible; your body tells you it's not just possible, but "I'm doing it, I've just done it."

Then, you are made to feel the gap between that and stanza five. You move into thinking, generalization, and you're told, "What you're left with in this world—*in this world*—is all the ideas that this experience generated: the report of it, the large abstractions, 'loss' and 'contentment,' trade and sacrament. But remember that you were just in the presence of something apparently 'untrue' by the terms of your own thinking mind, the very conceptualizing instrument you're using in this last stanza: an almost bodily, angelic, manifestation; an annunciation. You were just annunciated-to, and you responded. You were—forgive me for using the term, but I really do believe it—you were impregnated with grace right there, at that moment. And you took it in. There's no thinking about whether it exists or not; you just underwent it here, and you are in the condition of being pregnant with, or 'full of,' it."

Now, it leaves and you stay behind, carrying the seed of that knowledge. There are Dickinson poems in which this *it* is enacted more fully, but in this poem it is as if the seed were planted in you. Then what you're left with is the thinking about it. And you *can* think about it; you can name it; you can interpret it; you can generalize about it, you can *report* it; you can know it. It is not the same as the feeling, but it is an *other* human force or capacity. The *feeling*, the annunciatory activity, the personage of presence, is so counterintuitive here that had she written this poem without that final stanza, you would have thought she had merely taken you through a little allegorical drama. You wouldn't know how to step back from it; you would have to drop it and say this is theater because there would seem to be no connection between *that* world and *this* world. There is no way back across the river if you're left on that side of it—in presence—if your way back involves language. There's no way back unless she says, "And now step back into the mind and feel the difference, the gap." It's like being abducted by an alien and then put back down. You know you were abducted because you can see the gap in the snow. If you were not put back down, you would think you had dreamt it. There's a way in which it is in the crashing difference between the sensation of part A of this poem and of part B of this poem that you know that part A is real. You were let back down on this very fine rope that said: and now think it, and now name it, and now land back on the generalizations that include it. Remember you still have your body. "Encroach" is there for you to use. You'll feel how the body, in doing "encroach," isn't being used to do the work it was doing in "almost speaks" or "waits." It can't do that work of embodiment or enactment because it's got "trade" and "sacrament" to enact and that requires *reason* or intellection. See how your body *here* is not your body *there*? Your body here is making metaphorical use of a physical term. Your body there was making physical use of a physical term. Because—(or is it *thus*)—there are different worlds that your body comes to know exist. The world of presence (of "feel") is so palpably real, and yet you can be let back down out of it. It therefore exists. It is linked to—or interfaces with—the other world. If you were just dropped off (as it were) at the end of it, it would have seemed like a dream or a parable. But because it has a rational laddering back down to the so-called real world of mind and thought, where the body is used as a metaphor-enacting, reasoning, and representing instrument, you can believe that the body, by reference to that, was used for a sacramental activity. Of course, there are many poems where she fails to do it. It's not an easy thing to do.

TG: What would be an example?

JG: Well, 311, "It sifts from Leaden Sieves." It's thrillingly written, but you can see that that activity of enactment is not possible because you're always having to use your mental imagination—your translation-from-figures of speech—to see the activity. She's not asked for enactment, not allowed you into a sacramental drama:

> It sifts from Leaden Sieves—
> It powders all the Wood.
> It fills with Alabaster Wool
> The Wrinkles of the Road—

As much as you want to do all that, you always feel the degree to which each image is a figure "of speech" for snow. All the way down, it's the same strategy. You're free to believe or not believe in "Celestial Vail."

TG: I notice there's no "you" or "our."

JG: The reason that there's no "you" or "our," this is my point at least, is that my body, my *here*, my *you*, cannot do any of these things. For example, I don't know where to put the "wool." I have a "road," I have "wrinkles," but I have a very hazy sense—too hazy—of how close, how far, how big. I don't know quite where to put the snow except sort-of-everywhere. You don't always need those coordinates—but you do when a scene is being set. Otherwise one just does the work "generally"—which in the visual realm turns into idea. So I tend to do it figuratively, with a certain amount of physicality. "It makes an Even Face / Of Mountain, and of Plain—" is so large and general: I summon up a mountain, I summon up a plain, and I have to make them even-faced. But my body can't quite do that, because a mountain is high and a plain is low, and so the even face is slightly off. I know what she means; I substitute the meaning. She means she's evening it out in color, not in height or texture, but my body can't quite do completely all the work. It has to exclude a lot of bodily information that contradicts it. I don't undergo it; I translate it, which is a very different use of imagination. She writes, "It reaches to the Fence—," but "it" hasn't been made creaturely in the way that presence (as light) summoned itself from an "a" to an "it" in 812 and just became creaturely. In this case, she tells me it has agency, "it reaches," but I restore it to the other use of "reaches," which is just "gets as far as." When she writes "It deals Celestial Vail," the fact is that anything celestial there is a figure of speech because I have not been made to be in the presence of anything but "sieves" and "wool" and a "face" and things that have not built up into something supranatural or even supradomestic. And therefore my body can't build. And if I can't build, then *you* can't be real, and the *we* will never come about and the communion and sacrament won't happen.

Or take the beginning of a great poem, "After great pain, a formal feeling comes." This is like the end of 812 and the notion of contentment. I don't know what the "formal feeling" is that comes. She's going to have to make the whole poem do this work for me. This is what I can no longer accept in my own poems. As a reader, I go, "Okay, I have to put in pain. How formal? I'll just have to make a formal feeling for myself." It's abstract. It might be a beautiful idea. People tend to say, "I know exactly what she means: after great sorrow, I pull back into myself." But everybody means something different by that; it's not a communion. It's not grace-filled. It's not an indication that there's a reality that bonds us all so vividly in this world, a reality that is not rational— a mystery.

TG: Your language is certainly religious here. Would you talk for a moment about your religious position?

JG: I don't believe in an afterlife with heaven and angels and gods. I believe that the notion of community, not the political and aesthetic notion of community but the notion of a community of souls that actually, in this world, have a capacity for interaction, or a feeling of the *we* that transcends bodily difference, is a condition of grace. Being able to feel that is what many religious ceremonies—whether they're tribal or the Catholic Eucharist or singing in unison in a Protestant church—try to trigger in people. But I think if you can find a way in which to ask people to use their bodies— for example, song and dance in a Baptist revival or certain tribal actions—you can bring yourself to your communal creature, you can be allowed to break out of the singleness of your predicament. At that moment, you are not a dying creature. At that moment, you are part of a fabric, of a coextensive, continuous form. I think it's a moot question as to whether that could ever replicate the thing that afterwards it all feels "like," or whether that's a condition only present in a state of . . .

TG: Finitude?

JG: Finitude. I don't believe in heaven or hell, but I don't know what happens to the human spirit and I'm not sure that I believe any longer that it is extinguished with death. I don't know. Either that sense exists only in those conditions of grace where you actually lose separation, or it is a premonition or prefiguration of something else. That's as religious as I get. But I think you can have it in certain experiences in nature, which is why "A Light exists in Spring" is so extraordinary. It's harder to have with people. What's extraordinary about that poem is that she makes contact in it with the *genius* of the place—in the traditional Romantic sense. It's the *place* that summons its figure up for her. It's just light, but it becomes so annunciatory and so embodied that it can wait and have agency and almost speak and beckon. It becomes like what an ideal love relationship would be, and when you look at the love poems, you can see that the absence/presence of the loved one—a loved one who was definitely present, just also definitely absent—is such a precondition of her actual mode of experience.

TG: So, you think there *is* a specific lover?

JG: I think she's deeply in love with a person who is going to be forever absent, and that the "door ajar" that separates them is the single syllable that involved her saying "yes." The man she would have been with needed her to be a public religious person or he could not be with her. She needed to say "yes" when asked "Do you take Christ as your personal savior?" in the public forum of the Revival. She refers over and over again to that *single syllable*. She can't take Christ as her "personal" savior; she can only take whatever it is as a communal or *we* savior. But saying "no," the person who is her presence, her beckoner, her other, her thing that makes her a *we*, becomes forever absent from her, although they communicate. The "door ajar" is a metaphor for that.

There is a great deal to what that love implies as a metaphor for the relationship between the reader and herself. Because the fact that she uses the imagination to constantly summon an absent human . . .

TG: In her poems?

JG: Yes. She's constantly summoning a man she loves to the imagination. She can summon him very physically—so physically she wants to make love to his body when he's dead. She wants his body back! The muscle in her that involves using the body to physically summon an absent thing and make it present is so strengthened in her by this particular autobiographical condition that it ends up being able to summon for her annunciatory presences as well. The knowledge that the annunciation brings is that she's a *we*. The only point in 812 where it changes is when "It almost speaks to [her]" and then "It passes and *we* stay—." It's extraordinarily strange that we've been turned into a "we." It's because she knows the reader was with her. She was talking *to* the reader until she suddenly knew the reader had done the body work with her, and if you have done the body work, then you are one body. The physical work that we've been doing makes you and me and her and all of us find the place where we are identical. We have a place where senses and sense data unite us so vividly that the difference that we would call identity disappears. There is presence and you feel the we, but then we become "I" again and we each come back with a different account of it. If that's religious . . . Well, I believe in that mystical knowledge; it *is* the knowledge most mystics desire to find: in *this* world the sensation of unified presence. It's what Teilhard de Chardin calls a "numinous envelope" of the communal us that hovers over the whole globe. And whether that is eternity, immortality— whatever it is, it's not rational, it's not reached by reason, it can only be felt.

TG: When do you have these experiences? When you write?

JG: When I read. Issa is particularly extraordinary because he leaves no room for me to do anything other than exactly what he is undergoing physically. There is no interpretation possible. He's not dead, or I am not alive. Whatever the gap is between us, it's shut. And that sensation is one of the most profound ones I feel. It would be captured by the terms "I got it," but better yet, closer, "I did it" or "I'm here, I'm doing it." I'm actually again under the moon with the saucepan and the pond snails. I'm not elsewhere. I'm not dispersed. I'm a *here*.

TG: Bishop's "Why, why do we feel / (we all feel) this sweet / sensation of joy?"

JG: Oh yes, that! Or the end of O'Hara's "The Day Lady Died," which is another poem that does this completely for me: "and everyone and I stopped breathing." Everyone and I: it's one of the most mysterious phrases, coming at the end of this communion with the world, the circulatory system of trade and commerce and New York along which the whole poem has taken its journey. Using spatial and temporal markers is one of the ways in which you disorient (in order to reorient) your reader. Bishop obviously does it. You ask your reader to use their body in so many different ways that at a certain point they realize they have a body that has *so much more than body* in it. Or you shut down. Think about the beginning of "The Day Lady Died." It's Friday, it's three days after Bastille Day, it's 12:20, it's 1959—there are so many different kinds of time marked out there you've used most every part of your conceptual intellect, physical intellect, bodily intellect. You've used every part of your sensibility in such a way that—I was going to say, you're using parts of your body you didn't know you had. I could put it another way. A theologian (whose name I can never recall) said that the only religious instruction that he believes one can actually be sure of is that what is required of us is *presence*. The only religious instruction that we should count on as a sure obligation is to be present. Out to the outer reaches of our bodies. Perhaps it really is like we were all dead and these poems are waking us up. If you can become awake, born again into your body, being given your body back, then you are not alone, in the mystical sense. The we in 812 comes in as one of the loudest motions in the history of her poetry for me. "We stay": where did "we" come from except that it's "you and I, reader." There never was anybody else there. We only become a *we* when God leaves. We know *we* were here because he stepped away. "It passes": it was never meant to stay. It came that we become *we*.

TG: Can we go back the issue of Dickinson's love poems and the poetic importance of the "door ajar" between her and the lover? You make a good deal of use of Dickinson's 640, the poem that phrase is drawn from, in *Swarm*. And the body seems very much on your mind in that book.

JG: I was quite involved with her poems in the 600s (of course Johnson's arrangement). It seems to me that they can be read as a kind of sequence about the lover-relationship. I'm not sure the exact order matters all that much. In the early poems, she talks about him metaphorically before she takes the subject head-on—with her body, as it were. In 598, she calls him breath: "Three times—we parted—Breath—and I— / Three times—He would not go— / But strove to stir the lifeless Fan / The Waters—strove to stay." Or 601: "A still—Volcano—Life." There are memories of him in 603: "He found my Being—set it up— / Adjusted it to place—." The first place which is not just memory and talking about the grief, where it actually, I think, strikes her that they're going to be continually apart is 611. As I was saying, the fact that she can summon him physically, as a presence, prepares her for metaphysical summonings:

> I see thee better—in the Dark—
> I do not need a Light—
> The Love of Thee—a Prism be—
> Excelling Violet—
>
> I see thee better for the Years
> That hunch themselves between—
> The Miner's lamp—sufficient be—
> To nullify the Mine—
>
> And in the Grave—I see Thee best—
> Its little Panels be
> Aglow—All ruddy—with the Light
> I held so high, for Thee—

She really has to imagine she will only see him again in death, so death becomes an actual locale—a lover's meeting place.

I think it all turns at 632 when she decides she can hold the whole thing in her mind, in the way we were just talking about in 812: "The Brain—is wider that the Sky— / For—put them side by side— / The one the other will contain / With ease—and you—beside—." For me, in 636, there's a narrative of receiving a secret letter: "The way I read a Letter's—this— / 'Tis first—I lock the Door— / And push it with my fingers—next— / For transport it be sure—." She opens it and can "Peruse how infinite I am / To no one that You—know— / And sigh for lack of Heaven—but not / The Heaven God bestow."

TG: Can you talk me through that last stanza?

JG: "I am infinite to you, but not to anyone else, not to God. I lack heaven." *He* has heaven, but she said *no*. The heaven that she possesses is not the heaven belief gives, it's the heaven the letter brings: the heaven of 812, the heaven the written word brings.

Then there's 640. The reason the sexton keeps the key to the life over there is that her *he* has to be of the cloth: "I cannot live with You— / It would be Life— / And Life is over there— / Behind the Shelf / The Sexton keeps the Key to—." The wish for their simultaneous death, which overtakes the poem, gets translated into a desire for the same kind of union with the reader. If she and I (in 812) can be one, then we are dying at the same instant into a we. This is the autobiographical problem that leads to the aesthetic or poetic solution: "I could not die—with You— / For One must wait / To shut the Other's Gaze down— ." If we were both of the identical body, we could die at the same instant—die into grace—but not here. "So We must meet apart—": and I think meeting apart is what the strategy of that first poem we looked at is. The apartness of humans, and the meeting that can be done: "You there—I—here—." There's the word that to me is so crucial—*here*. "With just the Door ajar / That Oceans are—and Prayer— / And that White Sustenance— / Despair—."

TG: Is that why you write so many poems that are "Prayers"?

JG: They're that kind of prayer. Also they involve similar despair. The sensation of being "ajar." Despair is a place where the body can feel another body. It's a unifying experience. Or it can be.

TG: To go back to your sequence.

JG: Well, in 644, she speaks directly to him, and there's an anger that comes after abandonment: "You left me Boundaries of Pain— / Capacious as the Sea— / between Eternity and Time— / Your Consciousness—and Me—." And I think it's the reparation of this gap that her poetics then undertake, at a different level, with the reader.

That gives me a context, then, for 657, "I dwell in Possibility—," which seems to indicate that "I can summon you in the dark, through the door ajar." And what we make is: "A fairer House than Prose— / More numerous of Windows— / Superior—for Doors—." The imagination is this extraordinary, suprarational tactile, physical place where . . . Well, we've been over it! From that point forward, paradise, for her, I think, is an alternative paradise to his. His is the religious paradise. Hers is the imaginative, summoned one, which has grace in it. I don't think she's areligious, but it's a sacramental *here*, a house of *here*. It has windows and a door: "Of Visitors—the fairest— / For Occupation—This— / The spreading wide my narrow Hands / To gather Paradise—." I think that's also the context of "One need not be a Cham-

ber—to be Haunted— / One need not be a House— / The Brain has Corridors—surpassing / Material Place."

All those summonings. She has decided to build an actual alternative
home, a chamber. She's living with him—and he turns into the reader. Or,
perhaps they slur. At a certain point, he starts to matter less than what he
summons up as a stand-in for himself. Look at 701: "A Thought went up my
mind today— / That I have had before— / But did not finish—some way
back— / I could not fix the Year—." This relationship through a door ajar
recedes as a physical event, but leaves its imprint as a habit of consciousness. What I'm trying to say, I guess, is that you can have a life experience which, if you live through it, in as marked a way as she has done here,
creates a template forcing you to use your imagination in a particular way,
such that, when the life experience abates—this is probably true with a great
many poets—the template of what you had to use to engage and survive that
experience, the particular psychic musculature you developed to lift and put
down that particular experience becomes, by habit and by technical gift, the
musculature you use to pick up every other kind of experience. It's a funny
thing to remember that you had an emotion but to not have it any more. If
you're a poet, you're very greedy for summoning up that emotion over and
over again, and I think that creates a need for materiality in imaginative
summoning or writing; you keep wanting the experience not to recede into
abstraction or mere memory—you want it to stay physically in the room;
hell, you want it to make you turned on; you want it *there*. You start to use
sense data in such a way that it keeps remaking a physical world, something
present to you, and *that* slides over into realizing you can make others have
that experience as well. At that point, it leaves behind its original impulse.

What's intoxicating is moving from I-you to we, realizing that she can
have a different kind of heaven—the kind of heaven I was describing before
when I suddenly have the "I have it, I am it" emotion of loving (living with?)
a dead soul through language.

TG: And this takes us back to accessing the silence or the invisible?

JG: She's developed a capacity for summoning first a man, then an imagined
creature, then a memory, and then eventually what is both a resurrection and
an annunciation. She's resurrecting from the invisible or from the afterlife
into the here and now of her personhood this person. She learns to port—
to carry, portage—in her body the information. When she says "plashless
noon" in 328, it would be a noon where the bullet of the instant of the *now*
or the *here* would have no splash—no report or aftermath. It is a portage,

a resurrection, a bringing forward, a summoning up of a figure at a rate of sensorial accuracy where *we* are doing it so much *with her* that it doesn't end up being (even though after all a piece of light stands there and almost speaks) personification, because we have done the "carrying-over" simultaneously. She has been able to find those ligaments, those parts of the sense instrument, to build the creature with . . . A summoning is a resurrection of something which is already there, or it's a haunting, or it's an annunciation. All of them have information on the other side, in silence. And it's in silence that, if she waits at the portal of it and she uses her capacity for picking up sense data and doesn't force it or rush in or overwhelm it or overtake it but rather tries to "port" what's over *here*, that all this action results in our being able to port with her. And in the end we will have something which is not a report but a plashless noon.

The summoning of this presence/person out of the silence and into manifestation is not something that can be willed. It's something that your body has to be ready for. It's like Teresa of Avila, if you will. You have to wait for the Christ to appear. He appears, but it takes many days; you wait for portions; if you are given a shoulder you have to know how to bring it in to you. You have to respond to a shoulder with a shoulder, metaphorically. You don't go with your brain to try to get it, because the thing will disappear. And it's that kind of mystical activity that crosses over into eros which Dickinson then has with all of nature, and then with things larger than nature, and eventually tries to have directly with what's in the silence—with God or whatever. She writes to get to that *here*.

I'm not sure that she feels that you can go back the other way—in other words, that you can cross from *here* back to the *there* or the *elsewhere* that it comes from. There is probably no way to go in that direction. All you have is the quality of loss. You have an afterwards, a hereafter, or what most of the endings of her poems make me feel, which is a "for now," a "from this point forward." You're *left* in the very *here* ["we stay"] you have achieved. But it is from *here* that you can intuit a *there*. It's from the particular kind of heaven or presence that you can intuit what that presence is an ambassador from. It's not that the light approaches and then goes back in order to bring information. It approaches like a messenger, like the opening of *Hamlet*, and then it leaves. And what is the message that it gives? The message that it gives is that you were there for where it . . .

TG: Touched down?

JG: Yes.

TG: Now, how does this connect with *Swarm*? Lines from Dickinson run throughout the book.

JG: I'm not sure. In *Swarm* I was obsessed with "I know that He exists. / Somewhere—in Silence—." I was interested in how to be in conversation with what exists in the silence—how much speech you can put into the silence in order for the silence to begin to speak too. Everywhere in the book there's an image of a mouth over an ear . . .

TG: Yes, and a hand over the throat.

JG: Yes: the feeling is that the poem is (to a certain extent) dictated, that it's an inspiration taken in through the ear, as with the Greeks. That it's whispered to you. The poem comes from a lover's mouth over your ear. It goes into your "underneath," the cavity of your subjectivity, your inwardness. It goes into the place where the transmuting from the individual that you are to universal utterance occurs. As Eliot would have it, and I think the direction is right, you go down through personality in order to transcend personality. You go down into a subjective place, into a place that is so subjective and so personal, so much the I, that you then cannot but stain it with what he calls the "collective emotive." (I do think it's still a really good formula.) You want to stain it with something that when it comes back up, even if it's spoken as an I, it's filled with the knowledge of a *we*.

TG: But the hand is on the throat. Why is that?

JG: The utterance is being silenced. It's being choked off. It's as if a communal utterance can't come back out of a singular utterance. "I" couldn't get to a "we" anymore. I felt like I was having an experience (or a set of emotions) that were probably outside the bounds of the social contract. I couldn't find an addressee—a *you*. One major reason that 812 is so moving is that the *I* has the experience—once the you is finally summoned—(as you pointed out) that a *we* is possible. If there is no you, it is as if there is a hand on the throat. You remain an I. An "I" even looks like a throat, and you remain strangled at the first person, at the singularity, at the total subjectivity, and you can't get back out. In *Swarm*, the struggle is to get back out, but when it gets back out the chorus is always speaking. And the I often dissolves to multiplicity rather than commonality. There are many moments of acute singularity in that book: noon; the actual moment of noon repeated over and over again; atemporality sought again and again; places that are outside of time—underneath. The trial is to find a way to move from inspiration back into expiration. And to feel unable to do so any longer.

TG: And that's why there's so much emphasis in the book on trying to wake him up.

JG: Yes.

TG: The king, the wounded figure. That's why you use that "explain *this!*" tone.

JG: Yes, yes. He won't answer. If he *would* wake up . . . Obviously the you is a "You" and a "you" in that book. You need a you that is either the community or a large Other, *and* a very personal other. But it has to be very much also a not-I. The other has to be so real that it can summon the I's utterance up towards itself. And if shared—and that means the body is not strangled off but can be used—then a we can occur. And that *we* is a different social order than what the chorus has in mind. So the issue looms: then what guides one? Does that make sense?

TG: Yes. That makes *Swarm*, with all its fragments and silences, very much a Dickinson book, the dark Dickinson.

JG: I can never quite squint in "influence"—especially this close to a book. But it seems very much like the Dickinson of that period we were reading in: the anger, the bitterness, moments of luminous happiness. . . . It's as if the speaker wants to enter into a zone which you can call the *here* or the atemporal present—a zone which has fascinated me in both *Swarm* and *Never*. I'd say I've tried to enter it in different ways. One is by shortening—almost withholding speech—so that one's utterances are always of a level of duration that doesn't seem to become temporal, to last long enough to be carried on the spine of temporality (syntax, sentences, etc.). In my introduction to *Best American Poetry 1990*, I described this as a belief that spirit exists most truly in silence, life can be "captured" only in silence, and that speech trammels that very thing the poet wants to get to, and port to an other. Such are poets who don't believe in or expand easily into sentences. The puritanical dream it is that you could make a poem completely silent . . . It involves a distrust of language, and of the body, and the feeling that if language comes into play it will immediately become temporalized, and the minute it becomes temporalized it takes on desires of a certain kind that are of its own making. Desires that (obviously) bring the body to bear on the spirit's work. That's why (in *Swarm*) the sentence gets so important in "Fuse," the Agamemnon watch. It has desires of its own. The fires will suddenly come down like a fuse. The sentence itself is like a fuse, and it will burn for destination and destination will be massacre. Destination will also be meaning which might trammel the very much more important wisdoms that would have been available had the sentence not forged forward at all cost towards meaning. I stress this again, because it seems so obvious, it is also a relationship with the flesh, the relationship one has with the sentence. It's the belief that language trammels essential utterance, or distorts it—as flesh trammels "pure" spirit—by allowing those energies of desire to come in. So one breaks the line after one stress or two, breaks open sentences, makes the poems feel built of fragments. And whether it's Williams or Issa or Creeley or Niedecker, there are a great many poets for whom if the spirit could really live it would have to be disincarnated. Knowledge could ideally just leap across from spirit to spirit. It wouldn't have to go down through incarnation, senses, speech. So, yes: one of the things *Swarm* was trying to do was get to utterances that were small enough to not become (if that's possible—it's a large field of inquiry—which includes how much time an image takes versus a statement for example—what a verb does to time and so on) temporalized. It's not just that they didn't accrue with the catapulting energies of sentence-making that take on (as waves do in the new book) an energy of their own—each wave producing a new wave as in any evolutionary motion. But rather the ambition was that they stay on this side of those desires. It's as if the book were trying to speak, in a way, not just without a throat but without a body. As if it were trying to try to sequester the body and the body's desires and impulses and to speak as "spirit."

TG: How do all the references to the "underneath" in *Swarm* fit into this sense of something withheld?

TG: During the early moments of *Swarm* I had begun having vivid memories of playing as a child in the Roman Forum. Then I was astonished to discover, as I was doing reading during the time of that book, how full of soil the now mostly emptied Forum had been—so full in fact, that when the German archaeologists first came down to see it they just planted hydrangea, hyacinth, wisteria on the very "top of" that dirt. It wasn't just time that had filled the Forum with dirt, as I had always imagined. But, rather, all the excavations for each next incarnation of the city of Rome used the site as a dumping ground. In the German imagination, underneath the constructed self—or surface of the present—as if in the psychic imagination—there was a "Forum," an ancient Rome ("Rome Antique") in which all the different parts of the "original"—columns, steles, stairs, pediments—were held afloat, each fragment in its place, yet broken, albeit distinct, as if in amber, or in dirt. Intact, but broken. Still in their right places (making the whole) but broken. A kind of imaginative holding ground. If you went and dug them up (which is what the English and French imagination wanted to do and eventually literally did) the temples—the unity or wholeness of the past—of origins—that were being "held" aloft would collapse.

These seemed to me two interestingly differing notions of how the past can be dealt with. Either you hold it in imagination, untouched . . . That's one of Dickinson's "door ajar" situations. (When she summons him in the dark, he's never present again, but everything that she summons—the chamber and so forth— *can* be kept intact: it has rooms; it has articulations; it is a complete world as long as it's not lived in, not touched.) That imagined place becomes the understructure or underneath of her whole current existence: an entombed place which albeit very still is nonetheless very much a home *because* untouchable, unlived-in, undug-up. The French and English—in their own differing ways (Rousseau, Wordsworth)—want to dig the unfree structure up. They did not want (in the ways German Romanticism at its origins did) a whole *based* on fragments. They wanted to dig up the psyche of the *child* and make the adult's present be an outcome of his experience of the world in childhood. They wanted the underneath excavated.

TG: The dirt covers everything?

JG: The dirt was keeping the underneath, made of fragments, intact. Columns were held intact, as entire units, because dirt, the passage of time, the invisible (imaginary) status of their being, was holding them. The minute you go down and take the dirt away, the parts of the columns fall down and what you have is ruins—which are now "fragments" as opposed to an intact—so called "broken"— past.

TG: So, what were you were doing in the writing in relation to this notion of the underneath?

JG: In the writing . . . From Dickinson, I had this haunted house, this place underneath. I read that series of poems and I felt, "Ah, I've found the trauma experience here in this group of 'love' poems." In the work that followed, I found chamber after buried chamber: him imaginatively summoned up, over and over. I felt, ah, as long as it's not "lived in," it's alive. As long as it's not excavated, as long as its life is in imagination, it's real.

TG: More than if it's "lived"?

JG: Yes, there, yes. It's this substitutive life—no less life for it—"The Brain is wider than the sky"—which holds intact the "Forum," if you will, more vividly than if you had gone and dug it up. I come from a tradition that believes in the opposite of all this: that it's in getting to the root of the matter that we find the substructure to build from again. But . . . I didn't dig up the Forum in that book. I kept the parts intact apart. Silence might as well be the dirt holding the fragments between them. I kept everything in place, via an imagination of it rather than an enactment of it. That's why, I think, *Never* comes forth as through this broken seal and rush of enactment.

TG: Eurydice or Daphne, who come back into your work in *Swarm*, would seem to be voices from the underneath.

JG: Well, yes. Your home is in the grave; your home is underneath; your home is in the past; your home is in fragments. And you don't go there. I was writing that book with a feeling that history in the world I was watching unfold before me had become disconnected from the past in every single possible way. I was experiencing the degree to which we're in a virtual reality "America." The theme park of emotions. Many critics pointed out the book didn't seem to know who it is addressing. Didn't know whom to speak to. Who is listening anymore? Who knows what the poem is for?

Many of these strategies, these questions, constitute for me, attempts to correlate the act of making poems to a society which is increasingly no longer connected to the knowledge of the past. The idea that the past could be held in mind, could be made psychically operative again—it's not that I believed that, but that I was going to trawl through that . . .

Dickinson's turning point, her *no*, is, in many ways, for me, a truly singular moment in the era of the Civil War. It's as if the Civil War comes down to this one strange syllable, uttered in a public room by this near-child. There are many ways in which America said no at a certain point and everything after that that was built was an imaginary structure. The haunted house. It's as if almost all poetry written after that moment reenacts a house they could have built. That house that could have become America. That house with its heart a loaded gun. That home with the power to have grace occur in it. It's a tomb, but it's a house too. It's the aftermath. She's trying to rebuild, via an act of *imagination*, a house that's been divided. Perhaps as the fall is said to be "fortunate," the division is as well. As Bishop would have it—the being "halved" such a signal condition of hers—in the obvious "Man-Moth" or "Gentleman of Shallot," but also in the poetic strategies that tug us in and out, as readers, of states of "commerce" or "contemplation." "The Monument" is in many ways about this sense of division and how lucrative it is—they both (Dickinson and Bishop) admonish us to "watch it closely." I don't know. That was probably connected to it as well.

TG: This must be connected, as well, to the "Underneath" series.

JG: "Underneath I" was probably the most important poem in the book for me. There's this terrible submission to mastery in the book, picked up from Dickinson but also from my life. It's a submission to fate as a kind of absolute force, as in "Yes Sir," but it's also . . . Is this a moment here that's, for me, the "Dickinson" moment—maybe?

> Near noon all the tall grasses for an instant stiff at
> attention,
>
> then a sturdy nervousness from left to right—
> deep bending of the light—
> light carried across on the backs, in on the tips—
> the screengrid forced so deep into the eye it's in
> disappearance—or the mind—

It's in disappearance or in the mind: either he's gone, or he's in the mind, as in:

> you will
> have it
> No where
> No two
>
> slivers alike although all bendings or bowings
> identical
> except for the fact of
> difference
>
> As in
> Yes Sir

TG: The poem just before this, "The Swarm," about listening to "the long ocean between us" seems very much like a response to 640's meeting apart, its "Door ajar / That Oceans are—and Prayer— / And that White Sustenance— / Despair."

JG: You mean where the speaker's arm is holding the phone out, so that church bells ringing vespers in central Italy could still be "sent back" across the ocean from the old world to the new? Yes, it's a love poem: "you without eyes or arms or body now—listen to / the long ocean between us." Sort of along the lines of: yes, you can start living completely in the imagination and the following can occur: (a) you can love, (b) anything can happen, (c) you can kill everything. It obviously goes in all directions. I think in *Swarm* I tried to take to the maximum the deletion of the material world and still maintain the fabric of reality. The two lovers are not together. No one's even speaking on the receiver; the receiver's held midair. What's going into it is blue and air and church bells and, as you say, the ocean. You see, I know what I was reading and I know what I was writing, but sometimes it's hard to put them together in this way . . .

TG: Can you try?

JG: Let me try. It's clear that if something of you dies, something else of you will live. That's her transaction. In 812, the thing that will live will make you unified with others. In other poems, it will make you a haunted ghost. And in yet further poems, it will make you a source of great danger. And there's a way in which, once you have no eyes or arms or body now, you can listen to "the long ocean between us," but then, as it goes on to say, there are "no parts of me you've touched, no places where you've / gone—." In other words, you're the untrammeled earth and everything's in the underneath. It makes you free—it makes you free to invent. But there's a difference between invention and imagination and grace. You're also free to murder and to kill. I think the book was just horrified in some ways at finding out you have to have "the" body back. When Dickinson says "If I may have it, when it's dead" (577), it started to mean something very different to me. You have to have *your* body back. That's why 812 became this crucial, signal poem to me. Because it was the poem that not only took the body back for the writer, but it required the body back of the reader. In *Swarm*, the problem of having or not having a body—as a speaker—is explored.

TG: It's gone, but then it comes back.

JG: Yes. At the very end. As Eurydice. She comes back up. She says, "in this dusk   face me, / with   our muscles' work, extravagant." "Berries eaten": (she's Persephone too). But she comes back up. "Once I thought to think till opened-up," as another poem puts it. I thought thinking could do this.

I thought, let's be either all body or no body, but there's no way to reconcile thinking and the body—they come apart from each other. And that's why 812 brought me—brings me— back together. Many great poems do this: 812 is the site where, without a body, I can *use* a body. She's dead. I don't even have a body. I'm "reading." And yet, she'll bring my body back together with her body and together we can "have" presence. Then we can see where *thinking* is located, what work thinking can do. Thinking reports.

TG: Did 812 hit you at the end of writing *Swarm*?

JG: Well—these things are hard to pinpoint. You could say 812 rescued me from *Swarm* and took me to *Never*! One of the things that I realized is that I don't believe you can bypass the problem(s) of incarnation—morality, choice, longing, loss, absence. Yet the attempt is to keep them at bay in that book. To try to experience the body as just a piece of matter. The erotic acts in *Swarm* are places where the body might as well *be* a wall, might as well be a problem that has to be gotten through. The speaker (the person) of that book wants to reach the spirit, which is on the other side, which is why even the sexual acts in it have to do with mortifying the flesh, or getting rid of the flesh altogether, so that the thing on the other side can be gotten to—not unlike what's on the other side of a ruin, or what's underneath. But to get *through* what's materially given at the present, to what it's theoretically holding hostage as incarnation, is something many poets must have heard in Dickinson. Often it seems, in her poems, that if she could have written these poems with even fewer words, with fewer sentences or *less* rhetorical structure, she would here. She is not a poet to trust the desires of forwardness, the desires of incarnation, very much . . . What I first discovered in 812 was that it was much more complex than that, and that when she went into the encounter with her subject with her imagination (as with the incarnating in those four stanzas)—our bodies not just resurrected but incarnated—an actual annunciation could take place. And that's among her most sentence-driven (action-driven) poems.

There's a way in which the poets that distrust language also distrust flesh. When Roethke says "it is the body makes the spirit visible," what he's talking about is the body as the *only* way spirit can be visible. So, after *Swarm* I guess I went back to the Whitmanian side of things, which, naturally, put me in the body, put me in the contradictions and paradoxes of desires, of sentences. I keep using the term *sentences*; I could use *time*, which would make this thought: "Take me outside time, put me in fragments, let my utterance be such that it need not cross through the flesh or, if passing, pass through in installments so small they don't get temporalized, so they can't be mortal." As opposed to: "Put me back in the body, put me back in the desires of temporality and of time, and if we're going to be back *in* time, let's go back to evolution, let's track it and see not only what this single existence is, but try to figure out what 'existence' is and how we're supposed to be connected to the *here*." That book is desperate for a *here* which could be provided by the natural world.

TG: *Never* is.

JG: Yes. A *here* (as the one in 812, for instance) but which turns into a *now* by the end of the book. It's very interesting that the moment it finds the *here* most vividly is the moment when it's not just going inside a church, but when it's going inside the "going inside of a church" by trying *to represent* that action further on the page, and then having trouble figuring out when it's *inside* and when it's *outside* . . . and so on.

TG: That would be "The Taken-Down God." As in:

> You are not supposed to write in the presence so I can't really do
> this task [*for us*] in there [feel fear when I feel for my pen] [in
>   pocket] [have
> come outside, sit on the steps, people watching me as they
> go in] [remember]: in there: children who can't see told to kiss a
> wooden hand: me watching them feel for it:

JG: It doesn't know how to *report* an event, It's trying to both *port* and *report* it, if you will. It finally has to give up reporting it and start porting it. So, by the end of the poem what's being asked is a literal carrying of a body.

TG: By a *we*.

JG: By a *we*. The speaker asks the reader to come in. He says, "You can do it. Will you do this with me?" Once we become this *we*, we can carry the god and we can actually put him back up. The poem says *now* over and over again and it says *here* over and over again, as if to keep recreating right there on the page the fact that it's made out of words, it's made out of *these* words. It brings the scratching sound of the pen in along with the birds and the further scratching sound of the money going into its box. They're all equivalent transactions. They're all these trades made with time in order to get to the moment outside of time, which the *I*, the reader, and the writer, who are not theoretically in this same place, and this puppet whose function it is to bring the reader and writer together . . . Putting him back up is not the point. The point is it takes two of us, he's that heavy.

TG: And what we're lifting is something "taken down"—in a sense, taken down in writing. So, we're lifting the poem.

JG: Yes, that's what we're doing. We're lifting it. By my writing and your reading. . . . That *we* in 812 comes in as one of the clearest actions in my "private" history of poetry. "*We* stay": Where did *we* come from, except that it's you and I, reader. Who else was here? There never was anybody else here. We only become a *we* when God leaves. We know we were *here* because he stepped away. "It passes": for a moment it was more than an it then it's back to being "just" an it. It never was meant to stay. It came that we become *we*.

February 22–23, 2002
Cambridge, Massachusetts

CONCLUSION ⌀'

Hart Crane's 1927 sonnet "To Emily Dickinson," a powerful, ground-breaking response to the poet, strikingly dramatizes the drive to speak back we have been examining. It begins:

You who desired so much—in vain to ask—
Yet fed your hunger like an endless task,
Dared dignify the labor, bless the quest—
Achieved that stillness ultimately best,

Being, of all, least sought for: Emily, hear![1]

As with the other writers we have looked at, Crane calls attention to Dickinson's unfulfilled "hunger." Reaching for something she could never possess, Dickinson "bless[ed]" and "dignif[ied]" the experience of coming up short by taking it as poetry's "endless task." Within that experience, Crane's speaker goes on, she achieved a kind of "stillness"—writing herself into a position where desire's cogs stopped grinding and were converted into something new. I have called that her broken responsiveness—a relation to the world in which what was "sought for" is abandoned and a stilled openness takes its place. Eager to associate himself with Dickinson's achievement, seeking a blessing from the poet whose generative sense of longing he clearly understands and shares, Crane's speaker calls on Dickinson to "hear" him: to acknowledge his presence beside her.

But that is not exactly what happens. As he continues describing her accomplishments, he is gradually overwhelmed by them:

O sweet, dead Silencer, most suddenly clear
When singing that Eternity possessed

And plundered momently in every breast;

—Truly no flower yet withers in your hand,
The harvest you descried and understand
Needs more than wit to gather, love to bind.
Some reconcilement of remotest mind—

Leaves Ormus rubyless, and Ophir chill.
Else tears heap all within one clay-cold hill.

Dickinson's silences, he repeats, are the source of her power. They are her clearest representations of "momently" possessing and losing Eternity—possessing it by losing it. And these representations, her flowers and poems, have lasted. They have not withered. Rather they point to a harvest far beyond what the speaker is able to "gather"—a harvest beyond the reach of "love" and "wit," the speaker's own finite and suddenly inadequate tools. To reach such a realm, to be "reconcile[d]" with it, would involve the unfolding of one's "remotest mind"—a reconciliation so powerful in its effects that it would dwarf the heaped-up treasures of the earth; a reconciliation so piercing in its denial that its being withheld would "heap all" within the grave's "clay-cold hill." And this denial is just what occurs: Dickinson tantalizes him with the mind's remotest reaches and then abruptly pulls him up short with a reminder of his mortality; she becomes, for the speaker, a "sweet, dead Silencer."[2]

Crane, I want to suggest, has said "Hear me" in two different ways. In the first five lines he describes Dickinson's voice, but in the lines that follow, he enacts it. If Dickinson's hunger drove her to a place where her voice was silenced by what remained stubbornly inaccessible, Crane, in the poem's concluding lines, answers in that voice. He says "Hear me" in her language, establishing a pattern that much contemporary writing follows. Charles Wright, for example, in language much like Crane's, writes that, although "no one could answer back from the other side. / Still, I'd like to think I've learned how to speak to them, / I'd like to think I know how to conjugate / 'Can you hear me?' and 'What?'" (W, 91–92). Conjugating the portion of Dickinson's language each of them hears, enacting its possibilities and implications, contemporary writers continue to engage Dickinson's responses to what can't be fully known. Robinson's fragile, attuned analogies; Wright's luminous, shifting glimpses; Howe's straying, accidental connections; Graham's muffled exchanges with what exists in silence—each of these offers a different account of the "Odd secrets of the line" (160, F132) Dickinson draws our eyes toward. And yet, once one realizes that Dickinson's chastened attentiveness lies behind their positions, one sees that they, and others, have been participating in a larger, more inclusive conversation all along, a conversation which their at times opposed aesthetic commitments must have blinded us to.

Let me bring out the portion of that conversation that the four writers I have concentrated on give voice to. Marilynne Robinson's Ruth is, in Robinson's terms, "abandoned into a new terrain without being able to use [her] old assumptions about how to find [her] way."[3] Stripped of everything but a few shards of memory, some remembered texts from school, and what she observes around her—things "by their nature fragmented, isolated, and arbitrary as glimpses one has at night through lighted windows" (H, 53)—Ruth uses this material to speculatively re-create her world. In doing so, she creates a language that, in Robinson's words, both acknowledges "the continuous sense of failure, of falling short, that makes meaning float beyond the reach of language"[4] and finds in that brokenness a way to be "attuned" (H, 85) to a world that remains dark and overpowering. Speculatively extending a series of Dickinson's figures in an attempt to make sense of her world—the "Enlarging Loneliness" one experiences in encountering "Druidic Difference" (J1068, F895); the "Odd secrets of the line" (J160, F132) or barrier apparently sealing one off from a world beyond report; the house of "Possibility" (J657, F466) within which one might dwell in inhabiting that line—Ruth conjugates, by enacting, a portion of Dickinson's way of speaking. She reproduces what Robert Weisbuch has called Dickinson's use of a language whose authority has been stripped—a language "not mimetic but illustratory, chosen, temporary."[5]

Charles Wright is drawn to what he describes as the "unseen" or the "invisible," seemingly located just outside the range of his senses. His poems record and engage the moments when "the windows into the invisible are [briefly] lit" and "lifelines to the unseen" (H, 9) seem accessible. Those moments, of course, are as fragmentary and inadequate as Robinson's nighttime glimpses. Over and over in Wright, "Something infinite behind everything appears, / and then disappears" (W, 79), those brief glimpses no more than "dissolving images after the eyelids close" (W, 122). Wright draws primarily on one Dickinson image—her "slant of light," which, coming and going, offers a glimpse of a world other than gray New England but holds it at an impossibly great remove. He conjugates and enacts this aspect of Dickinson's voice by, first, concentrating on the briefly lit windows of landscape and memory and, second, "attacking" the unseen with them by means of a journal-keeper's ongoing, never-arriving commitment to looking and losing and glimpsing again. Where Robinson's paragraphs extend Dickinson's poems into intricate, speculative probes, Wright's circling journals use them to batter and tap against an unyielding surface.

Susan Howe, like Robinson's Ruth, describes herself as wandering in a wilderness—part of some "infinite mystery [which is] in us but beyond us" (B Int, 21). As with Robinson's tenuous analogies and Wright's too quickly shuttered windows, Howe engages "unrevealedness" (B, 4) or "the inapprehensible Imaginary" (B, 29) with the very forms left broken in its wake: "Narrative expanding contracting dissolving. . . . No hierarchy, no notion of polarity. Perception of an object means loosing and losing it. . . . Hush of hesitation for breath and for breathing. Empirical domain of revolution and revaluation where words are in danger, dissolving" (My ED, 23). But where Robinson and Wright build new, responsive forms out of the dissolving remains of observation and memory, Howe—and the Dickinson whose lead she is following—engages a more textual wilderness: "Her talent was synthetic; she used other writers, grasped straws from the bewildering raveling of Being wherever and whenever she could use them. . . . Forcing, abbreviating, pushing, padding, subtracting, riddling, interrogating, re-writing, she pulled text from text" (My ED, 28–29). Like Crane, Howe in her two books of prose first describes Dickinson interrogating and rewriting Brontë and Dickens and Edwards and then enacts what she sees, following Dickinson into that wilderness and, in her own uneasy, interrogative collages, grappling with the "bewildering raveling of Being." If Dickinson led Crane to a world that "Needs more than wit to gather, love to bind" and silenced him, she draws Howe to the same world and liberates her: "I am pulling representation from the irrational dimension love and knowledge must reach" (B, 83).

Jorie Graham would agree with the other three writers that the Dickinson who most speaks to her understands that one comes closest to the unknown in those moments when thinking or remembering or being at home breaks down. She calls attention, in Dickinson, to her

> use of order and its breakdown, senses and their extinguishing, imagery and its obliteration, rhyme and its increase or failure, the speaker moving from an active to a passive stance, remembering and then forgetting, narrative that breaks off into silence . . . attempts at letting the timeless as experienced in extreme states of being—anguish, despair, for example, or in the presence of death—penetrate the language in order to stain it.[6]

"To all except anguish the mind soon adjusts," Dickinson writes in a phrase that Graham quotes in *Swarm* (5). In those moments of vertigo, the mind no longer able to adjust or stabilize itself, Graham sees Dickinson "undermin[ing] any stable understanding of what's in the silence in order to be able to inhabit it fully."[7] Where the Graham of *Swarm* parts company with the other three writers is in her response to those broken, unsettled fragments of "the crashing of mind." Where their language becomes more free or more fluid or more expansively attentive, remaking itself, hers becomes muted and broken off and hushed, erasing itself: "Burn all the letters. / Look in the ashes with both hands. / . . . feel further round for fragments, / for any last unburnt / piece of / the crashing of mind" (S, 25).

Unfolding Dickinson's lament to a lover that "I cannot live with You— / It would be Life— / And Life is over there—"and her conclusion that "We must meet apart— / You there—I—here— / With just the Door ajar / That Oceans are—and Prayer— / And that White Sustenance— / Despair—," *Swarm* enacts a Dickinson most alive to the revelatory charge of anguish or despair as she holds herself "apart" from the complication and betrayals of time or bodies or speculation. In a sense, Graham speaks back to Dickinson the drive to get past or underneath the material:

> To get *through* what's materially given at the present, to what it's theoretically holding hostage as incarnation, is something many poets must have heard in Dickinson. Often it seems, in her poems, that if she could have written these poems with even fewer words, with fewer sentences or *less* rhetorical structure, she would have.

Underneath the mind, outside of language, *Swarm* proposes, is where one dwells in Possibility.

If Dickinson and the writers I have examined here have demonstrated the power of inviting tentativeness or brokenness or chance or surprise into one's text, privileging variants over single vision and the word made flesh over the word held apart, then it would follow that a criticism attempting to engage these might want to explore those formal possibilities as well. The four interviews I have included here attempt to do just that. Conducted after I had written each chapter, they press, sometimes forcefully, against my initial arguments—putting back in play what the conventions of critical prose would seem to have declared settled. Combining chapters and interviews is a way of acknowledging that language must fray, must hesitate and interrupt itself, in order to be fully responsive. To return to Crane's poem, the juxtaposition of chapters and interviews allows the reader to not just understand Dickinson but, in some senses, to enact her way of writing and thinking.

For example, what Robinson does in our interview is dramatically expand the context within which one might approach her novel. Ruth's being stripped of conventional means of approaching reality and then being led out into an open space where she is forced to "reconceiv[e] reality into larger terms that diminish her" is, Robinson agrees, a version of Dickinson's "stepping over a threshold . . . from normal religiosity . . . into something much more intense," an experience of self-diminishment prompted by "the other com[ing] close to you." But, she argues, Dickinson (and by extension *Housekeeping*) needs to be seen as a participant in Puritan or Calvinist culture—in particular, in that culture's emphasis, in Jonathan Edwards's terms, on the "arbitrary constitution" of reality," the sense that it "is in a constant flux . . . renewed every moment." If, as Robinson puts it, this leads to "the sense that the materiality of things can be understood as a part of contact with something utterly beyond the material," it also leads to the self-correcting, self-transforming uses of language displayed by a Melville or Thoreau or Dickinson as they stand before a world "continually made new, a new world . . . being spoken all the time." Robinson's "undefended" Ruth, then, might be seen as a strong argument for the continuing, and surprisingly various, extension of this tradition.

If the Robinson interview opens my chapter up by placing Dickinson within a larger, still-vital tradition, Wright's interview goes the opposite way, focusing and making more precise my remarks about landscape and memory. They are broken forms, Wright insists, "stand-ins . . . [or] simulacra for . . . something behind both of those things." Their luminous glimpses seem repeatable, but aren't. Memory, like the landscape of the back yard, "is always the same and always different"; it seems a stable reference, but nothing could be further from the truth. Memory is "a river rather than a lake" with "different aspects" of "something condensed and withheld and unknowable" coming into view depending on one's angle of response. Because it foregrounds its partiality, never letting the poet think he has returned to some lost wholeness, memory becomes for Wright "a kind of attack vehicle to get at things, to get at the point where you're open to . . . possibilities." In its beckoning partiality, it forces one to listen and be attentive. Wright calls this attentiveness not "memory . . . as remembering" but "memory in the present tense—talking about the memory." In the poem's present, reading and observation and speculation pursue the radiating implications of memory's momentary unveilings, the poet thereby reworking Dickinson's broken encounters with the unknown.

In her interview, Howe not only draws the reader into a deeper or more precise version of her Emily Dickinson, she draws the reader into its per-

formance. If Dickinson's manuscript pages are records of wilderness jour-
neys, if they "open fields of connections" and function as "sacred space[s] of
saved intensity," so, too, do the pages of Howe's interview. Our conversation
records what Howe would call a "spiritual improvisation," the poet "open
to [the] order which chance creates," focusing on particulars in an attempt
"to go back to a beginning. One has to go farther and farther back. I always
want to go back. . . . You might not have an answer at the end but you keep
trying, now this way, now that way. It's not the finding. It's the searching."
In the wilderness of her study, Howe, in Wright's phrase, concentrates and
listens hard. She draws us into a space where "love and knowledge" (B, 83)
weave together the sound of words read aloud and the sound of words singing in the head; words marked, saved, inscribed, pinned, drawn, made palpable and material. We are drawn into a community piecing out "an undeciphered form still unknown to us."

What's fascinating about the Graham interview is that we are invited to
listen in as she works away from, all but disavowing, her initial response to
Dickinson. The Dickinson she presents in her long opening reading of poem
812 is a significant modification of the poet *Swarm* imagines itself in conversation with. If the other three interviews unsettle and recast my chapters by
expanding or focusing or reenacting their issues, Graham's interview unset-
tles my work by, without comment, leaping beyond it, temporarily stripping us of location and returning us to the vertiginous position her poems
are consistently drawn to. Poem 812, she argues, "A Light exists in Spring,"
puts us in a position where the mind can no longer process the information
directed at it and instead gives itself "over to the body's sensations which
keep replacing each other." That awakening of the body eventually results
in the reader's experience of "an annunciation," the reader "using the body
to physically summon an absent thing and make it present." If *Swarm* and
Never, the book just completed as we conducted our interview, both attempt
to enter the same unknowable space ("the *here* or the atemporal present"),
they do so in two different ways: "One is by shortening—almost withholding speech . . . It involves a distrust of language, and of the body, and the
feeling that if language comes into play it will immediately become temporalized." The other is by returning to "the problems of incarnation—morality,
choice, longing, loss, absence . . . the contradictions and paradoxes of desires,
of sentences . . . [of] time."

Graham remarks that a version of Dickinson prompted both approaches
to the unknown. If *Swarm* enacted a Dickinson trying to move past the
problem of incarnation, poem 812 showed the poet "that it was much more
complex than that, and that when [we] went into the encounter with . . . our

bodies not just resurrected but incarnated—an actual annunciation could take place." What this suggests, and what this book has sought to demonstrate, is that Dickinson's legacy will remain a vital and continuing one, will continue to take shape, as long as her poems are taken up by and tested out in the work of practicing writers. An end to *this* process seems "Beyond the Dip of Bell—."

NOTES

INTRODUCTION

1. Lucie Brock-Broido, *The Master Letters* (New York: Knopf, 1997), vii–viii.
2. *The Letters of Emily Dickinson*, ed. Thomas H. Johnson (Cambridge: Harvard University Press, 1958), 2:333 (letter 187), and 2:375 (letter 233). Cited by letter number.
3. Gerald Bruns, *Heidegger's Estrangements: Language, Truth, and Poetry in the Later Writings* (New Haven: Yale University Press, 1989), 67.
4. See Sheila Coghill and Thom Tammaro's anthology *Visiting Emily: Poems Inspired by the Life and Work of Emily Dickinson* (Iowa City: University of Iowa Press, 2000) for some indication of the range of responses by poets. See my review essay dealing in part with this volume, "Dickinson and the Unknown," *Review* 25 (2003): 163–73. "Titanic Operas: A Poet's Corner of Responses to Dickinson's Legacy," ed. Martha Nell Smith, as part of the *Dickinson Electronic Archives,* available at jefferson.village.virginia.edu/dickinson/titanic/table_of_contents.html, is a valuable collection of tributes and essays. See also Susan McCabe, "Poets: Influence on," in *An Emily Dickinson Encyclopedia*, ed. Jane Donahue Eberwein (Westport, Conn.: Greenwood Press, 1998).
5. Joyce Carol Oates, "Soul at the White Heat: The Romance of Emily Dickinson's Poetry," *Critical Inquiry* 13, 4 (summer 1987): 824.
6. Hart Crane, "The Broken Tower," in *The Complete Poems and Selected Letters and Prose of Hart Crane*, ed. Brom Weber (Garden City, N.Y.: Doubleday, 1966), 193.
7. On this pattern, I have found most valuable the following works: Richard Wilbur, "Sumptuous Destitution," in *Emily Dickinson: A Collection of Critical Essays*, ed. Judith Farr (Upper Saddle River, N.J.: Prentice Hall, 1996), 53–61; Robert Weisbuch, *Emily Dickinson's Poetry* (Chicago: University of Chicago Press, 1975), and "Prisming Dickinson, or Gathering Paradise by Letting Go," in *The Emily Dickinson Handbook*, ed. Gudrun Grabher, Roland Hagenbüchle, and

Cristanne Miller (Amherst: University of Massachusetts Press, 1998), 197–223; Jane Donahue Eberwein, *Dickinson: Strategies of Limitation* (Amherst: University of Massachusetts Press, 1985); Elisa New, *The Regenerate Lyric: Theology and Innovation in American Poetry* (Cambridge, England: Cambridge University Press, 1993), *The Line's Eye: Poetic Experience, American Sight* (Cambridge: Harvard University Press, 1998), "Awe, Wonder, and Wit: Elizabeth Bishop and the Modernization of Calvinist Mood," in *The Calvinist Roots of the Modern Era*, ed. Aliki Barnstone, Michael Tomasek Manson, and Carol J. Singley (Hanover, N.H.: University Press of New England, 1997); James McIntosh, *Nimble Believing: Dickinson and the Unknown* (Ann Arbor: University of Michigan Press, 2000). See my comments on New, Eberwein, and McIntosh in "Dickinson and the Unknown." For an example of a contemporary poet's work with this issue, see Charles Simic's account of Dickinson as "visionary skeptic," in "Visionaries and Anti-Visionaries," in *Wonderful Words, Silent Truth: Essays on Poetry and a Memoir* (Ann Arbor: University of Michigan Press, 1990), 72–81.

8. Gary Lee Stonum, *The Dickinson Sublime* (Madison: University of Wisconsin Press, 1990).

9. Sharon Cameron, *Choosing Not Choosing: Dickinson's Fascicles* (Chicago: University of Chicago Press, 1992), 182–83.

10. The poet Heather McHugh in "What Dickinson Makes a Dash For: Interpretive Insecurity as Poetic Freedom" makes a similar point. In Dickinson, she writes, we see "an energy outbounding its visible materials, and referring through every construction (in-, con-, de-, and decon-) to the uncontainable, that intuited spirit or gist or Geist we sense as living's ungraspable essential" (105). Dickinson puts aside the "single exclusive Sign" (107) as broken and inadequate and in its place employs "sentences and lines . . . designed (in judicious ellipses, elisions, contractions, puns, and dashes) to afford the greatest possible number of simultaneous and yet mutually resistant readings . . . directing us to what is irresoluble, or unsaid" (105). Through "the incompletion figured in the dash" and other features of her language, the reader is "freed from meaning as monolith, meaning in the narrow sense . . . [to] meaning that incurs its own undoing" (113). See her *Broken English: Poetry and Partiality* (Hanover, N.H.: Wesleyan University Press, 1993), 99–113.

11. Adrienne Rich makes a similar point in her well-known 1975 essay "Vesuvius at Home: The Power of Emily Dickinson." Dickinson was writing about her "relationship to her own power" (165), Rich argues—an inner power often represented as a "daemonic force" (170). "To say 'yes' to her powers" was Dickinson's "major act of nonconformity" (183). It meant "enter[ing] chambers of the self" and engaging "a part of yourself that you perceive as the essential, the creative and powerful self, yet also as possibly unacceptable, perhaps even monstrous" (175). In such an exploration, one must "relinquish control" (175), acknowledging that the terms and tools with which one turns to such a task are charged and deeply limited ones. Dickinson's "blurring erotic with religious experience and imagery" (165), then, her "poems of possession by the

deity, or by a human lover" (170), were attempts, using the language she inherited—"the language of heterosexual love or patriarchal theology" (170)—to get at something that remained, in some senses, always on the move: "her own active, creative power" (170). See *On Lies, Secrets, and Silence: Selected Prose 1966–1978* (New York: Norton, 1979), 157–83.

12. *The Complete Poems of Emily Dickinson*, ed. Thomas H. Johnson (Boston: Little, Brown, 1955). Because the writers I examine would have used this edition, I cite it throughout, as J. I also cite the recent Franklin edition number, for ease of reference, as F. See R. W. Franklin, *The Poems of Emily Dickinson* (Cambridge: Harvard University Press, 1998).

13. Annie Dillard, in her senior thesis at Hollins College, "The Merchant of the Picturesque: One Pattern in Emily Dickinson's Poetry," an essay that stands behind her *Pilgrim at Tinker's Creek*, notes how consistently, in Dickinson, "Things move away from the poet's range of vision and out towards infinity, the circumference of the natural world." Quoted in Nancy C. Parrish, *Lee Smith, Annie Dillard, and the Hollins Group: A Genesis of Writers* (Baton Rouge: Louisiana State University Press, 1998), 148. I thank Clay Delk for pointing this out to me.

14. Alec Marsh, "A Conversation with Alice Fulton," *TriQuarterly* 98 (winter 1996–97): 31.

15. Cristanne Miller, *Emily Dickinson: A Poet's Grammar* (Cambridge: Harvard University Press, 1987). See also Alice Fulton, interview by Cristanne Miller, *Contemporary Literature* 38, 4 (1997): 585–615.

16. Alice Fulton, *Sensual Math* (New York: Norton, 1995), 56.

17. Kathleen Fraser, *Notes preceding trust* (San Francisco: Lapis Press, 1987).

18. Kathleen Fraser, interview by Robert Gluck, April 2002, *Studiocleo* 4 (2002), available at studiocleo.com/cauldron/volume4/features/fraser/int/.

19. Kathleen Fraser, *Translating the Unspeakable: Poetry and the Innovative Necessity* (Tuscaloosa: University of Alabama Press, 2000).

20. Kathleen Fraser, "Notes on Poems," in *il cuore: the heart, Selected Poems, 1970–1995* (Hanover, N.H.: Wesleyan University Press, 1997), 195.

21. She notes in the Gluck interview: "Lyrics also entered my life almost every night when my parents would sing us to sleep with poignant (at least to my ears) duets from Jeanette MacDonald and Nelson Eddy musicals, standing in the door of our bedroom with their arms around each other."

22. Robert Hass, *Sun Under Wood* (Hopewell, N.J.: Ecco, 1996).

23. Recall Dickinson's well-known "I dwell in Possibility— / A fairer House than Prose—" (J657, F466).

CHAPTER 1

1. Marilynne Robinson, "The Hum Inside the Skull: A Symposium," *New York Times Book Review*, May 13, 1984, p. 30.

2. Marilynne Robinson, *Housekeeping* (New York: Farrar, Straus and Giroux, 1980).

3. Tace Hedrick, "On Influence and Appropriation," *Iowa Review* 22, 1 (1992): 1. For a recent listing of criticism devoted to this novel, see Lisa Durose, "Marilynne Robinson: A Bibliography," *ANQ* 10 (winter 1997): 31–46.

4. Thoreau, for example, writes: "Not till we are lost, in other words, not till we have lost the world, do we begin to find ourselves, and realize where we are and the infinite extent of our relations." *Walden* (New York: Vintage, 1991), 139.

5. Marilynne Robinson, interview by Thomas Schaub, *Contemporary Literature* 35, 2 (summer 1994), 240–41.

6. Marilynne Robinson, "Language Is Smarter Than We Are," *New York Times Book Review*, January 11, 1987, p. 8. Focusing in part on this essay, Thomas Schaub, in "Lingering Hopes, Faltering Dreams: Marilynne Robinson and the Politics of Contemporary American Fiction," claims that "*Housekeeping* is a brilliant, meditative resurrection of American romanticism. It is a resurrection that is thereby also nostalgic" (310). He goes on to describe the novel as a "withdrawal into language" (312) or into art. But as I will attempt to show in this chapter, the view of language that the novel works out is quite different from the one Schaub sketches in which "natural and spiritual fact" correspond "in behalf of [the narrator's] totalizing desire" (311, 312). See *Traditions, Voices, and Dreams: The American Novel Since the 1960s*, ed. Melvin J. Friedman and Ben Siegel (Newark: University of Delaware Press, 1995), 289–321.

7. Robinson's collection of essays *The Death of Adam: Essays on Modern Thought* (Boston: Houghton Mifflin, 1998) takes up these ideas at length. In contrast to much "contemporary discourse [which] feels to me empty and false," the essays in this book investigate many of the ways "the arts and sciences [have] declare[d] the strange exhilarations of our strange life on earth" (2). Such declarations are, at their best, aware of their own limits: "our best information about the planet has been full of enormous lacunae, and is, and will be. Every grand venture at understanding is hypothesis, not so different from metaphysics" (72).

8. Robinson, "Language Is Smarter Than We Are," 8.

9. Gerald Bruns, *Heidegger's Estrangements: Language, Truth, and Poetry in the Later Writings* (New Haven: Yale University Press, 1989), 66, 67.

10. Marilynne Robinson, "My Western Roots," in *Old West–New West: Centennial Essays*, ed. Barbara Howard Meldrum (Moscow: University of Idaho Press, 1993), 166.

11. An early, influential discussion of this pattern is Richard Wilbur, "Sumptuous Destitution," in *Emily Dickinson: A Collection of Critical Essays*, ed. Judith Farr (Upper Saddle River, N.J.: Prentice Hall, 1996), 53–61. For Wilbur, "the frustration of appetite awakens or abets desire" (56). In "the vaster economy of desire . . . the object is spiritually possessed, not merely for itself, but more truly as an index of the All" (58). For a contrasting view, arguing that deprivation leads in Dickinson to "the extinction of appetite" (63), see Vivian R.

Pollak, "Thirst and Starvation in Emily Dickinson's Poetry," in the same volume.

12. See also poem J718 (F881), in which Dickinson writes: "To wander—now—is my Repose—."

13. In an important early essay on *Housekeeping,* Joan Kirkby notes not only that the novel "evokes and improvises on recurring motifs and whole structures and patterns of resonance from the works of those earlier American writers also preoccupied with the interaction of nature and art, Dickinson, Thoreau, Hawthorne, Emerson, Poe" (92–93) but also that the book, at least in its final pages, "shares something with the persona of so many of Dickinson's poems, a voice speaking from another dimension" (106). As my chapter will demonstrate, however, I don't share the view that Ruth is simply "de-civilized and . . . drawn back into primal relation with the natural world" (97). See "Is There Life After Art? The Metaphysics of Marilynne Robinson's *Housekeeping,*" *Tulsa Studies in Women's Literature* 5 (spring 1986): 91–109.

14. Marilynne Robinson, "Psalm Eight," in *The Death of Adam: Essays on Modern Thought* (Boston: Houghton Mifflin, 1998), 230.

15. Robert Weisbuch, *Emily Dickinson's Poetry* (Chicago: University of Chicago Press, 1975).

16. As Weisbuch has recently reformulated the idea, "each apparently mimetic scene in [a Dickinson] poem is revealed to be a choice from an infinitude of potential examplings of the poem's unifying proposition. The scenes are not concrete but mentalized, illustratory, chosen, temporary, analogous." The poem is "sceneless" because we are pointed to the mind at work, not the originating scene or occasion. See "Prisming Dickinson; or, Gathering Paradise by Letting Go," in *The Emily Dickinson Handbook,* ed. Gudrun Grabher, Roland Hagenbüchle, and Cristanne Miller (Amherst: University of Massachusetts Press, 1998), 200.

17. For recent work on this idea of limits, see E. Miller Budick, *Emily Dickinson and the Life of Language* (Baton Rouge: Louisiana State University Press, 1985), who writes that for Dickinson, "without symbols there can be no access to any knowledge whatsoever, even if the knowledge obtained points to the ultimate fallibility of the symbols that communicate it" (167). For work on analogy and speculation, see Suzanne Juhasz, "Costumeless Consciousness," in *The Undiscovered Continent: Emily Dickinson and the Space of the Mind* (Bloomington: Indiana University Press, 1983). She remarks: "speculation is a kind of knowing which must include uncertainty in its aptness" (145).

18. We hear such language throughout the novel: "Imagine my grandfather reclined how many years in his Pullman berth, regarding the morning through a small blue window" (150); or "Say that water lapped over the gunwales, and I swelled and swelled until I burst Sylvie's coat" (162).

19. "The First and Second Epistles General of Peter," in *Incarnation: Contemporary Writers on the New Testament,* ed. Alfred Corn (New York: Viking, 1990), 310.

20. Jane Donahue Eberwein, *Dickinson: Strategies of Limitation* (Amherst: University of Massachusetts Press, 1985), offers a valuable, book-length examination of Dickinson's probing of this boundary. She writes: "Guessing at the secrets God had hidden beyond circumference constituted the essential work of Emily Dickinson's life, the resolution of riddles the impelling drive of her imagination. Discontented with the routine answers that seemed to satisfy most people and unwilling to rest in the uncertainty that sufficed for others, she concentrated her intellectual and emotional energy on the effort to make connections between 'this side' and the other, the finite and the infinite, time and eternity" (225). For Eberwein, this probing involves a "deliberate cultivation of limitation" (272) that then "fired her longing for unbounded ecstasy beyond her mortal circuit" (261).

    In the opening paragraphs of *Housekeeping*, Robinson introduces the Dickinsonian image of circumference, commenting that from within the grandfather's childhood home in the Middle West, "a house dug out of the ground, with windows just at earth level . . . the perfect horizontality of the world in that place foreshortened the view so severely that the horizon seemed to *circumscribe* the sod house and nothing more" (3). On moving to Fingerbone and the west, he found himself in a place where those margins seemed to have shifted: "It seems there was a time when the dimensions of things modified themselves, leaving a number of puzzling margins, as between the mountains as they must have been and the mountains as they are now, or between the lake as it once was and the lake as it now is" (4–5). In fact, those various circled margins are everywhere apparent to Ruth: "At the foundation is the old lake, which is smothered and nameless and altogether black. Then there is Fingerbone, the lake of charts and photographs, which is permeated by sunlight and sustains green life and innumerable fish, and in which one can look down in the shadow of a dock and see stony, earthy bottom, more or less as one sees dry ground. And above that, the lake that rises in the spring and turns the grass dark and coarse as reeds. And above that the water suspended in sunlight, sharp as the breath of an animal, which brims inside this *circle* of mountains" (9).

21. See "My Western Roots," 171.

22. See Weisbuch, "Prisming Dickinson," 197.

23. One can feel this poem shaping Ruth's description of her first encounter with Sylvie as references to Sylvie's hands and the word *narrow* play back and forth across each other for several pages. For example: "I imagine her with her grips in her bare *hands*, walking down the middle of the road, which was *narrowed* by the banks of plowed snow on either side, and *narrowed* more by the slushy pools that were forming at the foot of each bank" (48).

24. In the interview included in this book, Jorie Graham speaks at length about the distinction between thinking and feeling in Dickinson. See Dickinson's poem 812: "A Color stands abroad / On Solitary Fields / That Science cannot overtake / But Human Nature feels."

25. As we'll see in chapter 5, Susan Howe develops this idea at length, describing, for example, the way Dickinson and Robert Browning (in "Childe Roland to the Dark Tower Came") see themselves as "alien explicators of ruin after the Tablets of the Law were broken," each of them having "unselved identity, memory, poetic origins," "wander[ing] a wilderness of language" (69, 70). See *My Emily Dickinson* (Berkeley: North Atlantic Books, 1985).

26. Some of these fragments include the stories of Cain and Abel (192–93) and Noah's wife (172).

CHAPTER 3

1. Charles Wright, *Halflife: Improvisations and Interviews* (Ann Arbor: University of Michigan Press, 1988), 54. Cited as H. In an interview with Sherod Santos, Wright expands on this essay: "With the exception of Dante—who is ultimately, for me, unapproachable—she is the 'What.' The others are the 'How.' She was never a technical influence on me, other than in the idea that shorter is just as good as, if not better than, longer. Her disquietudes are my disquietudes" (H, 179). Other Wright titles will be cited as follows: *Country Music: Selected Early Poems* (Middletown, Conn.: Wesleyan University Press, 1982)—C; *Negative Blue: Selected Later Poems* (New York: Farrar, Straus and Giroux, 2000)—N; *Quarter Notes: Improvisations and Interviews* (Ann Arbor: University of Michigan Press, 1995)—Q; *The World of the Ten Thousand Things: Poems 1980–1990* (New York: Farrar, Straus and Giroux, 1990)—W.

2. Bonnie Costello, "The Soil and Man's Intelligence: Three Contemporary Landscape Poets," in *The Point Where All Things Meet: Essays on Charles Wright*, ed. Tom Andrews (Oberlin, Ohio: Oberlin College Press, 1995), 149. This collection will be cited as P. Costello extends this idea in "Charles Wright's *Via Negativa*: Language, Landscape, and the Idea of God," *Contemporary Literature* 42, 2 (summer 2001): 325–46. She writes: "Ideas of sin and limit particularly distinguish Wright's visionary poetics from the Romantic and Emersonian traditions that have continued to dominate American landscape poetry in the twentieth century" (331). Elisa New, *The Regenerate Lyric: Theology and Innovation in American Poetry* (Cambridge, England: Cambridge University Press, 1993), examines the idea that "Growing up beside the mainstream tradition we call Emersonian was another tradition, call it anti-Emersonian . . . [which found] language itself structurally resistant to . . . 'transcendence'" (3). In a second book, *The Line's Eye: Poetic Experience, American Sight* (Cambridge: Harvard University Press, 1998), New importantly qualifies this argument by distinguishing the earlier and later Emerson. The Emerson of "Experience," she notes, joins Dickinson, Crane, Stevens, and Frost in "discover[ing] fallenness more usable, more responsive, to Being than the pre-lapsarian innocence the Emerson of *Nature* thought poetry's enabling condition" (3). David Baker, in a review of Wright's *Chick-*

amauga, usefully links Wright to the Emerson who "knows the winding destination of language is also its extinction." See "Chickamauga," *Poetry* 168, 1 (April, 1996): 33.

3. For an important exploration of Wright's interest in Morandi, see Bonnie Costello, "Charles Wright, Giorgio Morandi and the Metaphysics of the Line," *Mosaic* 35 (March 2002): 35, 149–71. "In Morandi," she writes, "Wright found an imagination akin to his own, interested in 'the metaphysics of the quotidian,' and drawn to the everyday for the sense of mystery it arouses. He traces disappearances to awaken a sense of 'what's not there'" (153).

4. In a recent interview, he notes "a deep yearning, a deep desire for something that's beyond one's control and one's grasp, and beyond one's comprehension. This is nothing new, obviously, but it is the movement my whole project has been tending toward all these years." See Ernest Suarez, *Southbound: Interviews with Southern Poets* (Columbia: University of Missouri Press, 1999), 57. Cited as S.

5. See, for example, Helen Vendler's discussion of seasons and earlier writers in Wright's landscapes in "Charles Wright," P, 13–20; discussions of landscape and memory in J. D. McClatchy, "Under the Sign of the Cross," P, 72–85, and Julian Gitzen, "Charles Wright and Presences in Absence," P, 172–83; and Bonnie Costello's analysis of Wright's vision of "landscape [as] an unreadable, undecodable text" (332) in "Charles Wright's *Via Negativa*."

6. Marilynne Robinson, interview by Thomas Schaub, *Contemporary Literature* 35, 2 (summer 1994): 241.

7. Dickinson, of course, is present in Wright's other books. Calvin Bedient discusses a number of references in *The Southern Cross*. See "Tracing Charles Wright," P, 28–30.

8. Mutlu Konuk Blasing, "The American Sublime, c. 1992: What Clothes Does One Wear," P, 199. See her entire discussion of Wright's approach to "those 'zones' we can get at only through such self-erasure" (201).

9. In a more recent formulation: "The world is a language we never quite understand, / But think we catch the drift of. Speaking in ignorance / And joy, we answer / What wasn't asked, by someone we don't know, in strange tongues" (N, 23).

10. See Bonnie Costello's discussion of "the process of articulation and erasure" (342), in "Charles Wright's *Via Negativa*." I have made particular use of her description of Wright's "darker vision in which the infinite burns into the finite and consumes it, leaving its trace as a charred notation" (345).

11. New, *The Regenerate Lyric*, 161–62. See also her discussion of Dickinson's poem 258 and the way the slant's resistance causes "orders [to] unfix themselves and drift. Hitherto unimpeachable Chains of Being reveal the fragile contingency of their organizations. Experience in the poem makes possible a re-cognition of a profounder, more surprising, Creation than reason allows"; *The Line's Eye*, 165.

12. Calvin Bedient, in "Tracing Charles Wright," quotes Wright in conversation in similar terms: "What I see I really want to do is be Emily Dickinson on Walt Whitman's road—that is, to have his length of line and expansiveness of life gusto with her intelligence walking along, and her preoccupations, which are my preoccupations," P, 27.

13. For a discussion of these frescoes, see Vendler, "Charles Wright," 17–19.

14. Wright echoes Ezra Pound's "The Return': "See, they return, one, and by one, / With fear, as half-awakened."

15. She writes: "Could you believe me—without? I had no portrait, now, but am small, like the Wren, and my Hair is bold, like the Chestnut Bur—and my eyes, like Sherry in the Glass, that the Guest leaves—Would this do just as well?" See Thomas H. Johnson and Theodora Ward, *The Letters of Emily Dickinson*, 3 vols. (Cambridge: Harvard University Press, 1958), 2: 411 (letter 268). For a discussion of this letter, see Jane Donahue Eberwein, *Dickinson: Strategies of Limitation* (Amherst: University of Massachusetts Press, 1985), 3–20.

16. In an interview with Elizabeth McBride, Wright formulates this idea slightly differently. Asked if he thinks of his work as engaged in a search, he responds: "Constantly. A search for the small, still center of everything. It's what one looks for. I don't know whether that exists. . . . A lot of what I want to say changes but the place I want to get to never changes. There are different ways of approaching it, through language, metamorphosis, other changings, but I do want to get to that still, small pinpoint of light at the center of the universe, where all things come together and all things intersect" (H, 128).

CHAPTER 5

1. Susan Howe, "Encloser," in *The Politics of Poetic Form*, ed. Charles Bernstein (New York: ROOF, 1990), 192. Cited as Pol. Howe has also used this notion of "another language" in talking about dreams: "another language, another way of speaking so quietly always there in the shape of memories, thoughts, feelings, which are extra-marginal, outside of primary consciousness, yet must be classed as some sort of unawakened finite infinite articulation. Documents resemble people talking in their sleep." See "Either Either," in *Close Listening: Poetry and the Performed Word*, ed. Charles Bernstein (New York: Oxford University Press, 1998), 111. John Palattella in "An End of Abstraction: An Essay on Susan Howe's Historicism," *Denver Quarterly* 29 (winter 1995): 74–97, writes that "Howe's poetics stutters to sustain an ongoing redefinition of a polyphonic American voice . . . a particular, dissembling voice" (97). See the entire essay. Peter Nicholls, "Unsettling the Wilderness: Susan Howe and American History," *Contemporary Literature* 37, 4 (winter 1996), 586–601, writes that in the writers Howe is drawn to, "The failure to speak

fluently becomes a strength as it sets up a resistance to conceptuality and dialectic" (597); see 596–98. For a discussion of the link between "an other voice" and the feminine, see Lynn Keller's chapter on Howe in *Forms of Expansion: Recent Long Poems by Women* (Chicago: University of Chicago Press, 1997), esp. 191–92.

2. Susan Howe, *The Birth-mark: Unsettling the Wilderness in American Literary History* (Hanover, N.H.: Wesleyan University Press, 1993), 181. Cited as B.

3. Susan Howe (with Tom Beckett), "The Difficulties Interview," *Difficulties* 3, 2 (1989): 21. Cited as B Int.

4. Peter Quartermain remarks of Howe that "Her writing is essentially religious, devoted to a lively apprehension of the sacramental nature of our experience of the world, and of the sacramental nature of the world." See *Disjunctive Poetics: From Gertrude Stein and Louis Zukofsky to Susan Howe* (Cambridge, England: Cambridge University Press, 1992), 194. Susan Schultz, in "Exaggerated History," *Postmodern Culture* 4, 2 (1994) makes a similar observation, though she is more uneasy about this aspect of Howe's work. See especially paragraphs 9 and 10.

5. Susan Howe, *My Emily Dickinson* (Berkeley: North Atlantic Books, 1985), 117–18. Cited as My ED.

6. Fiona Green, "'Plainly on the Other Side': Susan Howe's Recovery," *Contemporary Literature* 42, 1 (spring 2001): 78–101.

7. See Rachel Tzvia Back, *Led by Language: The Poetry and Poetics of Susan Howe* (Tuscaloosa: University of Alabama Press, 2002), 21–22, esp. fig. 2.1, in which she reproduces the page from *Webster's Third New International Dictionary* Howe used, marking the words drawn from this text. For her reading of *Secret History of the Dividing Line* as a whole, see 19–37. Green also was led to Howe's source in *Webster's*; see 86–87.

8. For an instructive demonstration of the way Howe brings out the stutter in another text, see Peter Quartermain's analysis of her work with *Billy Budd: The Genetic Text*, in "Scattering as Behavior toward Risk," in *Disjunctive Poetics*, 183–92. Quartermain describes this as "throwing a halo of wilderness" about a source text.

9. Susan Howe, *Secret History of the Dividing Line* (New York: Telephone Books, 1978), 1.

10. Susan Howe, *Articulations of Sound Forms in Time*, in *Singularities* (Hanover, N.H.: Wesleyan University Press, 1990), 5. Cited as A.

11. For readings of this poem, see Back, *Led by Language*, 39–44; Palattella, "An End of Abstraction," 88–92; Nicholls, "Unsettling the Wilderness," 593–96; and Marjorie Perloff, *Poetic License: Essays on Modernist and Postmodernist Lyric* (Evanston, Ill.: Northwestern University Press, 1990), 297–310.

12. George Sheldon, *A History of Deerfield Massachusetts*, vol. 1 (Deerfield, Mass.: Pocumtuck Valley Memorial Association, 1895), 161–66. Nicholls's discussion of this source, "Unsettling the Wilderness," 593–96, is quite useful.

13. Sheldon, *History of Deerfield Massachusetts*, 166, 167.

14. Line 1, for example, is from a letter found in another chapter of Sheldon's book, while line 4 is from yet another. See 185, 189. Line 5 splices two phrases from an Atherton sentence, 166. On the muffling of polyphony that occurs here at the end of the poem, see Palattella, "An End of Abstraction," 92.

15. Susan Howe, *The Nonconformist's Memorial* (New York: New Directions, 1993), 6. 7. For a reading of this entire sequence, see Back, *Led by Language*, 162–80. In an interview with Lynn Keller, Howe makes a number of revealing remarks about how she reads, or voices, these upside-down and scattered lines. See pp. 9–13 of "An Interview with Susan Howe," *Contemporary Literature* 36, 1 (spring 1995): 1–34. Cited as K Int.

16. See also her remark on influence in the Keller interview: "Virginia Woolf and Emily Dickinson were there as the two completely necessary guides in ways that were immediate—absolutely necessary, not at a remove, but in me" (K Int 20). George Butterick, in "The Mysterious Vision of Susan Howe," *North Dakota Quarterly* 55 (fall 1987), 312–21, writes: "She is one of the new American poets *not* descended from Walt Whitman—though she follows Jonathan Edwards, Emerson, Melville, and of course Dickinson. Dickinson is her fore 'father,' her protogonic spirit, matrix" (317). Susan Schultz, in passing, describes *Singularities* as "almost a work of poetic ventriloquism (Dickinson writing through Howe)," "Exaggerated History," paragraph 15.

17. See my comments on Fulton in the introduction.

18. Being cut off from home produces, for Howe, a voice in American poetry "that seems (sounds) stilted and wild at once" (Pol, 192).

19. John Taggart suggestively gets at the outsidedness of Dickinson's speaker in Howe's account by describing the movement of a hunter/composer "in a wilderness of language." See "A Picture of Mystery and Power," in *Songs of Degrees: Essays on Contemporary Poetry and Poetics* (Tuscaloosa: University of Alabama Press, 1994), 168–78.

20. For example, Howe compares early American captivity narratives to the rich accumulation left behind by drained beaver ponds, suggesting that writers like Dickinson and Melville drew on that material: "During the 1850s, when the Republic was breaking apart, newly exposed soil from abandoned narratives was as rich and fresh as a natural meadow" (B, 51). "Thinking about her poetry and her letters led me" (B, 155) to those voices, Howe notes in an interview.

21. See Back, *Led by Language*, 121–23, for remarks on the link between Dickinson and antinomianism.

22. For a different reading of what this inside narrative reveals, see Palattella, "An End of Abstraction," 80.

23. "A Narrative of the Captivity and Restoration of Mrs. Mary Rowlandson," *The Harper American Literature*, ed. Donald McQuade (New York: Longman, 1999), 127. Cited as MR.

24. Nicholls describes this as Rowlandson's "narrative seeming to work against itself"; "Unsettling the Wilderness," 590.

25. For a thoughtful weighing of the claims Howe and others have made for Dickinson's manuscripts, see Cristanne Miller, "The Sound of Shifting Paradigms, or Hearing Dickinson in the Twenty-First Century," in *A Historical Guide to Emily Dickinson*, ed. Vivian R. Pollak (New York: Oxford University Press, 2004), 201–34.

26. Susan Schultz remarks: "She takes as a given that our histories and literature have already been written, and makes it her task to alter rather than to reinvent the record. As editor, however, she does not seek to purify her source texts, but to re-complicate them, implicate them in the 'wilderness' that was overrun by European immigrants, as by white male editors"; "Exaggerated History," paragraph 3.

CHAPTER 6

1. I will refer to the following Graham texts in this essay: *Erosion* (Princeton, N.J.: Princeton University Press, 1983), *The End of Beauty* (New York: Ecco Press, 1987), *Region of Unlikeness* (New York: Ecco Press, 1991), *Materialism* (Hopewell, N.J.: Ecco Press, 1993), *The Errancy* (Hopewell, N.J.: Ecco Press, 1997), *Swarm* (New York: Ecco Press, 2000).

2. In *The Breaking of Style* (Cambridge: Harvard University Press, 1995), Helen Vendler notes in passing Graham's "descent from Dickinson at her most metaphysical and Moore at her most expansive" (93). For Graham's response to Bishop, see "An Interview with Jorie Graham" (229–32), in my *Regions of Unlikeness: Explaining Contemporary Poetry* (Lincoln: University of Nebraska Press, 1999).

3. Jorie Graham, "Some Notes on Silence," in *19 New American Poets of the Golden Gate*, ed. Philip Dow (New York: Harcourt, Brace, Jovanovich, 1984), 409, 411.

4. Jorie Graham, introduction to *The Best American Poetry 1990*, ed. Jorie Graham and David Lehman (New York: Collier Books, 1990), xxvii.

5. Jorie Graham, reading at the Folger Library, December 13, 1994.

6. Jorie Graham, reading at Harvard University, August 13, 1999.

7. Graham, introduction to *The Best American Poetry 1990*, xxviii.

8. *The Letters of Emily Dickinson*, ed. Thomas H. Johnson (Cambridge: Harvard University Press, 1958), 2:444, letter 311.

9. Some of the comments that follow rework readings of Graham's early work in my *Regions of Unlikeness* (166–213).

10. In *The Breaking of Style*, Helen Vendler writes that "a poetry of middleness, of suspension, is Graham's chief intellectual and emotional preoccupation in *The End of Beauty*" (80). She discusses "the moment of suspension" in Graham in broader terms in *Soul Says: On Recent Poetry* (Cambridge: Harvard University Press, 1995), 224–27.

11. In *The Given and the Made* (Cambridge: Harvard University Press, 1995), Helen Vendler notes that this opposition is at work even in Graham's earliest work: "How to give bodily perception its due in thought is a question already vexing Graham's verse," 96.

12. In *Soul Says*, Helen Vendler describes the poet moving in this poem "toward the overwhelming metaphysical question: . . . What is Being *like*? In what words, in what symbols, can it be made intelligible?" (230).

13. Helen Vendler writes in *The Given and the Made* that in this volume Graham "attempt[s] to describe the material world with only minimal resort to the usual conceptual and philosophical resources of lyric . . . and to make that description a vehicle for her personal struggle into comprehension and expression,'" 129. Willard Spiegelman, "Jorie Graham's 'New Way of Looking,'" *Salmagundi* 120 (fall 1998): 244–75, offers a strong essay-length discussion of the way Graham enacts description and its limits as part of a quest to know and see.

14. I have in mind Bishop's story "In the Village" and the mother's scream "alive forever" in the narrator's Nova Scotian village. See my discussion of this story in *Regions of Unlikeness*, 63–64. In "Some Notes on Silence," Graham writes of Bishop that "the scream is in fact the voice of the silence—its foray into, possession of, speech—silence made audible," 410.

15. See, for example, Bishop's "The Man-Moth," who "always seats himself facing the wrong way," and my discussion of this poem in *Regions of Unlikeness*, 34–35.

16. See also letter 892, where Dickinson remarks "'So loved her that he died for her,' says the explaining Jesus." Among the cries taking this form are several baffled responses to Dickinson's poem 640: "Explain   *and were you lost /* Explain   *and were you saved*" (50); "Explain   door ajar / . . . Explain   saturated. / Explain   and I had no more eyes" (55).

17. "Underneath (Always)" (30–31) borrows the agonized phrasing of Dickinson's second Master letter—"A love so big it scares her, rushing among her small heart"—to get at this near wordless anguish:

> But, master, I've gone a far way down your path,
> emptying sounds from my throat like stones from my pockets,
> emptying them onto your lips, into your
> ear warm from sunlight.
> Not in time. My suit denied.
> What is lateness my small heart asks.

18. In an excellent review essay focusing on *Swarm*, "To Feel an Idea," *Kenyon Review* (winter 2002): 188–201, Joanna Klink writes at length about the relation of body and mind in Graham and in this volume in particular. She summarizes her argument this way: "To bring together what I experience of the world in my body, and the ideas by which I understand this experience, or to

restore the body and senses to the mind, is the 'Dream of the Unified Field,' the prayer behind every poem" (189).

19. In the interview that follows, Graham talks at length about the expansion of her view of Dickinson that occurred as she finished *Swarm* and moved into the reader-oriented descriptions of a disappearing world in *Never* (2002). Particularly interesting in this regard is the powerful crisis poem "High Tide," which forms part of the book's conclusion. Its central moment, when the speaker touches the face of a homeless woman and discovers a representation and not a person—"it is a puppet: it is a place / holding a place: it is an eclipse of"—recalls the account in Dickinson's poem 1084 of the disappearance of a bird whose "silver Principle" had "Supplanted all the rest": "At Half past Seven, Element / Nor Implement, be seen— / And Place was where the Presence was / Circumference between."

20. On the importance of suffering, see "Underneath (Libation)" where Graham quotes the chorus speaking to Orestes in the *Oresteia*: "The one who acts must suffer" (72). In a note on the poem "Fuse," Graham refers the reader to Robert Fagles's translation of the *Oresteia* as well as his introduction to the work. Fagles calls attention to the "bloody wedding" (18) that frees the swarming furies who must be embraced in order for regeneration to occur. For Fagles, Orestes—who avenges his father's death by killing his mother, suffers the onslaught of the equally vengeful furies, but then is led by Athena's powers of persuasion and compassion toward restoration—is the key figure. He writes that Orestes "must suffer for 'the race of man,'" through madness being granted "the power to suffer into truth" (63). See Aeschylus, *The Oresteia*, trans. Robert Fagles (New York: Bantam Books, 1982), in particular "The Serpent and the Eagle: A Reading of the *Oresteia*" (1–99).

21. Graham may have in mind here Dickinson's poem 664, where the speaker imagines a future outside of time and mortality in which "this brief Drama in the flesh" has been sifted and a more fundamental relationship is revealed: "Behold the Atom—I preferred— / To all the lists of Clay!" Sharon Cameron, in *Lyric Time: Dickinson and the Limits of Genre* (Baltimore: Johns Hopkins University Press, 1979), comments that this poem "reduces human form to the essence of an 'Atom,'" imagining an "immortality purified of all but created soul," 3. The first poem in *Swarm* seeks to move toward such a reduction: "Give me the atom laying its question at the bottom of nature / . . . the atom still there at the bottom of nature / that we be founded on infinite smallness" (4–5). This final poem, then, moves back to the "clay" and to time's complications.

CONCLUSION

1. *The Complete Poems and Selected Letters of Hart Crane*, ed. Brom Weber (Garden City, N.Y.: Doubleday, 1966), 170.

2. Elisa New, "Hands of Fire: Crane," in *The Regenerate Lyric: Theology and Innovation in American Poetry* (Cambridge, England: Cambridge University Press, 1993), is the best account of Crane's version of these issues I know. Crane is for her "Dickinson's greatest heir" (184), "describ[ing] a broken world in broken language" and drawing a poetically rich "regeneracy" out of "the lyric's reservoir of sin and limitation" (224).

3. Tace Hedrick, "On Influence and Appropriation," *Iowa Review* 22, 1 (1992): 6.

4. Marilynne Robinson, "The First and Second Epistles General of Peter," in *Incarnation: Contemporary Writers on the New Testament*, ed. Alfred Corn (New York: Viking, 1990), 310.

5. Robert Weisbuch, *Emily Dickinson's Poetry* (Chicago: University of Chicago Press, 1975), 16.

6. Jorie Graham, reading at Folger Library, December 13, 1994.

7. Jorie Graham, reading at Harvard University, August 13, 1999.

INDEX ✍